Popular Injustice

Popular Injustice

Violence, Community, and
Law in Latin America

ANGELINA SNODGRASS GODOY

STANFORD UNIVERSITY PRESS

STANFORD, CALIFORNIA

2006

Stanford University Press
Stanford, California
© 2006 by the Board of Trustees of the Leland Stanford Junior University.
All rights reserved.

Printed in the United States of America on acid-free, archival-quality paper

Library of Congress Cataloging-in-Publication Data
Godoy, Angelina Snodgrass.
Popular injustice: violence, community, and law in Latin America/Angelina Snodgrass Godoy.
   p.   cm.
Includes bibliographical references and index.
ISBN 0-8047-5348-2 (cloth : alk. paper) – ISBN 0-8047-5383-0 (pbk. : alk. paper)
1. Lynching—Guatemala. 2. Guatemala—Social conditions—20th century.
3. Lynching—Latin America. I. Title.
HV6471.G9G63 2006
364.1'34—dc22   005028102
Original Printing 2006

Last figure below indicates year of this printing:
14 13 12 11 10 09 08 07 06

Portions of chapter one originally published in *Theory and Society*, 2004. Reprinted with kind permission of Springer Science and Business Media.

Typeset by G&S Typesetters, Inc. in 10/12.5 Palatino

Para el colocho de allá arriba.
Gracias.

Contents

Acknowledgments

WRITING THIS BOOK HAS BEEN a labor of love, and not only my own. Though it deals with violence, death, and other dark topics, it is the product, more than anything else, of countless acts of kindness, support, and intellectual and political camaraderie, and it is in this light that I would like to acknowledge those who helped bring it to fruition.

First and foremost, I am grateful to those who go unnamed in these pages: the individual respondents who shared their stories with me, sometimes through tears; the human rights groups that facilitated portions of my research and whose members inspired others through their tireless dedication to social justice, even at great personal risk; the friends and family members who lent me advice, vehicles, places to stay, and emotional support throughout the research process. Particularly enormous thanks are due to Estuardo Godoy Pineda and Mynor Melgar, whose contributions are far too numerous to name here.

I have also benefited beyond measure from intellectual encouragement, professional mentoring, and personal support from a range of esteemed colleagues and friends. I owe a tremendous and eternally unpayable debt of gratitude to Peter Evans, whose thoughtful and considerate guidance over the years has contributed immensely to my development as a scholar—and to this work's progress from nagging curiosity to research project to dissertation to book. At Berkeley, I was also fortunate to work with Beatriz Manz, Harley Shaiken, Laura Enríquez, and Laurie Edelman. During my graduate studies at Berkeley, I received financial support from the Andrew W. Mellon Fellowship in

Latin American Studies, the National Science Foundation, and Berkeley's Human Rights Center.

At the University of Washington, I am fortunate to be surrounded by an unusually supportive and stimulating community of colleagues, all of whom have contributed in one way or another to the development of my work. I am especially grateful to Katherine Beckett, Mary Callahan, Rachel Cichowski, Alexes Harris, Steve Herbert, George Lovell, Jamie Mayerfeld, Michael McCann, Joel Migdal, Arzoo Osanloo, and Jonathan Warren, many of whom read drafts of chapters, and in some cases the entire manuscript, and provided very helpful feedback. I have also been blessed with generous and gifted students, among them Oscar Barrera Núñez, Cameron Herrington, Phil Neff, and Karen Rosenberg, whose comments on my work have enriched it in many ways. I am grateful, also, for the support of the University of Washington Graduate School Fund for Excellence and Innovation.

Special thanks are also due to a wide range of scholars at various institutions who have on one or another occasion provided me with advice or support related to this project. These include Javier Auyero, John Comaroff, Tamara Kay, Heinz Klug, Carlos Mendoza, Sally Merry, Gay Seidman, Jonathan Simon, and Erik Olin Wright. I served as a visiting fellow at the University of Notre Dame's Kellogg Institute for International Studies for one semester while developing this work and benefited from interactions with numerous colleagues there, especially Iván Orozco. Similarly, I would also like to thank friends and colleagues at Amnesty International, especially Christina Albo, Barbara Bocek, Meredith Larson, and Tracy Ulltveit-Moe, for sharing with me so many insights about Guatemala over the years. Ian Malcolm, at Princeton University Press, and Amanda Moran, at Stanford University Press, supported this project in pivotal ways over the course of several years, and I am grateful, too, for that.

And lastly, I am grateful to Natalia, my daughter; to my parents; and to my brothers and their families.

MUCH OF THIS BOOK DEALS WITH the phenomenon of lynchings in contemporary Guatemala. In recent years, accounts of these events have been splashed across newspaper headlines and beamed around the world by sensationalist television shows, and commentators of all stripes have offered their analyses, usually based on scant empirical evidence, of what the lynchings mean. If residents of the communities in which lynchings occur are given a voice at all in these discussions, it is but a sound bite, used only to underscore previously drawn conclusions about these people and places on the margins.

Yet if I understand anything at all about the lynchings, it is thanks to the people who took the trouble to explain their worlds to me, thanks to long and sometimes painful conversations, careful examples, deliberately chosen phrases. It seems only fair, then, that in a book that draws so extensively on their experiences, those who have so frequently been judged for these episodes should have the chance to speak for themselves. I attempt to share the sensitivities and ambiguities of their words with readers in these pages. Some may find this makes for interrupted reading: at times respondents' words are rough and unpolished, and the emotion with which they were spoken may translate into awkward syntax on the printed page. Often, I include lengthy interview excerpts to allow an appreciation of the ambiguities they contain. Sometimes, too, translation into English fails to capture the multiple meanings at play in any given phrase; in cases where particularly idiomatic language was used or multiple translations of the same words might be equally legitimate, I included the speaker's original Spanish. Although summarizing respondents' expressions in my own words might shorten this text, ultimately I seek to ground my analysis in the words and understandings of those who made this research possible.

I would like, then, to approach this topic through the words of one particularly eloquent woman who shared her story with me. Doña Laura is a Maya K'iche' woman who had served as my interpreter for many previous interviews;[1] when she began to speak for herself, her words fell like a torrent. They remain in my mind the most complex and articulate account I have heard of a lynching.

DOÑA LAURA: I would like to share with you the information that I have regarding the lynching that happened in San Jacinto. Maybe it's not much since I wasn't there at the time, but it's what they've told us by cellular phone and what I've been told.

On Thursday, last Thursday, tomorrow it'll be a week ago, around one in the afternoon, one of the men who was lynched came to town to process some documents, and when he returned [to the village], they were waiting for him on the way. In other words, before he arrived at his house, they were waiting for him—not like an ambush, but like a gathering, the people were waiting on the way. When he arrived there, he was on a bicycle, and they told him to get off the bicycle and to accompany them, that they had to take him somewhere. So he got off the bicycle and they tied his hands with wire, and one of them took the bicycle. When they passed by his house, he said, "I only want to leave the bicycle in my house, just permit me to put the bicycle inside." And they said, no, we are going to call your family [to come out]. And they did, they called the family, they called his wife and they told her to take the bicycle, to take it into the house. He said to her, "I have to go with these people; just put my bicycle away for me." So the [man's] father, since he was home—he lives in a separate house, not with his parents, but his father was there and since he saw him, he followed him for a time and then went to call the brother-in-law—in other words, [the father] called the husband of the sister of the man who was lynched—and he told him, "Go call the police, because the community's grabbed my son and I don't know what for, who knows what they're going to do with him." So the brother-in-law got on his bicycle and went off to get the police. He arrived in San Jacinto [on the bicycle].[2] So, since every Thursday all of us on the [mayoral] council have our meeting, and since that Thursday was our regular meeting—we start at around 2:30 and go to 6:00 or 7:00, depending on the agenda—he arrived when we were in the middle of the meeting.

But before the meeting, I had already received word that they had grabbed the man—his name was Pedro López Jolón—that they'd grabbed him and a *compañero* and that it was not known what was going to happen to them. I heard this before starting the meeting. But I already had a certain, a certain, what's it called, a certain feeling, because those two people were *compañeros* in the struggle,³ they participated in the struggles, earlier, in the past, in the time of the violence and all that, and ever since then they had been organized. They were part of the committee to bring electricity to the community. They aren't criminals, they are members of a committee; you have to understand that. They grabbed them because they accused them of being thieves. They gave them three days—they gave them a period of time—to produce a report, a financial report, to account for their expenditures [*rendir cuentas*], and it seems that the numbers didn't match up, a certain quantity was missing, and that was why they grabbed them; the people say that they stole that money, the money that was missing. So that day they grabbed them and told them to say where they had the money hidden, but he said, "No, no, there is no money, our committee already spent the money," because they had already spent it on the committee's activities. But the people became furious. "There's no money," they said. "We already told you what we spent the money on, we had to buy this and that, we had to pay the company a certain amount in order for them to approve the project . . . ," but their explanations were not satisfactory for the people.

So I think then [the people] told them, "No, we're going to burn you right here, because if we take you to the courts, we already know they won't do anything to you, they'll just lock you up for two or three days, that's it. So right here we're going to make justice," the people said. "We have justice right here in our hands and if we take you there, they won't make justice. No. It's better to do it right here." So they started to pour gasoline on them, the whole mass of people that were there present—men, women, children, young people—and they also poured gasoline around them and then they set them on fire.

The police arrived late. Because, as they told us, it's very difficult [to get to] that place so far out where the community is, there's still no telephone in the community, and there are no numbers to call the police,⁴ so there's no way to call them in an emergency, so the person—the man's father—had to walk about half an hour in order to tell the brother-in-law, and that man had to take another fifteen minutes or so on his bicycle to get to the police station in San Jacinto. The mayor had already received information, because someone in the community has a cellular phone—a *compañero* of ours, who worked with us on the political campaign of [political party], because that's the party that won there in San Jacinto, so he warned us, "They've grabbed a *compañero*, his name is such and such, what can we do? We don't know what they're going to do with him but they've gotten him and they have him tied up. So please send someone to call the police immediately."

So the mayor, when he heard that, he contacted the police and he told them, "A young man is going to come to lead you to the place where these problems are happening." So after a short while the young man arrived at the police station, and he led the police to the place where this was going on. But they didn't arrive in time to help; by the time they arrived it was too late. The *consejal segundo* and the *consejal primero* were also on their way,⁵ but when they were on the way [the man from the community] called them on the cellular phone to tell them that it wasn't worth it for them to go anymore, and that it would be better for them to pull over to clear the road for the police because they [the police] were on their way back [from the community], bringing the burned men. So [it was better to pull over so] that the police could pass quickly without stopping on the road. And that's how they arrived, and the *consejal segundo* and *consejal primero* came in the vehicle behind the police, who brought the burned men.

That Thursday, it was about 3:30 in the afternoon when the lynching occurred. About 4:30, the lynched men passed through the town, the police were bringing them here [to Santa Cruz del Quiché], and since there were two of them, and the car that one of them was being brought in, it seems that car didn't really work, it had some sort of problems with one of its tires, so they barely got to the town, and since they were worried that maybe the people of the community were following them to finish the job, they barely arrived in the town and changed cars, passing both men to another car. Then, since our meeting had been interrupted, I was in the municipal building, when suddenly I heard a lot of noise and commotion outside, and I felt, in that moment I felt like someone had doused me in cold water, that's how I felt. I ran outside. All the employees in the municipal building ran outside, and since it's on the second floor—maybe you don't know the building, but it's on the second floor—so we ran out [onto the balcony] and we were looking down [into the street]. I saw one of the men when they transferred him to the other car, but he was all burnt, and you couldn't recognize that it was him, because the poor man was completely burnt, without clothing, without anything.

At that moment, when I saw that, I thought many things. First I thought, how must the community feel? . . . Do they feel happy, or . . . how do they feel? Because when the police arrived, they couldn't even enter the community because the road was blocked. The people had knocked down trees [to block the road], and for that reason the police couldn't arrive quickly, and they couldn't rescue the men right when they'd set them on fire, but rather once the poor men were already burning. They say there wasn't any water, and when the police arrived, the crowd came down on the police, and the police thought that at any moment they might set fire to their cars, they had that concern. "And who sent you?" the people shouted at the police. "You don't have any business here. We're making justice here because no one else will." That's what the people said.

So the police said, "Just a moment. Here the job we've come to do is to rescue these people, because you all don't understand that they are people, and they have rights. That's why we're here," said the police. And then apparently the police started to shoot tear gas, because the people didn't let them enter. So then the people cleared the way to the place where the men were burning up. And the police did what they could to put out the fire, but they couldn't touch the men because they were burning, so they threw dirt on them, they did what they could, and I even heard that the hands and clothes of the police got burned too. But like that, throwing dirt on the fire they were able to put it out, and they untied them and got them out of there. But the police were also hit with rocks, because the people were throwing rocks and everything. They [the police] had to fire—it wasn't that they wanted to kill anyone, but that they had to rescue the men.

I was left very affected by what I saw, because it brought back everything, everything that happened in the time of the1980s—I saw that, because I am also a survivor of the massacres and all the repression that happened. So it felt like that time had returned, I felt that I was living again in that same time of the '80s.

. . . In relation to the lynched men, they arrived here [in Santa Cruz del Quiché] at the hospital, but since there are no materials here to treat people who've suffered third-degree burns, they were transferred to the capital. They took them away alive. They took them to the Roosevelt [Hospital]—in the early morning hours they arrived at the Roosevelt Hospital [in Guatemala City]. And there, the morning of the next day, one of them died, and the day after that, the other one died. So now you could say that tomorrow it will be a week ago that they died.

On Saturday, [the body of] one of them arrived back at the parish house [*parroquia*], because nobody else in the community was willing to receive the body, but thank God the priest did allow the corpse to be taken there. The body arrived on Saturday and they kept it in the church, and in the afternoon they buried it. But that's only because the parish staff was willing to accompany him to the cemetery, because the community was like, how would I say . . . well, they were happy that he had died. And Sunday, in the early morning, the other one arrived, and that same Sunday afternoon they buried him, again only because the parish priest took charge of doing this, of taking him to the cemetery.

. . . That Saturday was very difficult, it was very hard. I had to travel to the capital, and all I heard was that one of the men had returned dead, but I had to travel anyway—I had to travel. So that weekend I was in the capital, but I was still in touch with what was going on, and I heard that the two had died there in the capital. Well, anyway, that Saturday, the official secretary [in the mayor's office], who works half a day on Saturdays, he was working that day, and a group of those people—of the lynchers—went there [to his office] to say, "We've brought a statement [*un acta*] and what we want is for you to type it up and put a seal on it."[6] Like that, they gave him orders, very forcefully. "I'm sorry," he said, "I'm going to do you the favor of typing up your statement, but I'm not going to seal it, because I don't have the orders, I don't have an order from the municipal council to do so." So then the people were not satisfied; even though they'd already done it [killed the men], now it seems they wanted to finish off their families, so that's really serious.

Another thing: according to what those lynchers said, they trace the problem to the municipality. They say that the two men, since they're members of committees and had a lot of dealings with the municipal council, of course the municipality is in favor of them [the victims], so they're saying, or I've heard anyway, that maybe we are at risk because of them. I really don't have anything against anyone, but I am also afraid, because like I told you, the situation right now is extremely delicate. So it seems like what's happening is like what happened in Chichicastenango, in Xalbaquiej,[7] as if people are learning this thing of the lynchings, as if it were something common. Since there's no justice for the lynchers either, it's like every week, a new community [lynches], another month, another community. It's already become kind of contagious. I don't know what would have to happen to stop this, but it worries me very much. In this case, two widows are left. What are the two widows going to do? The two widows are afraid to demand that the lynchers maintain their families [financially], because, well, who's going to demand that? On a national level, I want to know, what's being thought of to end this sickness?

. . . But also, it shouldn't be confused with Mayan law, because Mayan law is not this. The lynchings are learned; the lynchings began when the violence happened, in the time of the '80s, because the army was the one who began to burn people alive around here. And that happened close to the community where this lynching was, and they saw it, the people lived it. Even minors, children, were burned alive by the army. The army piled cornhusks on top of a girl and there they set her on fire. Because they thought that even children, even dogs were part of the guerrillas. So they were the ones who were burning around here.

In my village there never had been a lynching, and I'm worried because this had never happened. Whenever we got together with the municipal council we would talk about the theme of the lynchings, but in general, in order to reflect upon it, not because it had touched us. And we always talk about lynchings as a question of crime, not for misuse of funds. That's completely different. You have to differentiate crime from misuse of funds. Because there was never any investigation to see if they really stole or invested those funds badly. I don't know how they might have managed those funds, I couldn't tell you if they were innocent or not, but I do know that they were people who had worked with us for years, and who collaborated on the electoral campaign of the [political party], that's how I knew them, they were very active people. Sometimes there are conflicts between sympathizers of the different parties, and they could take advantage of a situation like this to get rid of some enemies, I think. . . . If they invested those funds badly, I don't support that and I think it's important. But, well, they shouldn't pay with their lives. There are problems behind this that have a political character, there are hidden forces, there's something more than that going on.

I can't get over it. For me, it traumatizes me to think that those men who were such hard workers have had to pay like this for what they did. I was left traumatized also from those days [during the war], after they kidnapped my uncle, and the army took away my father, so all my family was affected. And now that I see another similar thing happening, I feel like I'm going back to the same thing again, going back to what was the time of the '80s. It's sad, it's terribly worrisome, but anyway, some people are working with the [victims'] families to demand justice from the Public Ministry.

Q: And is it known who the leaders of the lynch mob were?

DOÑA LAURA: Yes, it's known, because they told a son, a son of one of the victims—one of the men who died has an eighteen-year-old son and he was there close to his father. Because of that, they also beat him, and they almost set the boy on fire, too, because he didn't want that to happen to his father, and while they were preparing everything the boy was crying. "No, no, don't do this," he said, but they didn't pay him any attention, and then afterward, when they had already started the fire, one of the lynched men said to his son, quietly, "So-and-so tied us up, so-and-so was the one who sent them after us." So the son knows who was responsible, and they have their names there in the municipal building. Also that Thursday the mayor got [angry] because they told us that one of the lynchers announced in the community, "We are going to do this because the mayor authorized us to"; that's what one of the lynchers said. The families of the burned men heard that, but they didn't believe it. They knew that the people had planned to lynch them beforehand and that the mayor had nothing to do with it.

On Friday we continued our meeting of the council, and the family arrived that day, I mean the [families of the] victims, and they told us how everything happened, what happened, what they did to them, and they told us that they [the lynchers] had told them [the family members] that if they got close they were going to kill them too. So then, since one of the women has a nine-month-old baby, they couldn't get any closer, and they said that one of the women was beaten up because she wanted to get close to her husband and they wouldn't let her, they told her that they were going to burn her too because her husband had shared the stolen money with her. So she went away, and . . . only saw from a bit of a way off how the huge cloud of smoke went up when they set them on fire; [she] felt that her own life was ending too. But when the police arrived, the mother of one of the lynched men approached, and since the police saw her, when they took away the lynched men they took their families too, they brought them here, and the women stayed here. It was really sad.

Q: And were the lynchers from a different political party?

DOÑA LAURA: That's what we still have to find out; they're investigating. They say that the priest is also very worried for that reason. They say that on Sunday he didn't celebrate Mass, because when the people arrived he said, "I'm sorry, ladies and gentlemen, but today there is no Mass. Why are we going to have Mass, if there is no tranquility, if there is no peace? There's a man here. Why was he killed? What law allowed him to be killed?" So the people went away without receiving communion.

The violence left this sickness. This is sown here; it didn't exist before, but it's a legacy of what we have lived. All those who participated in the massacres of the 1980s, those are our people, Maya people, campesino people. Those were the people who came after us to try to kill us. And those people, *our* people, were left deeply affected; our culture, our society is affected. That doesn't get erased by a signing of the peace.

Popular Injustice

CHAPTER 1

Examining Popular Injustice

HARROWING INCIDENTS OF MOB VIOLENCE like the one recounted in the opening to this book are not uncommon in contemporary Guatemala, where an average of nearly ten *linchamientos* (lynchings) per month were reported during 1999 (Misión de Verificación de las Naciones Unidas en Guatemala [MINUGUA] 2000b).[1] Between 1996, when the government and guerrillas signed the final peace accords to bring the country's thirty-six-year civil war to a close, and the end of 2002, the United Nations Verification Mission in Guatemala reported 482 such incidents; many more have likely gone undocumented. In the incidents the mission was able to verify during this period, 240 people were killed and 943 injured; yet only thirty-nine defendants had been brought before the courts, twenty-four of whom were found guilty (MINUGUA 2002).[2]

In a country the size of Tennessee, with a population of roughly 11 million, these numbers suggest the emergence of an alarming trend. Although Guatemala's history has long been scarred by violence, incidents of this sort are unprecedented; under authoritarianism, the grip of military repression made such open, independent forms of collective action simply unthinkable. The lynchings began as the war ended; in Guatemala, as in Brazil (Holston and Caldeira 1998; Caldeira 2000), South Africa (Comaroff and Comaroff forthcoming), and other parts of the postcolonial world,[3] extralegal violence in the name of justice has been a disturbing dividend of democracy.[4] Today, lynchings occur in urban and rural settings alike, among indigenous and mestizo (*ladino*) communities, and they target individuals from within the community at least as often as they do interlopers. And although in the United States the word "lynching" conjures up images of racially motivated violence, in Guatemala I found no evidence for such a dimension to the phenomenon. Indeed, although collective violence is often assumed to be targeted against members of an identifiable out group, defined in ethnic, religious, cultural, or other terms, in the dozens of Guatemalan cases I investigated the only common thread linking the victims was the accusation of criminal activity.[5] In the context of a very serious contemporary crime wave, many Guatemalans openly support vigilante behavior: one recent survey found that 75 percent of the population expressed at least partial support for these killings in the name of "justice" (Ferrigno 1998).

I first became aware of the phenomenon on a 1996 human rights research trip to Guatemala. I was instantly curious: unlike the state-sponsored repression that had shaken the country for decades, this appeared to be a new kind of abuse—one that rose up from below. If the struggle for democracy had for so long been a battle against the oppressive state, what did it mean when previous victims of state violence were the ones doing the killing?

Of course, I quickly learned that it was not so simple. Like virtually every case of violence in Guatemala, the lynchings are open to multiple readings. By 1996, although the trend had yet to take off in earnest, there were various interpretations of early incidents swirling about, and I soon learned that the analysis offered by any one commentator often said more about his or her political sympathies than it did about the incident in question. As with so many other things in Guatemala, the hard facts were elusive, and the answer often simply came down to whose rendering of events one chose to believe.

As in other cases of human rights abuse in Latin America, the best-documented cases are often (though not always) those where the victims are foreigners from wealthier countries.[6] When I first began asking people about lynchings, in 1996, the best-known incidents were a series of mob attacks and attempted attacks on U.S. citizens falsely accused of stealing Guatemalan babies. The most serious of these incidents involved the Alaskan environmental activist June Weinstock, who was stoned, stabbed, and beaten nearly to death by a crowd in the rural village of San Cristóbal Verapaz in 1994. Accounts of her ordeal, pieced together from eyewitness accounts and two videotape recordings of the event, paint a harrowing picture. A tourist, Weinstock had spent the morning of March 29 strolling through the village market and taking pictures, including some of local children. But when a mother suddenly noticed her young son was missing, Weinstock was yanked off a departing bus by an angry crowd who accused her of stealing the baby. Not fluent in Spanish, Weinstock had no way of knowing what was brewing, but a missionary stationed in the town intervened to translate and, along with two policemen, to try to hold the mob at bay for as long as possible. These men hurried Weinstock to the local judge's office in an attempt to protect her, arriving at around 11:30 A.M., according to the U.S. Embassy. Tear gas was used in an attempt to disperse the crowd that gathered outside, and a priest from nearby Cobán attempted to mediate; one eyewitness reported that some in the crowd threw stones at him and yelled, "We don't want your blessings, we want blood." The judge eventually fled the building, as did the missionary, who was attacked and beaten twice before the police were able to escort him to safety; Weinstock was left alone to barricade herself in the bathroom. The mob shattered windows and tried to set the structure afire. Eventually, they used a bench as a battering ram, broke through the doors and, around 4:00 P.M., located Weinstock and brutally beat her with fists, feet, sticks, and stones; the attack only stopped after police convinced the crowd she was already dead. Although she was in fact still alive, her injuries were sufficiently grave that months after her return to Alaska, Weinstock had still not regained the ability to speak, walk, or respond to environmental stimuli (W. Booth 1994; Morello 1994).

Rumors of baby stealing and organ harvesting by foreigners posing as tourists have a long history in Central America (and beyond—see especially Scheper-Hughes 1996), but in these, as in many cases of violence in Guatemala, there were indications that the apparently spontaneous attacks may have been deliberately instigated to serve certain political ends. The attack on Weinstock came only weeks after another U.S. citizen, Melissa Larsen, was either arrested (according to some reports; see W. Booth 1994; Morello 1994) or "placed into protective custody" (Intelligence Oversight Board [IOB] 1996) by the Guatemalan authorities for a period of two weeks after a mob accused her of baby stealing in Santa Lucía Cotzumalguapa. At the same time, graffiti had appeared overnight in Guatemala City denouncing gringo baby thieves, the simultaneity of which, to some, suggested a deliberately coordinated campaign.

But who would stand to gain from such violence? These events took place during the negotiations between the government and guerrillas over the Global Human Rights Accord, one of the most significant and sensitive in the series of agreements that, in their entirety, comprise the Peace Accords that in 1996 finally ended the country's three decades of armed conflict. Among the points most hotly contested by the military and far right was the 1994 agreement to welcome United Nations personnel into the country to verify both sides' compliance with the peace process. In this context, there are indications that individuals linked to the armed forces may have concocted these incendiary rumors as part of an effort to create a climate of hostility to foreigners, thus undermining the U.N. mission's eventual ability to carry out its human rights work. Some observers spotted military men among the crowd at the lynching of Weinstock, and some villagers in Santa Lucía Cotzumalguapa reported that they had been warned about coming violence prior to the attempted attack on Larsen (W. Booth 1994).

The U.S. government, in its 1996 Intelligence Oversight Board (IOB) report detailing incidents of violence against U.S. citizens and their family members in Guatemala, lent some credence to these analyses, reporting intelligence information that suggested these acts had been promoted by forces associated with the Army and far right. But there was blame for the other side too: the report also noted that during the war, the guerrillas had deliberately spread rumors linking U.S. citizens to organ theft as a way to encourage opposition to U.S. policy, which had long supported the Guatemalan government in its struggle against "communism" (IOB 1996). Guatemalan government officials publicly attributed the attack on Weinstock to guerrillas trying to destabilize the country. And of course, the dozens of men arrested for the crime saw nothing, knew nothing, and had nothing to say about how it started (W. Booth 1994). As one Western diplomat told a *Washington Post* reporter in Guatemala who was investigating the incident, "Even when you think you know who is pulling the strings, you don't know . . . if you eventually find out who benefited from some act, you don't know if they pulled the strings to get what they wanted or whether someone else pulled the strings to make it look like they did it" (quoted in W. Booth 1994).

Today, most lynchings do not involve foreigners accused of baby snatching (and most do not result in international inquiries or dozens of arrests, either).[7] A surprising number are actually carried out against residents of the very community in which the lynching occurs. For the most part, those lynched appear to be more or less what their attackers say they are: suspected criminals.[8] They are most often accused of property crimes, sometimes no more serious than the theft of a chicken;

there are cases of attacks on accused rapists, murderers, and child mo-
lesters, there have also been attacks on alleged witches, public servants
accused of corruption, and those responsible for traffic accidents. How
do such accusations erupt in lethal violence?

The more I spoke to Guatemalans about the phenomenon of lynchings, the more it perplexed me. At one level, it was of course very plausible that politically motivated campaigns of misinformation fed into
this trend. But could they be its *cause*? Why would crowds sometimes
numbering into the thousands be persuaded to summarily execute
someone—even one of their own neighbors—to suit a national political agenda? Were people being forced to participate against their will?
How would anyone carry out such a massive campaign of coercion? Although the army's well-documented orchestration of a decades-long
counterinsurgency campaign targeting church workers, health promoters, literacy advocates, and unarmed indigenous villagers as threats to
national security certainly lowered the threshold of believability about
how far they might be willing to go to achieve their ends, it didn't make
sense to me that the army would mount such an elaborate effort to crack
down on chicken thieves. *Why?*

Furthermore, as I began investigating the lynchings, I became aware
that the apparent surge in collective vigilante practices was not unique
to contemporary Guatemala: extrajudicial executions of suspected
criminals at the hands of large groups of citizens were also being documented elsewhere with increasing frequency in the late 1990s. In
Venezuela, the human rights group Programa Venezolano de Educación y Acción en Derechos Humanos reported 164 lynchings between
October 2000 and September 2001 (Programa Venezolano de Educación
y Acción en Derechos Humanos [PROVEA] 2001); the rate of lynchings
in Caracas alone reached one death every three days in July and August 1999 (Luna Noguera 1999; Monasterios 1999). The anthropologist
Daniel Goldstein (2003) reports that more than thirty lynchings occurred on the outskirts of Cochabamba, Bolivia, in 2001. And in Mexico,
Carlos Vilas (2001) investigated some 103 lynchings between 1987 and
1998; other reports have suggested many more. Related incidents have
been reported in Ecuador, Peru, Brazil, and other countries. In many of
these cases, there was no plausible postconflict explanation, no way to
see things through the binary lens of "army or guerrilla" that so frequently tempts observers of Guatemala; rather, citizens and residents of
marginal communities (both urban and rural) appeared to be rising up
and taking justice in their own hands in response to a growing sense of

insecurity caused by rising rates of common—not political—crime. What was going on? How could it be that in so many communities across the Americas, people who had struggled for human rights for so long, many surviving periods of brutal state violence, could now themselves be carrying out acts of violence—even invoking terms (such as *mano dura*) that recalled authoritarianism, in deliberate defiance of the human rights discourse? Could this be a new form of poor people's "justice"?

What's more, within and beyond Guatemala, I soon learned that the lynchings were but the tip of the iceberg. Owing to their high visibility and visceral impact, they captured headlines, attracting press and would-be mediators (police, military, human rights professionals, and in Guatemala, U.N. personnel) who sought to intervene (sometimes successfully, sometimes quite heroically, almost always at great risk to their personal safety, but all too often in utter futility) to prevent or limit the bloodshed. Yet many respondents told me of similar practices—often called "social cleansing" or simply "cleansing" (*limpieza*)—whereby real or suspected criminals were summarily executed under cover of darkness, without witnesses, without spectacle. Bodies were often secretly disposed of, residents said; in any case, no one dared to ask what had taken place, although many were tacitly grateful that the "criminal" was gone. In some cases, people told me about death squads that were specifically constituted for the purpose of carrying out these executions; in others, people said, a locally powerful man (in rural areas, often a landowner) took the responsibility to do the "dirty work" upon himself (or to hire someone to do it for a fee); in others, particularly in urban Guatemala City, local drug gangs or other criminal organizations would "clean up" the neighborhoods in which they lived or operated.[9] Lynchings, then, were simply the most sensationalized, the most visible, and the best documented of a whole set of clandestine practices that claimed to crack down on crime by excising criminals from the body social.

Such behavior clearly defies the expectations of the many scholars, citizens, and observers who welcomed the recent "democratic opening" in Latin America. Democracy, many expected, would allow civil society to flourish, rising up to fill the gap left by the retreat from repression and bringing with it increased citizen participation. This was assumed to be a positive development; most believed this empowerment would serve as a check on violence, not a catalyst for it. Although *state* violence has indeed decreased in most cases, its replacement by violence at the hands of nonstate actors has therefore come as a surprise. As Dirk Kruijt and Kees Koonings observe, violence in Latin America has "ceased to be the resource of only the traditionally powerful or of the grim uniformed guardians of the nation. [It] increasingly appears as an option for a multitude of actors in pursuit of all kind of goals" (1999: 11). Some of this violence is undoubtedly attributable to petty crime, random acts of personal retribution, by-products of the burgeoning drug trade, or other developments; but some of it constitutes a new form of *counter-criminal* violence: organized and deliberate, though illegal, acts taken purportedly to stem the tide of common crime.

Moreover, this trend is not limited to clandestine or illegal behavior. Even where citizens did not take these sentiments to their most dramatic extremes, support for a new set of "hyperpunitive" criminal justice practices known as *mano dura*,[10] including the expanded use of capital and corporal punishment (sometimes administered in public view), the imposition of stricter sentencing guidelines, and a general rejection of rehabilitative programs in favor of "just deserts," also appeared to be on the rise. Though some people took the law into their own hands, others demanded that state wield the law in stricter, more repressive, or more visible ways—or even that the state violate the law, endorsing acts of police brutality as necessary tools in the fight against crime, a fight that is increasingly understood as an all-out war against a dangerous internal enemy. Fear of crime has taken a deep hold of many societies across the Americas, where citizens retreat behind ever-higher walls, barred windows, and armed guards, and/or enter into associations with neighbors aimed at protecting property, often through methods resembling vigilantism (or invoking its principles outright) (see Caldeira 2000; Briceño-León and Zubillaga 2002; Rotker 2002). And popular clamor for a "solution" to the crime problem has also provided a new generation of political *caudillos* (strongmen) with a platform ripe in populist appeal: during campaigns, candidates flex their *mano dura* muscles in attempts to outdo one another as "tough on crime." Perhaps most alarmingly, even former dictators and others with dubious democratic credentials have parlayed their past heavy-handedness into postauthoritarian political currency, as increasingly crime-weary electorates find renewed appeal in promises of security, even at the price of justice (on this point, see Chevigny 2003). In this way, the illegal acts of lynching, performed mostly by marginal communities, find their parallel in a discourse and set of practices both legal and illegal, supported and invoked by the middle and upper classes as well. The trend of *mano dura* thus includes both vigilantism and support for a hyperpunitive form of criminal justice meted out by the state.

Popular Injustice in Perspective: Why Lynchings Matter

In this book, I explore the rise in lynchings and the generalized support for *mano dura* in several Latin American nations, focusing most closely on the case of Guatemala. My research is motivated by a number of central questions: How can increasing democratization in the political sphere be reconciled with broad support for the denial of due process and other "core" civil rights? Why are these apparent disjunctions growing in contemporary democracies? And what are their consequences for political order and democracy itself?

These questions probe the *quality* of democracy in places like Guatemala. For although I use the term "democracy" in this text, as opposed to dictatorship, to connote the country's contemporary political system, many might reasonably question whether it is appropriate to apply this term to the contemporary Guatemalan regime. Although the system might meet the strictest Schumpterian definition of a democracy—elections are "free and fair," after all, and the constitution recognizes a full panoply of rights—virtually everyone acknowledges serious deficiencies in the functioning of Guatemala's institutions, such that, de facto if not de jure, basic citizenship rights are often compromised or denied, especially to women, indigenous peoples, the rural poor, and any of the other disempowered groups that in fact make up a majority of the country's population. Although the constitution confers formal political equality on all citizens, formidable barriers limit the ability of many to exercise their rights, making the law sometimes appear to be little more than a series of dead-letter promises and elegant proclamations bearing only scant resemblance to real life.

The existence of this gulf between democratic promise and real-life practice is not news to scholars of democracy (nor is it, certainly, to scholars writing in the law-and-society tradition, who have long argued that such gaps, in varying degrees, characterize all legal regimes). On the contrary, it has been widely studied and debated, and in recognition of its significance scholars have variously invoked such terms as "low-intensity citizenship," "illiberal democracy," "democradura," or "dictablanda," among others, to describe regimes in the region. Though experts agree on the need for these limiting qualifiers in Latin America, they do not necessarily agree on the definition of democracy itself—in other words, on when the qualifiers should come off. Some, following Joseph Schumpeter, suggest that democracy denotes a *process* of electoral competition, not a predetermined *outcome* in terms of specific policies or social characteristics: Diamond, Linz, and Lipset (1998), for example, define democracy as "a political system, separate and apart from the economic and social system. . . . Indeed, a distinctive aspect of our approach is to insist that issues of so-called economic and social democracy be separated from the questions of governmental structure" (xvi; see also Diamond 1990: 228). Adam Przeworski, similarly, considers democracy to be a political system centered on competitive elections (Przeworski 1988).

Others, such as William Robinson (1996), Atilio Borón (1998), and Augusto Varas (1998), suggest that narrowly procedural approaches may identify *polyarchies* but fall short of defining *democracy*.[11] Polyarchy is a system of government whereby popular participation is confined to the expression of preferences in elite-controlled electoral contests; it is premised on political equality but perfectly compatible with sharp social iniquities.[12] Democracy, on the other hand, requires something more: formal political rights must be accompanied by some measure of social justice.[13] Without such a social component, they argue, democracy risks being reduced to a meaningless charade.

Although these definitional questions have spawned a vigorous debate in the academic literature, there are some basic areas of agreement. Virtually everyone recognizes that endemic poverty and lack of education limit citizens' ability to exercise their rights; even those who define the political sphere alone as the object of inquiry have increasingly acknowledged the capacity for these social inequalities to effectively invalidate political rights.[14] Scholars disagree as to when the label "democracy" should be applied, but not on the relevance of extreme levels of social and economic inequality for the health or vitality of representative regimes. Similarly, polyarchy, even in the most limited and formal sense, is generally recognized as an improvement over authoritarianism because although it may fall short of some expectations, it provides a framework of citizenship rights that can be mobilized and expanded by civil society. Once granted access to political institutions, the argument goes, citizens can leverage their power to implement reforms to social and economic structures; once the polity is democratic, the economy can become so through concerted action. Thus democracy is a process that, though it may not dictate specific outcomes, permits popular participation that should—in theory—tip the balance in favor of social justice: as Rueschemeyer, Stephens, and Stephens, write, "we care about formal [political] democracy because . . . it tends to be real to some extent. Giving the many a real voice in the formal collective decision-making of a country is the most promising basis for further progress in the distribution of power and other forms of substantive equality" (1992: 10). The key to making democracy "real," then, lies in citizens' mobilization—not in the formal institutions themselves, but in the substantive struggles they enable.[15]

It is for this reason that *mano dura* makes for such a fascinating puzzle. In lynchings and other acts of *mano dura*, we see popular participation, both within and beyond the law, working not to expand rights but to constrain them. This is why, although lynchings are reminiscent of practices that various scholars have dubbed "popular justice" as an alternative to state legal systems (see Abel 1982; Merry and Milner 1993; Santos 1977), I deliberately avoid use of this term—first, because although in this case the state law is indeed arbitrary and infused with violence, its mimicry at the hands of mobs hardly represents an emancipatory event;[16] and second, because I insist that lynchings themselves must be understood as simply one manifestation of *mano dura*, distinct in form but not so much in function from "zero tolerance" criminal crackdowns, expedited deportation of petty criminals, erosions of due process, "social cleansing," and other measures supported by a range of social actors and in many cases involving the harnessing of official criminal justice institutions. In all these examples the very civil society that scholars expected would breathe life into formal structures has mobilized—through public demonstrations, petition drives, political pressure campaigns, paid advertisements in public fora, and other tactics often considered the core of democratic participation—to promote a rollback of rights for certain groups, a suspension of key human rights provisions, and a remilitarization of societies struggling to emerge from state repression.[17] *Mano dura* forces us, then, to reconsider what has often been an assumption in democratization theory: the notion that civil society itself is an inherently democratizing force, that unfettered popular participation will in fact produce socially just outcomes.

In this book, rather than proposing a new means of classification by which to decide whether countries are or are not democracies, polyarchies, or some other new subspecies, my purpose is to examine the nexus between popular participation and injustice, to probe the ways ostensibly democratic institutions can be inhabited by profoundly un-

(and even anti-) democratic forces, and specifically to suggest that this propensity grows as societies become more socially and economically polarized. In deeply unequal societies governed by the political economy of neoliberalism, criminal justice becomes increasingly prominent as a mechanism for sanitizing socioeconomic exclusion and shoring up the status quo. Crime fighting is thus deeply politicized, even as the language and logic of *mano dura* strive to define the issue as one of social and moral decay, void of political causes or consequences. Politics itself is vilified in a discourse that promises to transcend differences of class, race, gender, or social position, but that in its effects reifies them by reinforcing the mechanisms of exclusion that limit citizens' ability to exercise the rights they have been formally granted.

As societies are pushed toward the poles,[18] then, law—and particularly criminal law—becomes a central staging ground for struggles to define citizenship, justice, and order. For although *all* liberal democracies are characterized by tensions between the formal equality of all citizens before the state and the real inequality of citizens' vastly different positions of power, what knits these contradictions together is law. It is no secret that those adversely affected by substantive inequality—the poor, the marginalized, the downtrodden or dispossessed—experience deprivations that effectively neutralize the equal rights promised them under their constitutions. But law provides the framework through which such individuals can seek redress (at least in theory); its existence and availability confer legitimacy on this system of inherent contradictions.

It is not surprising, then, that law becomes the central site for contestation as gaps between haves and have-nots grow wider. Santos (2000) and others have referred to this as the "judicialization of politics." But here I mean not only the increasing prominence of courts, but law in the broadest sense—for although some contestation takes the form of lawsuits, reform campaigns, or other attempts to work within the framework of liberal legality, some takes the form of illegal, even violent, attempts to subvert that very system, laying bare its contradictions and denouncing its compromises with the mechanisms that maintain mass exclusion. As John Comaroff writes, "When they begin to find a voice, peoples who see themselves as disadvantaged often do so either by speaking back in the language of the law or by disrupting its means and ends" (1994: xii). As violent, public expressions of resistance by marginalized populations in isolated rural hamlets or urban shantytowns, lynchings provide a perfect illustration of this point.

But it is not only the disadvantaged who see the law, and matters of criminal justice, as increasingly important arenas in which issues of practical and moral import are negotiated. Extreme inequality also leads those with considerably more resources to turn to the law as a means of protecting their property and power from a growing under-class often perceived as increasingly restless. So not only lynchings, but also other expressions of *mano dura* such as "social cleansing," vengeance killings, public support for police brutality against criminal suspects, expedited routes to capital punishment, or other forms of un-dermined due-process rights, are characteristic of deeply unequal societies.[19] As Holston and Caldeira explain:

Among all social classes, the everyday experience of violence and of the institutions of law leads to a pervasive and comprehensive delegitimation of the rule of law. Poorer people are victims of arbitrariness, violence, and injustices committed by law institutions. As a result, they feel that they are left without alternatives inside the law. In contrast, the rich find it in their best interest to take advantage of the failures of legal institutions. They have the privilege of being able to choose to ignore the law and do what they think is personally more appropriate. What is similar for both groups, however, is that their reactions tend to be framed in private and frequently illegal terms. (1998: 278)

If law is what holds together the contradictions of liberal democracies, in deeply unequal societies it is stretched, like a taut rubber band, across an ever wider divide. *Mano dura* emerges like a fissure in that elastic, a sign that it is stretched too thin. This is why *mano dura* reflects deep socioeconomic inequalities, and why its emergence is among the hallmarks of our neoliberal era.

The bulk of scholarship on democratization and development, however, does not recognize law's role as a democratic binding of this sort. In fact, the literature on democratization has historically focused on the development of political, rather than legal, institutions, in a way that may unwittingly reinforce the perception of their separation. In recent years, however, many scholars have begun to identify crime, or the ill-functioning of legal institutions, as a threat to democracy in Latin America and an emergent priority for research. Felipe Agüero and Jeffrey Stark (1998) define the weak rule of law as among the principal "fault lines" of democratic consolidation in Latin America. An expand-ing list of authors cites the region's increasing tide of criminality as evidence of weak states' inability to govern effectively and uphold the rule of law across the national territory (O'Donnell 1993, 1999, 2001; Méndez 1999; Prillaman 2000). Larry Diamond (1999) suggests that this danger has been largely overlooked by theorists of democracy, despite its gravity: crime destabilizes democratizing societies, discourages the expansion of their embattled economies, and dismantles the rule of law, encouraging illegal behavior by the state and its citizens. Indeed, the "rule of law" became the new buzzword in the policy circles of the 1990s, and at the behest of such organizations as the World Bank, the Inter-American Development Bank, and especially the United States Agency for International Development (USAID), millions of dollars have been pumped into judicial reform across Latin America in an effort to shore up the region's ailing judiciaries and to respond to, among other things, the anger embodied in lynchings (Jarquín and Carrillo 1998; Carothers 1998; Santos 2000).

Yet although scholarly interest in Latin American justice systems is growing, much of today's rule-of-law approach effectively depoliticizes crime, taking it largely at face value as a naturally occurring fact. Perhaps because most of those tackling this topic are lawyers, jurists, or practitioners seeking tangible solutions to a very pressing problem, much of the literature tends to depict crime as largely exogenous to the political system and to focus on concrete ways to reform state structures to better combat it: modernization of justice systems, professionalization of police and judges, institutional streamlining, and other measures.[20] Little attention is given to the social and political causes (or ramifications) of the perceived crisis. Why is crime seen as a crisis in certain settings and not in others? What social forces drive this perception? Who defines acceptable solutions? Where lynchings, *mano dura*, and vigilantism are mentioned, it is only to underscore the urgency of justice-sector reforms such as those currently under way;[21] it is assumed, in other words, that the lynchings express discontent at precisely the deficiencies identified by international assistance programs. But how do we know that? In this book, I argue that these trends, rather than being a technical question of the maladministration of justice, are a bitter manifestation of the neglected intersection of law and politics as it plays out in situations of extreme polarization.

For this reason, lynchings speak to more than grim rites of death on the margins; they provide a window into the possibilities for civic life in a region struggling to weather dramatic social changes while preserving, for the most part, an economic and political system controlled by a very few. This is a story of fragmented solidarities, of identities and institutions under assault and enduring values that rise in violence in response to specific perceptions of power and powerlessness. It is a story told, in these pages, through lynchings, yet also spoken—very differently—through attacks on foreign banks and government institutions in Argentine riots (Auyero 2001); witch burning in the "new" South Africa (Comaroff and Comaroff 1999); ethnic cleansing abetted by state inaction in India (Varshney 2002); and other bottom-up eruptions of anger at historic inequities. This book is about lynchings, but it is also about the contentious politics of community belonging and control in settings of institutionalized mistrust, and about the meanings of justice and security in the increasingly polarized world that is characteristic of our times.

The Commonsense Consensus on Lynchings

Most Latin Americans today can recount a tale or two of lynchings or social cleansing, whether culled from rumors, reports in the mass media, or firsthand experience. The region, of course, has a long history of behind-the-scenes extralegal "justice," and many assume today's lynchings are simply the latest wrinkle in this long and lamentable tale. Perhaps as a result, very little scholarly attention has been focused specifically on these incidents: explanations for the phenomenon may appear obvious to many observers. After all, it is no secret that in recent years criminal violence has skyrocketed in such countries as El Salvador, Guatemala, Mexico, Colombia, Venezuela, and others; it is also common knowledge that in these and other contexts, state judicial systems are notoriously weak and unable to enforce the law across vast swaths of the national territory. (For a particularly convincing and influential exposition of this problem, see O'Donnell 1993.) In this context, lynchings are assumed to be an indication of citizens' desperation at an appalling situation: confronted with widespread crime and woefully inefficient state justice systems in regimes crippled by legacies of authoritarianism, some people take the law into their own hands; it may be unseemly, but ultimately, it is unsurprising. As William Prillaman writes, "The void created by weak, inefficient and inaccessible courts has been filled by a combination of mob action, vigilante justice, and law-and-order politicians tapping public frustration and exposing some of the more base impulses of society" (2000: 172). Though the human tragedy inherent in these executions should be immediately apparent, they might seem to challenge few of our assumptions about life in what Guillermo O'Donnell (1993) has called the "brown areas."

Everyday citizens echo this view, offering a commonsense explanation for the phenomenon: in Guatemala, for example, virtually everyone told me lynchings happen because crime is out of control and the justice system is at a standstill. Faced with the immediacy of the problem and the inadequacy of the state's solution, the story goes, communities are forced to take the matter into their own hands. This position resonates in the words of government officials and educated residents of the capital as well as those of citizens of the marginal communities where lynchings have occurred.

A *ladino* salesman from a lower-middle class area of Guatemala City articulated this perspective well:

Lynchings . . . are savagery. But they're an understandable savagery [*Los linchamientos . . . son una salvajada. Pero es una salvajada comprensible*]. A while ago in the neighborhood [*colonia*] where I live, [the residents] caught a thief, they beat him up, then let him go again and hunted him down, like a sport, and beat him up again, then let him go again, and they'd caught him again a third time when the police showed up. The police said, "What did he steal? Where is it? Listen gentlemen, you all can be sent to jail for this, the man doesn't have anything on him." "But we caught him inside one of the houses." "Which house?" "That one, it's empty." "Then there's no plaintiff [*parte pidiente*], no no no. Look, next time you find a thief around here, just kill him at once" [*Miren, si alguna vez encuentran otro ladrón por acá, mátenlo de una vez*]. It has a certain logic, no? Now, imagine, if you live in [the rural and primarily indigenous department of] Totonicapán, where there's a tiny little station of a few police who basically just patrol up and down the highway. Someone rapes one of your daughters. You know who it was. You know you don't speak enough Spanish to . . . be able to express yourself sufficiently before a judge, and you know that a trial could take years and lots of money. See what I mean? Lynchings are an understandable disgrace. They're deplorable, but understandable.

Former Guatemalan President Alfonso Portillo, in an interview with the journalist José Zepeda, explained it thus: "The people are desperate because they see that there are rapists, that there are robbers, that there are murderers, and that the police come, they take them to court and then two weeks or a month later they're released for lack of evidence. So this desperation, this anguish in the people is making them take these measures."[22] A Mayan peasant from Chimaltenango described the phenomenon to me in similar terms: "Lynchings . . . are an action that the people take when they know who it is, and that person steals, steals, steals, or kills, kills, kills, and the police don't do anything, so in the end the community explodes." And the executive director of CACIF (Comité Coordinador de Asociaciones Agrícolas, Comerciales,

Industriales y Financieras), the country's powerful private-sector coalition of agricultural, commercial, industrial, and financial leaders, told me, "A culture of violence sown by thirty-six years of armed conflict, a very weak, very fragile judicial structure, and a vacuum of power: it's a recipe for the lynch law."

Others, frequently alluding to the concentration of lynchings in remote areas—and particularly among deeply impoverished indigenous communities—tend to regard lynchings as something of a vestigial throwback to the premodern period. This argument is offered by those who decry lynchings, seeking to blame them on "backwardness" (often, but not always, by invoking unambiguously racist discourses about indigenous cultures and peoples), but it is also put forward by apologists for lynchings, who would justify them as an element of local tradition or the time-honored practice of "frontier justice." In Guatemala, for example, newspaper columnists have described lynchings as an "ancestral inheritance" tracing back to ancient Mayan traditions.[23] And in Mexico, in response to a 2001 lynching in Mexico City, Mayor Andrés Manuel López Obrador declared, "This is the Mexico that never ends, that remains alive in its traditions and customs, above all in small towns and communities; and with the beliefs of the people, it's better not to interfere" (*con las creencias del pueblo, más vale no meterse*).[24]

A related, though perhaps more sophisticated, argument blames the state for its failure to provide an adequately functioning legal system in such communities, citing the monopoly on the legitimate use of violence as a basic precondition for the modern state and suggesting that its absence here reflects not indigenous barbarism but state failure. The problem, in other words, is that these communities lack access to justice. In Guatemala, the administration of Alvaro Arzú (1996–2000), for example, responded to the lynchings as primarily indicative of an absence of state institutions in the areas where these incidents have been concentrated.[25] The chief of the United Nations Development Programme noted in 2002 that "the lack of presence of the justice system and of all other state institutions in ample rural areas is a decisive influence" in the phenomenon of lynchings (Montoya 2002). Ultimately, whether one blames indigenous communities for their savagery or the state for its exclusion of the poor and underprivileged, the answer is the same: bring in the law, for these territories exist outside it. Lynchings are assumed to be a vestige from an incomplete process of assimilation (if one adopts the cultural view) or state formation (if one takes the position that "access to law" is the problem).

If one accepts these "obvious" explanations, the "obvious" answer lies in improving—and extending—the reach of the law: hence the proposals to counter the lynchings by constructing new courts in rural areas, by incorporating new forms of dispute resolution into the formal legal system, or by improving the delivery of legal services to the non-Spanish-speaking population through the use of interpreters. On one level, such changes should of course be welcomed: they should bolster the effectiveness of the state's justice system, and this is undeniably important. Were state justice systems effective, lynch mobs would likely lack motivation to mobilize, and *mano dura* politicians would be without a platform; clearly and indisputably, these eruptions underscore the need for real reform of state structures.

But on another level, as Yves Dezalay and Bryant Garth (2002) remind us, the contemporary enthusiasm for judicial reform risks repeating the mistakes of the law and development movement of the 1960s and 1970s, when scholars and activists rushed to "modernize" developing countries' legal systems by exporting liberal legal models from the United States to Africa, Asia, and Latin America. Although the law-and-development movement is today largely considered to have been a failure (Trubek and Galanter 1974), one of its most important lessons was the need to study law in its social context—to understand the law's relation to social movements and political struggles, as well as its embeddedness in other structures of power dissymmetry in society. And it is in this regard that I suggest lynchings deserve closer attention. Drawing on such an approach, I argue that the commonsense consensus on lynchings misunderstands these acts in at least three ways: lynchings are not about crime; lynchings are not premodern; and the "answer" to lynchings (inasmuch as I have one) is not to apply law to this lawlessness, but to understand the lynchings themselves as profoundly political commentaries on the distribution of power and resources in these deeply unequal societies.

Lynchings Are Not about Crime

Lynchings are not about crime; at least, they are not *only* about crime. Today's lynchings occur in the context of widespread fear of crime and a pervasive sense that the authorities' response to crime has been unsatisfactory; without either of these conditions, there would quite likely be no lynchings. These incidents would not occur if a legitimate state with institutions of justice capable of responding to crime were present.

Yet such a system has probably never existed in Guatemala; lynchings are only a recent occurrence. Many suggest, then, that the contemporary crime wave has made the state's long-standing inadequacies all the more apparent; recent increases in crime, therefore, explain the rise in lynchings.

I disagree. Lynchings, I suggest, are more a reaction to fear and insecurity than they are to crime per se. Certainly, repeated incidents of criminal activity, or particularly brutal criminal acts, engender fear and disorder in affected communities, and contemporary events suggest that crime may be the most powerful of potential catalysts for mob "justice." Yet it is important to disarticulate widespread social anxiety from crime itself. The tenor of communities' responses to crime should not be expected to rise and fall in direct response to the gravity and frequency of actual criminal acts; it is a reflection of fear—an eminently social product—more than it is of crime itself. Though the two are often related and frequently conflated, they are not the same.

First of all, the lynchings do not occur in the areas where crime is at its worst. In Guatemala, although government figures on crime are unreliable, the problem is generally considered to be most severe in the port areas of Izabal and Escuintla and in the capital city itself (Centro de Investigaciones Económicas Nacionales [CIEN] 1999); lynchings, on the other hand, are concentrated in the western highlands. And although the poor functioning of the justice system is indisputable, there is no reason to believe that in the areas where lynchings do not occur, crimes are being dealt with through state mechanisms. State failure is a necessary component in the volatile cocktail that explodes in lynchings, but this alone is not enough to explain their present eruption; as corrupt and woefully inefficient as the formal legal system may be, it has never functioned any better for most rural residents.[26] The state's present-day failure to control crime, then, cannot explain the recent rise in lynchings.

Second, the crimes that contribute to the fear expressed in lynchings often do not correspond to the offenses allegedly committed by the person(s) actually lynched. When discussing the "crime problem" in their area, my respondents recounted in lavish detail spectacular crimes perpetrated with atrocious savagery and unrelenting regularity. Yet most of those lynched were accused, in fact, of relatively minor property crimes.[27] In the case of Mexico, Vilas (2001) notes a similar disproportionality between the gravity of the offense and the usually fatal outcome of the lynching; in Ecuador, Castillo Claudett (2000) finds that some

86 percent of those lynched were accused of theft, compared to 2.2 percent accused of murder, 3.2 percent accused of child rape, and 6.5 percent accused of assault. This frequent disparity suggests a need to disentangle explanations of lynchings from discrete incidents of real crime.

Not only political leaders, but also scholars and analysts, often read lynchings and other manifestations of *mano dura* as a reflection of crime and state performance, something we can measure through homicide rates and mitigate through reforms to the penal code. But crime is not—or not only—a technical problem. The perception of a crisis in crime is socially and politically mediated, and it has political consequences. Rather than "real crime rates" and "actual state performance," this trend is driven by fear of crime and lack of faith in public institutions. These are eminently social products, elusive to quantification and best understood through inquiries not into the technical nature of crime or its combat, but into popular perceptions of social life and attitudes on the ground.[28]

This is not to suggest that there is not a real and troubling increase in crime plaguing Latin America, or to dismiss citizens' fears as illusory; quite the contrary. I have spent too much time with people deeply distraught about crime to discount the urgency of their concerns. Nor is my analysis intended to underestimate the value of the many practical inquiries into ways to improve the functioning of state bureaucracies. My point here is to insist that we should not assume *mano dura* is somehow the "automatic" or "natural" response to crime, flaring up where crime levels cross some imaginary threshold of tolerability—and assume, therefore, that today's rule-of-law programs will, in and of themselves, prove capable of halting this trend. To understand the source of these manifestations, we must examine the larger assault on community and order from the point of view of those experiencing it.

As Richard Sparks et al. have written, crime "is something for which we seek explanation and accountability—and how we explain it and whom we blame may be highly symptomatic of who we are and how we organize our relations with others. In this respect, crime may be one of those forms of 'danger on the borders' which gives form to a community's sense of itself and its distinctiveness from others" (Sparks, Girling, and Loader 2001: 888). Moreover, concern about crime is often heightened at times when the community's sense of itself is under assault, as Erikson suggests in his famous (1966) study of crime "waves" in the Massachusetts Bay colony. Lynchings take place in communities in crisis—and that crisis is about more than crime.

Lynchings Are Not Premodern

The sociologist José de Souza Martins writes that lynchings in Brazil occur "on the 'razor's edge' of incomplete transition . . . the urban and political threshold of an unfinished intersection—where temporary and permanent migrants are gathered, and populations are barred in time and space from entering the modern world" (1991: 22). Yet though lynchings indisputably occur among populations largely excluded from the benefits of development and modernization—whether they are residents of isolated rural outposts or of the ramshackle shanty-towns that ring the region's major cities—we should be careful about describing these people as somehow trapped outside modernity. In fact, quite the contrary is true: the communities in which lynchings occur are fully inserted into the globalized political economy of late modernity—and what's more, it is precisely this insertion that causes the social dislocations of which lynchings are a particularly painful indicator. Rather than a remnant of traditional practices, lynchings are evidence of their erosion.[29]

In Guatemala, there is no evidence to suggest that lynchings have their roots in traditional mechanisms of indigenous justice. Lynchings are overwhelmingly concentrated in the western highlands,[30] where there is a well-documented history of Maya traditional justice (known locally as *justicia consuetudinaria, justicia Maya,* or *usos y costumbres*) by which communities resolve conflicts through informal practices outside the state legal system.[31] Though specific practices vary from group to group (the Guatemalan Maya population is comprised of some twenty-one different ethnolinguistic groups), in general the tradition revolves around restitution rather than retribution and communal consensus-building rather than adherence to legal code (see Defensoría Maya 1999; Yrigoyen Fajardo 1999; Coordinación de Organizaciones del Pueblo Maya de Guatemala [COPMAGUA] 2000). Maya have practiced forms of traditional justice for well over five hundred years, but lynchings did not occur in any regular fashion until the 1990s. Were such practices part of traditional Maya justice, they surely would have surfaced earlier.

Moreover, a significant number of lynchings have occurred in urban or semiurban areas where the state institutions *are* present (at least physically). An internal study of lynchings by MINUGUA found that more than half of the incidents investigated (58 percent) occurred in municipalities that had a justice of the peace (*juzgado de paz*); in somewhat less than half (40 percent) there was a police substation; and in total, 69 percent of the lynchings occurred in areas where some form of state authority was present.[32] Many lynchings have occurred in areas with full police presence, with a court open and ready to receive cases; and many others have occurred where a mob forcibly enters a police station to remove the criminal from police custody. These incidents have often been accompanied by clear reactions *against* the authorities, including the destruction of municipal property and police vehicles; judges and police officers have themselves been lynched. So where the state and its law are present, they have failed to solve the problem: at its core, lynchings are a problem of the legitimacy, not the presence, of law. Indeed, they are a commentary on that law and the social order it upholds; the exclusion of which they speak is embedded within it, not lurking somewhere beyond its gaze. As Daniel Goldstein writes of lynchings in Cochabamba, Bolivia, "Through such violent practices, the politically marginalized find an avenue for the communication of grievances against the inadequacies of the state's official legal order, while at the same time deploying the rhetoric of justice and law to police their communities" (2003: 23).

The Answer Is Not More Law

Among the lessons learned from the failure of the law-and-development movement, Yves Dezalay and Bryant Garth tell us, was that "law cannot be considered merely a matter of technology to be acquired off the shelf as the best or most efficient practice" (2002: 5). Yet such an off-the-shelf approach to law often seems to underlie contemporary judicial reform and rule-of-law programs. Though a strong and predictable legal framework (particularly as regards property rights) is the bedrock for the private investment and economic growth necessary to transform impoverished societies, a selective strengthening of certain legal mechanisms is not the same as ensuring "justice for all." To suggest that the solution to the widespread exclusion of marginalized populations is to grant them access to the institutions of state law — the very institutions that, in lynchings, they often attack (quite literally, with fists and feet and torches)—while at the same time reducing state spending for social policies and limiting the opportunities for political mobilization, is to propose a law-centered vision of social change that is entirely out of step with political reality.

This is, upon closer inspection, a vision that coincides neatly with the same neoliberal vision of governance espoused by the very lending institutions that often bankroll rule-of-law reforms. This is a vision in which problems such as poverty and social exclusion are to be resolved through market mechanisms, not redressed by redistributive policy. The formal legal system remains available to redress egregious wrongs, of course; but it is not intended, nor even empowered, to promote far-reaching social reform. Individual disputants can and do come forward with rights claims, but in the absence of other forms of political mobilization, litigation itself is ill equipped to achieve far-reaching social change (Scheingold 1974; Epp 1996). So although some Latin American jurists have applauded the rising protagonism of the courts in their countries (Jorge Correa Sutil, for example, touts the trend as the first sign of "modernization" [1998: 98]), others suggest that this law-centered vision of social justice, sometimes called "the judicialization of politics," only thinly conceals the failure or abdication of other institutions charged with important democratic functions.

Boaventura de Sousa Santos argues, for example, that the legitimacy of political leaders as reliable representatives of the popular will has been eroded by increasing awareness of powerful corporate influences, corruption scandals, and the like; with the welfare state lying in ruins, fewer and fewer everyday citizens see the executive or legislative branches of government as truly responsive to their needs.

The downsizing of the welfare administrative sector [has led] to the upsizing of the judicial system. . . . [But] by becoming more active in the area of administrative law and the protection of rights, courts contribute to diffusing the conflict that may arise in the process of dismantling the welfare state. The judicial system thus injects legitimacy into the democratic social pact of a state enfeebled by the erosion of the conditions that had hitherto sustained it. This judicialization of politics is not without problems: caught in the dilemma of having all the independence to act but no powers to enforce, the promise of court activism may soon prove to exceed, by far, its delivery. When that occurs—if it occurs—courts will cease to be part of the solution to become precisely part of the problem. (Santos 2000: 268–69)

Enhancing the efficiency of the courts while reducing the scope of state involvement in other aspects of social justice thus promotes a vision of law unlikely to confer more meaningful benefits on marginalized communities. Lynchers do not clamor for the vindication of their individual rights through the resolution of discrete criminal cases. What they seek is a broader transformation of their world, a fairer system in which the marginalized have a voice. This is not a call for more law, but a cry for justice. For in mimicking the state's law, lynchings denounce it; they clamor for order but deliberately subvert that order, which is premised on their exclusion. In their defiance they reveal the yawning gaps between the promise and reality of democracy in these deeply divided societies and the inability of law—*any* law—to bridge a chasm so wide.

Guatemala as a Research Site

I first became intrigued by this topic because of my long-term interest in human rights and democracy in Guatemala; indeed, although I posit a broad argument in these pages, Guatemala remains at the core of this work. For better and for worse, Guatemala is simply the best place to study lynchings, for two main reasons: first, the sheer frequency of these acts far outpaces that found in other settings; and second, the organized presence (and assiduous data-gathering) of the U.N. mission, which operated in the country from 1994 to 2004, enabled the documentation and verification of many incidents to a far greater extent than has been accomplished anywhere else in the Americas. My personal involvement in human rights in Guatemala made these topics more accessible to me in this context than they would be elsewhere. As readers will no doubt imagine, it is not easy to carry out research on these illegal and violent phenomena: contacts must be carefully cultivated; respondents are often reluctant to speak; conducting the research requires a deep sensitivity to local variations of things such as word usage (when discussing illegal phenomena about which they may be uncomfortable, respondents often resort to more oblique references and terminology); knowledge of political context and historical background is imperative (particularly in the postwar context, respondents' testimonies are colored by what they have experienced, often in ways they do not always consciously enumerate); and other factors. Despite my familiarity with the Guatemalan case, I cannot claim to have always mastered every subtlety, but my experiences there convinced me that to unravel these semiclandestine practices and somewhat-unspoken attitudes, it would be more fruitful to conduct an in-depth case study of a context I knew well than to attempt a broad multinational data-gathering exercise, which by virtue of necessity would sacrifice depth for breadth.

Furthermore, Guatemala's recent history makes that country particularly suited for a case study of this topic. Although the levels of past and present violence make the country something of an extreme, the patterns that undergird the Guatemalan experience of violence are not atypical for the region as a whole; they are simply more naked examples of trends that also occur elsewhere. During the long authoritarian period in Guatemala, the military dominated civilian institutions of justice and social control, leaving them woefully underprepared to assume the challenges of maintaining order at war's end. The system still lacks many basic capacities necessary for the successful functioning of an independent judiciary. At the same time, the complicity of the state in egregious human rights violations—and the ongoing unwillingness of the justice system to recognize and render judgment on state (and nonstate) actors guilty of these crimes—reinforce the extremely low legitimacy of the state, and most particularly its legal system. The state thus lacks both the moral authority and the institutional capacity to uphold the rule of law. Not surprisingly, rates of common crime have soared in recent years, and many observers place Guatemala (and neighboring El Salvador) among the most violent countries in the world, with homicide rates exceeding those of the United States—a country not exactly touted for its low crime rates—by as much as 1,500 percent (Buvinic, Morrison, and Shifter 1999).[33] In the context of such widespread cynicism about the state and the alarming rise of crime in the postwar era, *mano dura* proliferates in both the formal (on-the-books) and informal (popularly administered social sanctions) incarnations of the law. Formally, support for such measures as the expanded use of the death penalty, the restriction of rights to appeal, and the militarization of domestic policing has risen; informally, practices of *justicia a mano propia* (taking justice into one's own hands) have become common and are, in most contexts, widely tolerated. In this sense, in ways that are deeply painful for the Guatemalan people, their country constitutes perhaps the ideal laboratory for the study of what Guillermo O'Donnell (1999) has called the "(un)rule of law." The weakness and illegitimacy of the state, paired with the high levels of contemporary violence, make the country perhaps the best place in the Americas to investigate "self-help" remedies in the shadow of the law.

So, this book is very much a story about the Guatemalan experience. Its pages are peppered with the words and insights of Guatemalans, most of whom I cannot name but without whose help I could never have begun to write. It tells a particularly tragic story about recent Guatemalan history. But, I insist, this is not *only* a story about Guatemala—or even only about Latin America. Indeed, ongoing debates about the importance of preserving civil liberties or protecting due-process rights in the post-9/11 United States show that perceived tensions between security and justice are not unique to the developing world; now, more than ever, it is important for us to reexamine the recent history of counterterrorist excesses in Latin America (many of them carried out under the advisorship of U.S. government forces) and the legacies they have left for contemporary criminal justice and governance concerns. Though important differences remain between the United States and Latin America, recent years have witnessed an apparent convergence in penal policies across the Americas—and indeed around the globe. Popular injustice in the name of security and the widespread depoliticization of crime are among the hallmarks of neoliberal governance in our insecure world, increasingly representative of a new global reality perhaps most starkly sketched in settings of extreme marginality (such as rural Guatemala), but certainly not unique to these areas.

There are problems, no doubt, in letting any one country serve as our window on this global phenomenon; I am not unaware of these shortcomings. But without some initial attempts to illuminate these phenomena, based as they admittedly are on incomplete, partial information gleaned from glimpses of a very complex and contentious reality, we will never begin to understand this very important pattern of "justice" that is, itself, criminal. It is my fervent hope that this book might spark further debate about these issues and practices in this region and others, and that scholars, observers, activists, and justice practitioners might read it and come forward to comment on and contest the ways the initial postulates I put forth here explain, and undoubtedly also fail to explain, the realities in the contexts they know best.

Researching Popular Injustice

In part, shortcomings in existing understandings of *mano dura* stem from something of an epistemological blind spot. The academic literature on democratization is dominated by top-down approaches to the study of legal and political institutions. In policy circles, too, many inquiries into institutional functioning expose problems and propose solutions—and indeed, thanks to the support of international institutions, especially the World Bank and USAID, and the efforts of courageous justice-sector reformers in Guatemala and beyond, many of these solutions are being implemented today—but most note that it will, of course, take time before such reforms produce a democratic culture grounded in institutional trust and respect for the rule of law. The assumption here is that improved institutional efficiency and output will eventually lead to citizen confidence and a culture of legality—a sort of trickle-down democracy, so to speak.[34] Yet without specific research on the intangibles of trust, legitimacy, and law, we cannot know how such reforms are perceived or experienced. Clearly, if increasing numbers of Latin Americans are employing the very institutions of liberal democracy to elect authoritarian wolves in democratic sheep's clothing, then we must question the inherent transformative power of these structures and ask, instead, what is happening on the ground beneath these vaunted institutions. "Bottom-up" inquiries into the meaning of democracy in lived experience are best positioned to offer useful insights in this regard, and as a methodology, ethnography seems especially apt for getting at such perspectives.[35]

Of course, this blind spot is easy to criticize but hard to avoid: conducting research on lynchings and other aspects of *mano dura* presents serious methodological challenges. First, information about the actual incidence of lynchings or other incidents of semiclandestine "crime control" is hard to come by, and where it exists, it is often drawn from media reports that are unreliable at best. If anything, the available numbers are likely to understate the phenomenon: of the small number of cases I was able to personally verify, few were reported in the national media, and virtually none received the detailed investigative treatment necessary to get to the bottom of what took place. This lack of comprehensive figures goes hand in hand with a deeper problem: eyewitnesses' reluctance to speak. Although in some cases this stems from the illegality of the events in question (and the ambiguity about individual informants' potential responsibility for them), in others it is a direct result of death threats issued by those instigating the lynchings against anyone who would divulge information about them. Lastly, attempts to collect firsthand information about lynchings can compromise the personal security of the researcher because of such threats, and also, perhaps even more significantly, because most of these acts occur in the context of extreme social marginality, in settings where everyday violence often runs rampant; as the sociologist Carlos Vilas (2001) has put it, lynchings are certainly not "lightning striking on a sunny day."

It was partly because I myself was so daunted by these challenges that I initially undertook to gather opinions about crime, rather than eyewitness testimony about lynchings. I have been conducting fieldwork on issues of justice and human rights in Guatemala since 1996, spending many summers there and visiting the country for various lengths of time during the academic year as well. In initial research trips in 1996, 1997, and 1998, and then much more extensively in 1999 and again in 2000, I conducted interviews with over one hundred respondents, specifically on the theme of crime, democracy, and human rights. These interviews were mostly unstructured, relatively informal discussions, and I aimed to cast my net as broadly as possible in order to ensure representation of a wide range of sectors in my sample. Although the majority of the interviews were conducted in the capital, I also traveled to rural areas in eastern and western Guatemala and interviewed many people in the capital who were themselves from other departments. And I interviewed people from all walks of life: leading public figures, such as the executive director of the business association CACIF, to a former president of the republic to several sitting congresspersons; activists in various civil society groups concerned with issues of crime, human rights, and justice; and teachers, factory workers, campesinos, and housewives. In most cases, I made audiotapes of these interviews, although a significant number of respondents specifically asked not to be recorded and others expressed hesitance or discomfort upon seeing my tape recorder; in these cases I did not record the discussions but took careful field notes. Also, in some cases, I conducted group interviews, or focus group discussions; these were often necessary where circumstances (such as the physical space in which the interview was being conducted) made private discussions difficult; in addition, some interviewees expressed a preference for having family or friends with them during the interview. These collective discussions had not been part of my original research design, but they often opened a useful forum in which participants sometimes encouraged one another on in their stories, leading to revelations that might not have emerged in one-on-one interviews.[36]

I was initially surprised by how eager most respondents were to talk about crime, once I framed the topic as such. When introducing myself, I usually explained that I wanted to speak to them about *la violencia*, a general term that just means "violence" but that is often understood to refer to the country's armed conflict. If they didn't know me, this ambiguity often made respondents visibly uncomfortable; a frequent response was, "Which violence are you talking about?" or, more bluntly, "Is this political?" But once I specifically stated that I was primarily interested in their thoughts about *postwar* violence, most let their guard down, perceiving postwar crime to be an apolitical topic and thus something that was "safe" to talk about. In fact, this clarification often provoked a gush of relief and/or gratitude. As one woman told me at the conclusion of our conversation, "Thank God someone is doing a study of this, because it's horrible, what we're living is horrible. But it sometimes seems like foreigners are so interested in the violence that went before, like they don't notice we're getting killed here, today. Thank you so much for doing this study."

In fact, in the context of our conversations, many of which ended up being quite extensive and were continued over the course of secondary interviews, a large number of respondents ended up sharing insights and experiences that were extremely political. Most Guatemalans are abundantly aware that today's violence is linked to that of the past, so any serious discussion of contemporary crime inevitably touches on issues of accountability for wartime atrocities. Some respondents, once they got talking, were quick to make these connections. Others recognized when they turned this corner in the conversation by asking me to turn off the tape recorder, looking around before speaking, or sending children out of the room. Many used the passive voice and deliberately vague language to refer to the guerrillas or to the army when making statements about wartime violence, thus enabling them to talk about the war yet avoid the controversial step of attributing blame to one side or the other. Also difficult to decipher were terms such as the politically neutral *aquellos* (them), without specifying to whom the article referred, or *los grupos armados* (the armed groups), an ambiguous term that could mean either party. The use of more politically charged terms such as *delincuentes* (criminals) or *subversivos* (subversives) to refer to the guerrillas was often a tip-off to the speaker's political sympathies, although not always, and occasionally speakers used such language even as they expressed sympathy for such groups, revealing the extent to which language itself—even the language of resistance—was colonized during periods of state terror.[37] (General Efraín Ríos Montt, who presided over the country at the height of its genocide, at one point prohibited the press from using not only the word "guerrilla" itself, but also the names of the individual insurgent organizations, allowing only "terrorists," "subversives," and "delinquent bands" as appropriate terminology [Black 1984: 126].) In this charged climate, I also had to monitor my own language in the interviews so as not to give my respondents the impression that I favored one side or the other and thus risk coloring their responses. In some interviews, deliberate avoidance of controversial words on both my and my respondent's part turned some (in a few cases, all) of the conversation into an uncomfortable and excessively polite dance around an unspecified subject neither party would state.

Other interviews made me uncomfortable for quite a different reason. The deeply disturbing accounts of lived violence that so many respondents freely shared with me often left me feeling small and powerless, and sometimes afraid. From my experiences doing human rights work in Guatemala, I was accustomed to taking testimony about wartime atrocities, but I never expected to hear so many horror stories about the everyday experiences of life in postwar Guatemala. The topic touched a nerve. Many interviewees were tearful, others angry. I was unprepared to deal with the acuteness of many respondents' pain, or with the hope that many expressed that through my study I personally might find some solution to the contemporary crime problem. I tried to lend them the only support I could, by listening to their stories; after I carefully and regretfully explained that I didn't think the results of my work would be likely to point the way to a new crime policy for the Guatemalan government, one woman whose son had been kidnapped said, "Well, at least you came and asked about what happened to me. Because here, since we can't trust the police, when something like this happens, there is no one to tell. Except for your family, of course, but no entity, no organization—no one cares." The acuteness of that feeling— of a deeply tragic personal loss that was not valued by the state or society as a whole—was deeper and more frequent than I had imagined.

Though my initial snowball sample yielded a wealth of information and perspectives, it failed to provide me with much concrete insight into the phenomenon of lynchings. People were generally quite willing, even eager, to talk about lynchings that had happened elsewhere in the country, but the residents of communities where such incidents had occurred were, quite understandably, reluctant to share their stories with a stranger. Local leaders or human rights activists would talk, but not ordinary citizens, and most were hesitant to refer me to other potential informants: the snowball simply stopped rolling, often quite abruptly. In one rural municipality several hours' drive from the capital, for example, I interviewed the local human rights procurator about some lynchings that had occurred nearby. He was very helpful and forthcoming, but when at the conclusion of our interview I expressed interest in talking to some residents of the community, he became visibly uncomfortable, his expression darkened, and he warned me that for my own safety I should get back in my car and leave at once, without saying a word of this to anyone else. (I hastily obeyed.)

Indeed, among indigenous survivors of state violence in the highlands and *ladino* residents of the capital alike, the discussions I had were sometimes extraordinarily delicate in ways characteristic of postconflict settings—and particularly of settings such as Guatemala, where military intelligence agents have at times posed as survey takers to gather information about civilians that sometimes led to their later victimization. Though some researchers have surmounted local suspicions by maintaining a sustained presence in a specific locality, allowing villagers to gradually accept and trust them (see, for example, Manz 2004; Green 1999; Falla 1992), my research design relied on a sample larger than a single community. (Not only would establishing myself in a specific community and waiting for a lynching to occur have constituted a dubious ethical proposition, it would also likely have yielded data of questionable generalizability—useful in understanding the dynamics of a single case, undoubtedly, but I sought a wider lens on the phenomenon.)

Fortunately, I was able to collaborate with a Guatemalan human rights group organizing in highland communities affected by wartime violence.[38] Colleagues from this organization contacted members of several Mayan communities in El Quiché—some where lynchings had occurred and some where they had not—and invited them to speak to me at meetings they arranged in advance. Thanks to this support, I was able to interview more than fifty residents of several rural villages in El Quiché, many of them eyewitnesses to unspeakable atrocities during the war *and* to lynchings in the contemporary period. Though the majority of these interviews were conducted in Spanish, seven or eight were conducted in K'iche', with the aid of an interpreter. Given the topic of the interviews, for security reasons the group advised me to hold these interviews in the municipal centers of Chichicastenango and Santa Cruz del Quiché, rather than in the rural hamlets where the participants resided; thanks to a grant from the Human Rights Center at the University of California, Berkeley, I was able to cover the costs of respondents' bus fare and meals, enabling them to make the trip to meet me (although many still had to walk for hours to reach the nearest highway to take the bus and missed valuable work time in order to share their stories with me, a sacrifice for which I will be forever grateful.) I was also able to observe some of the group's meetings, although because the proceedings were mainly in K'iche', I relied on group members as interpreters.

Of course, it is impossible to discount the effect that my partnership with this organization may have had on the information I obtained.

I was only able to interview those who shared some affinity with this human rights organization. Not surprisingly, there were no army supporters among the group (though there were several former members of the paramilitary civil patrols). Clearly, it was a self-selected sample and not a random cross-section of highland residents.[39] At the same time, I was shocked how many of these respondents expressed unequivocal support for lynchings, despite the organization's open condemnation of such views (and even, at times, the interventions of its leaders to that effect in these conversations). If my involvement with this organization skewed the sample, it undoubtedly did so by yielding respondents *less* likely than the average resident to support lynchings. I am confident that if I found significant support for lynchings even among this group, this sentiment must be much more pronounced among the population as a whole.

Despite the facilitating influence of the human rights group, signs of fear and suspicion still cropped up in some conversations. Inevitably, perhaps, there were those who shifted uncomfortably in their seats when I asked certain questions; at times, even inquiries that seemed harmless or inconsequential to me provoked visible discomfort and reluctance on the part of some respondents. This was true among respondents in all my various research settings, including middle-class *ladinos* in the relative comfort of the capital city, but it was accentuated among those with direct personal experience of state repression. Although many of my informants were disarmingly frank and open, some spent much of the interview scanning my face to read my reactions (or the opposite: avoiding my gaze) and gave the impression that if I asked the wrong question or pushed too far in my inquiries, they might simply get up and leave. (I had, of course, assured everyone I interviewed that they were free to do so at any point.) Because of this, and, perhaps more important, because I was aware that the information I sought was sensitive and that providing it could have very real consequences in terms of respondents' safety, I did not push anyone to provide information he or she did not volunteer, nor did I try to pin them down to specific yes-or-no responses on aspects they preferred to leave ambiguous. I did not ask the exact same questions of everyone I met; and I did not request or compile biographic data on respondents.[40]

Clearly, this has consequences in terms of the data I can provide. I cannot, for example, quantify what percentage of respondents agreed with lynchings, or even how many had witnessed one, because few made unequivocal "yes" or "no" statements in this regard. I also cannot situate each respondent in terms of age, occupation, community of origin, or other background characteristics, although I provide this information in cases where I do have it. Some readers may find the ambiguities embedded in this data frustrating, but I suspect this research would not have been possible had I attempted to close those spaces that many respondents deliberately left open. These are the inherent challenges of social science research in politically contentious settings, where petty details of personal identity have made a life-or-death difference in the recent experience of many respondents. This book, like any research project, is a product of methodological compromises, many of them made to protect my own safety as well as that of my informants;[41] researching it has been a fascinating, and at times frightening, adventure. The more people I spoke to, the more stories I heard, the more nights I lay awake trying to wrap my mind around how these painful personal testimonies related to "the literature," the more convinced I became of the need to interrogate concepts such as democracy, human rights, and the rule of law, from a bottom-up perspective. But the longer I tried to do this research, the more convinced I also became of the inadequacy of my own efforts. Although there is no substitute for this kind of firsthand field research in analyzing such complex, confounding, and even contradictory phenomena, the limitations and constraints under which it must necessarily be conducted should be kept in mind by the reader.

Analyzing Popular Injustice

At this point, a brief foreshadowing of what lies ahead may help readers identify some of the central plotlines in this story.

In chapter 2, I explore the current violence in Guatemala both as a reflection of the country's extremely unequal social structures and as an outgrowth of the authoritarian period. During the series of military dictatorships that governed the country from the 1950s to the 1980s, the state's counterinsurgency machine set up a system of inverted legality, in which law enforcement became a deliberate exercise in terror and disorder, and everyday crime fighting overlapped with counterinsurgency as justification for the repressive state. Any discussion of contemporary developments can only be understood against this backdrop of profound mistrust.

In light of Guatemala's history, it may be tempting to ascribe contemporary trends to a culture of violence sown by decades of state-sponsored killing, but this underestimates the complexity of the phenomenon. *Mano dura* represents not a continuation of past practices or a reflection of some enduring element of political culture, but an attempt to import selected elements of dictatorship into an ostensibly democratic structure. Its appeal, in part, is a reflection of democracy's broken promises. More specifically, many respondents told me they supported such measures because concerns about human rights—the very ideas that most acknowledged were so important in breaking the deadlock of dictatorship—have become perversely twisted in the battle against crime. Although the human rights approach to crime parses out human suffering into complex categories—was it politically motivated? who pulled the trigger?—and treats cases differently depending on their strategic importance while insisting that everyone's rights matter, the *mano dura* response is seductive in its simplicity: crime is a reflection of moral decay, and no force should be spared in eliminating it from our midst.

There are practical and theoretical justifications for the selectivity of human rights groups' approaches to crime, but on the ground these policies mean that in the overwhelming majority of crimes (which are not politically motivated), mainstream human rights organizations will intervene only if the state, in detaining or prosecuting suspects, oversteps its bounds (as in cases of police brutality or capital punishment, for example). Explanations of these choices are often lost on grieving family members, who fail to understand why certain people's lives seem to matter more than others and in many cases express deep outrage that human rights groups should defend the rights of criminal suspects while remaining silent on the rights that were denied their victims. (This perception is not limited to Guatemala; see also Restrepo 2001 on Colombia; Caldeira 2000 on Brazil). This anger fuels allegations that human rights are "on the side of the criminals" and opens the door to politically motivated charges by the Right that the human rights provisions of the peace accords have effectively handcuffed the police and security forces, limiting their effectiveness in combating crime. Faced with such a situation, many Guatemalans endorse *mano dura* policies that roll back certain hard-won democratic rights—not because they reject democracy, but because they consider the erosion of security they have experienced under democratic rule to be a flaw that could be corrected by importing certain practices of the past into the present but placing them at the service of apolitical (i.e., purely crime-oriented) aims. Of course, crime fighting is itself inherently political, and these attempts to purchase security at the expense of rights represent a very real danger to democratic regimes, for reasons I explore in chapter 2 and then revisit in comparative perspective in chapter 6.

In chapter 3, I turn specifically to the question of lynchings, seeking to explain their postwar emergence as a legacy of terror tactics used by the state (and, to a much lesser extent, by the rebels as well) during the country's thirty-six-year civil war. In the Maya communities of the western highlands, the state's scorched-earth campaigns deliberately destroyed the social fabric, supplanting locally legitimate institutions with militarized alternatives that altered the very meaning of justice, community, and authority. Today, public executions and other violent rituals performed during wartime are reenacted in these communities—sometimes under the direct influence of former paramilitaries, but sometimes independent of such coercion. Although it is relatively easy to understand why forces linked to past violence might perpetuate such practices in the present and how communities might be forced to participate out of fear, it is this second category of lynchings—those that occur without paramilitary coercion—that are more sociologically interesting, more troubling, and less well understood. And although some histories of the highlands cast the Maya in the role of eternal victims, these lynchings reveal a more complex reality in which roles overlap and shift and yesterday's victims can become today's victimizers—not because of a repeating cycle of retributive violence, but because of the profound lack of the social capital that would allow communities to rebuild nonviolent practices.

Though human rights tragedies like the Guatemalan genocide are often quantified in terms of the number of dead or disappeared, this approach highlights the importance of sociological and anthropological inquiries into the effects of mass violence on the sometimes intangible but always critical institutions of collective life. For it is here—at the level of institutions uprooted, not of individual lives lost—that lynchings are born. They are testament to a devastating loss of trust. In the wake of genocide, many communities find it difficult to redefine collective norms through nonviolent means because language, dialogue, and shared understandings of the meaning and purpose of collective life have been decimated by the experience of intracommunity and even intrafamily violence. In *The Body in Pain* (1985), Elaine Scarry writes that torture destroys language itself, negating the ability of survivors to communicate with those who have not shared their experiences. In many postgenocidal Mayan communities, a related process occurs at the community level: it is the shared language of governance that has been destroyed, leaving in its wake only the blunt vocabulary of violence.

At the same time, however, lynchings reveal more than the devastation of war: how else can we understand their emergence in contexts where communities have not experienced massive state violence? In chapter 4 I explore some of the phenomenon's more subtle, but ultimately more generalizable, roots in the recent transformations of collective life occasioned not by militarization but by modernization. I suggest that lynchings reveal broader anxieties about change and disorder in deeply disempowered communities. In isolated rural hamlets or overpopulated urban slums, lynchings occur as a last resort when communities feel their very livelihood is under assault—by crime, certainly, but also by the ebb and flow of unreliable employment, the mounting pressures of an agrarian crisis, and the impersonal dictates of a transnational economy in which they have neither voice nor vote, despite a profound and growing sense of personal vulnerability. Add to this mix the concerns about generational differences, lifestyle choices, and, especially for indigenous communities, the perceived abandonment of traditional values, and the theft of a chicken is no longer simply that. In lynchings, communities in crisis seek to reassert boundaries through what is, to many, the only means of collective action left in a devastated toolkit.

It is a core contention of this book that lynchings and other elements of *mano dura* speak more to the character and quality of communal life than they do to the actual crime rate or to characteristics of the criminal justice system, strictly speaking. Just as Robert Putnam has famously argued that the vitality of democratic institutions lies in the ties among citizens that exist outside the institutions themselves, I suggest here that the effectiveness of the law, too, relies on the existence of social capital. The lynchings, therefore, reveal the absence not only of legitimate state institutions, but, more important, of horizontal ties of trust and tradition in deeply afflicted communities: without trust there can be no civil society.

The question of civil society is an important one, particularly for incipient democracies in the Latin American tradition. Most observers agree that the regimes of the region have adopted the formal framework of democracy—constitutions, courts, representative institutions in the executive and legislative branches—yet have failed to fulfill many of democracy's more transformative promises in the area of social justice and representative rule. Many theorists assumed that once the yoke of political repression had been removed, citizens would be free to organize themselves and reclaim these rights, transforming their societies from democratic in theory to democratic in practice. To be sure, this has occurred to some extent; there has been a much-celebrated flourishing of nongovernmental organizations (NGOs), religious groups, political associations, and other forms of collective citizen organization across the Americas (see, for example, Eckstein and Wickham-Crowley 2003). Yet, as I argue in chapter 5, lynchings and other eruptions of popular injustice suggest a need to reexamine the assumption that voluntary association, in and of itself, contains within it the virtuous kernel of democratic life. Under what circumstances is this true? Under what circumstances is civil society truly civil?

Often when political scientists find that expectations of liberal democratic theory map poorly onto the contemporary realities of a given context, they conclude that the country in question is not truly democratic and effectively demote it in considerations of democratic consolidation, whether by scoring it lower along a scale such as Freedom House's global survey or by applying a more ominous-sounding adjective qualifier.[42] But I suggest that these examples from Latin America should prompt us to question more fundamentally whether the liberal democratic project is compatible anywhere with the socioeconomic structures of mass exclusion that have been sharpened by recent economic trends. The much-celebrated "third wave" of democratization has been accompanied by a more diffuse wave of income and wealth polarization, which has had profound political effects. How significant is it that the poor are formally empowered to cast a ballot if most are too preoccupied with the immediate needs of satisfying subsistence to participate actively in politics? The contradictions between political inclusion and economic exclusion have become clearest in the countries of the global periphery, where more and more poor communities see their own marginalization as upheld by the very structures of democracy and more and more now turn to extralegal forms of collective action as resistance; but, I insist, these lessons should not be lost on more established democracies either.

In chapter 5, I also examine more conventional manifestations of civil society, exploring anticrime organizing in marginalized Mayan communities and among middle-class *ladinos* in the capital city. In the first case, I suggest that the lack of vertical bonds of trust and collaboration between Mayan communities and the state leads even those communities that have a high level of social capital to advocate "solutions" to crime that sidestep state involvement, such as the revitalization of traditional forms of customary law. Given the state's active involvement in the genocide that targeted precisely these communities, such suspicion is understandable, but without broader engagement with the state and its law, some communities' visions of reform may ultimately be shortsighted.

Among more powerful sectors of society with closer ties to the state, it is not surprising to see a different course of action on crime. In the second part of chapter 5, I discuss the anticrime efforts of organized groups in the capital, especially leading business associations, which are deeply concerned about crime. Even these sectors of society, despite their ability to bring organized political power to bear on state institutions, are so suspicious of these very institutions that they advocate policies to pare down their decision-making power. This suggests that not only the presence or absence of social capital, but also the existence of a legitimate and effective state with which civil society seeks engagement, is necessary to promote a vibrant, participatory democracy. Without it, civil society actors continue to join forces in advocating their collective interests, but measures such as *mano dura* gain ground, reducing the law to its repressive backbone. Violence, Hannah Arendt reminds us, is the failure of politics.

This brings to mind some reflections that should sound familiar to U.S. readers. In a time of sweeping changes to criminal justice institutions in the United States, of the dismantling of the welfare state and the criminalization of poverty, proponents of zero-tolerance policies in the United States and advocates of *mano dura* in Latin America have placed these two regions more on the same page than perhaps ever before. In chapter 6, I argue that the rise of penal populism across the Americas is in many ways a reflection of the contradictions of neoliberal policy: states must provide a stable climate for investment, which relies on political continuity and the reliable rule of law; yet such stability is difficult to reconcile with massive social exclusion without the exercise of widespread repression. As our societies become more unequal, preserving macroeconomic stability without resorting to overt, visible acts of repression means finding new ways to effectively control the poor. This is the genius of neoliberal penality: it imports elements of authoritarianism into ostensibly democratic structures, allowing the preservation of formal democratic structures while undercutting the truly transformative potential of citizenship rights.

Jonathan Simon (forthcoming) argues that the United States' war on terrorism has been structured in many ways by the preexisting war on crime. Though some critics have reacted with alarm to recent erosions (or erasures) of civil liberties, Simon reminds us that this form of governance through fear has long underpinned American society; terrorism merely introduces a new criminal "other" to be feared. In chapter 6, I argue that similar processes are underway in Latin America, but in reverse order: in Latin America, the war on terrorism, as it were, preceded the war on crime. The propaganda machines of authoritarian governments capitalized on fear of communist insurgencies to justify their iron rule, and today's democracies seek to deploy the same repressive structures against crime. And across the Americas, the new penality risks repeating errors of the past: specifically, it structures the world in terms of "us" and "them" and justifies the partial (or in some cases, complete) derogation of "their" rights in exchange for "our" security. Fear of terrorism led Latin Americans to consent to this transaction in the 1960s and 1970s; fear of crime leads many to return to it today.

But the success of this penality is built on two false assumptions: first, that we can reliably distinguish "them" from "us" (and therefore can adopt ever-looser definitions for "terrorism" or "crime," untroubled by the fact that these ensnare a disproportionately large number of dark-skinned young men and of individuals from specific religious or ethnic minorities in the criminal justice web); and second, that because there is a sharp distinction between "us" and "them," we can mete out ever-harsher treatment to "them" without any adverse consequences for "us." In the United States, we are told there is a bright future for security: ever-sharper scientific tools on the way to more reliably separate our societies into these two camps (including technologies that can examine DNA or scrutinize proto-criminal behavior to detect a threat before it happens); and an ever more invasive and aggressive state poised to strike more effectively at those we define as "other." And yet, in casting the net ever wider and turning the war within, we risk undermining the social fabric that forms the foundation of our democracy, trading diversity and tolerance for dread and fear. Thus we creep ever closer to a model of governance that is perhaps epitomized in the Latin American lynchings, themselves the ultimate expressions of "us" versus "them."

In the United States, of course, the task of policing this boundary is delegated to the state; lynchings and collective acts of vigilantism are largely a thing of the past, and most citizens recognize the state as the legitimate arbiter of order. In Latin America, the state's weakened legitimacy (and its low effectiveness, which makes prosecution unlikely) makes acts of vigilantism more attractive; but citizens also clamor for state enforcement in the form of zero tolerance. Though the means are different, the sentiments are strikingly similar.

I do not question any government's need to curtail terrorist violence, or for that matter to rein in violent crime; basic personal security and the right to life lie at the very core of citizenship rights, and states that cannot fulfill these most basic of compacts fail their peoples in the most profound of ways. But if this research teaches us anything, it should teach us the danger of structuring our societies along ever-sharper lines of exclusion and deploying collective resources to police these boundaries rather than to mitigate their effects. I therefore conclude this book with some reflections on the seductive but ultimately false opposition between human rights and security, arguing instead that the experience of nations such as Guatemala should remind us that there can be no purchasing security at the price of justice.

CHAPTER 2

Legacies of Terror in Postwar Guatemala

GUATEMALA IS A PHOTOGRAPHER'S PARADISE. Even a mediocre photographer like me has trouble taking a bad picture; the scenery is simply too sensational. Marked with majestic volcanoes, the skyline always makes a dramatic backdrop; the vegetation, thick and florid, lends color—hues so bright that they often seem to be false. And if one should ever be at a loss for subject matter, there is generally an abundant supply of adorable children who will smile for the camera the moment they spot it. Given such appealing raw material, it's hard to go wrong.

For the sociologist, however, Guatemala posits a more formidable challenge. The country's complexities are often difficult to grasp, much less describe in words. Guatemala is a country of contrasts, of at times spectacular dissonance; a country where currents of darkness, cruelty, and hunger, commingle with the irascible beauty of resistance, endurance, and strength in a broad river that sometimes descends into perilous rapids and sometimes, deceptively, appears placid. From the surface, it is hard to perceive the multiple undercurrents and easy to conduct a relatively simple sociology, one that would be the equivalent of my point-and-shoot photographic technique: of tyrants, soldiers, and a trembling population torn asunder by forces beyond its control, in which the advent of democracy saves the day.

Like the hasty snapshots I've taken out the windows of moving buses, this caricature captures some truth. Yet to truly understand the contrasts that make up Guatemala, one must steep oneself in the details. In this chapter, I scrutinize one aspect of this complicated, contradictory, often conflictive country. I aim to show that contemporary violence and counterviolence are legacies of authoritarian rule, but in complex and often unexplored ways. Although it may be tempting to view today's troubles as in some ways a return to the past, they are in fact testament to a new postwar challenge. The reinvention of democratic institutions is relatively simple, but their revitalization with legitimacy and efficacy is a far more subtle process, one whose importance is often alluded to in academic and policy writings on democratization but that has seldom been studied in its own right.

In this chapter, I argue that under authoritarianism, the institutionalized practices of state terror produced a functional inversion of the law in Guatemala, a system that justified (indeed, mandated) violence in the name of order and cast the formal law itself in a role of near irrelevance. In the postwar period, practices known as *mano dura* have prolonged this perverse marriage of violence and law, with devastating effects on democracy as a whole.

Guatemala's Human Geography

A Guatemalan friend once told me a joke about his country: When God was designing the landscape of Guatemala, he became impassioned, like the conductor of a great orchestra, and in his fits of inspiration he went too far. He sprinkled the countryside with so much natural beauty that Guatemala was unrivalled among nations, a virtual paradise on earth. Other countries' landscapes seemed paltry by comparison: a volcano here, a waterfall there, but nothing like Guatemala, the land of so many wonders. Recognizing his error, God decided to compensate when it came time to create the country's inhabitants. Instead of a peaceful people, possessed of a glorious, proud history, he etched Guatemala's human landscape with violence and grinding poverty, hunger and indifference, racism and war. In the end, the joke goes, the balance of beauty and butchery more or less evened out.

Many Guatemalans make similar jokes about their country's misfortunes; the depth of the disadvantage is often difficult to ignore. In many ways, Guatemala is a country of breathtaking precipices. Just as its landscape is studded by the silhouettes of proud volcanoes, their sharp sides sometimes seeming to rocket upward from the horizon at impossibly steep inclines, the country's human geography is marked by the almost incoherent coexistence of disparate social worlds connected by relations along a slope that cruelly approaches the vertical. Guatemala has the seventh highest degree of income inequality in the world, and the highest in Latin America (UNDP 2005);[1] in 1999, the World Bank estimated that the poorest quintile received only 1.9 percent of the country's total income (World Bank 1999). Some 83 percent of the population—and 90 percent of the indigenous population—lives in poverty (U.S. Department of State 2002)). And although most Guatemalans are poor, regardless of their ethnicity, the socioeconomic exclusion of the country's indigenous—mostly Mayan[2]—majority by the *ladino* minority has led to an especially notable disconnect between the few fairer-skinned elites who control the bulk of the country's resources and the mostly indigenous masses who toil in its fields and factories. Yet just as peasants often cultivate subsistence plots on the sides of volcanoes, the country's social and economic structure is pitched atop these unstable relations of mass exclusion. Like the land that occasionally rumbles beneath Guatemalans' feet, the nation they have constructed atop this precarious social scaffolding has been prone to periodic eruptions of brutal violence.

Guatemala is a poor country, yet it has sectors of extraordinary wealth. In an economy based on agriculture, the statistics on land distribution are particularly telling: according to a 2005 report commissioned by the United States Agency for International Development, Guatemala's "dramatically unequal pattern of land distribution constitute[s] one of the most unequal in Latin America and the world" (Brown, Daly, and Hamlin 2005: 2). Although the most recent national agricultural census was undertaken in 1979, the figures from that period show that 2.6 percent of farms occupied 65 percent of arable land, averaging 200 hectares in size, while 88 percent of the farms were less than family-subsistence size, together occupying 16 percent of arable land (ibid.). There has been no substantive land reform since this period, so current figures are likely, if anything, to reflect further concentration.

This inequality—and its mapping onto ethnic differences—dates back to the days of Spanish colonialism, when the Crown established a system of *latifundias* (large rural estates) and *minifundias* (miniature subsistence plots); the indigenous population was forced to labor on elite *latifundias* while eking out survival on the tiny surrounding plots of land designated for their subsistence. This maldistribution was only exacerbated by the introduction of coffee (still the backbone of the national economy) during the liberal period of the late 1800s, which required both larger plantations and greater quantities of cheap labor

(Jonas 1991: 17). Furthermore, in the latter part of the twentieth century, efforts to modernize the economy by expanding and diversifying agricultural exports triggered a rural subsistence crisis as many *minifundistas* were forced off their lands or obliged to abandon them to pursue low-paying seasonal wage labor. These economic transformations intersected with political transformations, fuelling mounting pressures for social reform that would eventually erupt in violence.

The country recently emerged from a thirty-six-year civil war. The conflict began with a 1960 barracks revolt by young officers upset over the egregious socioeconomic inequities and, especially, angered by their government's capitulation to U.S. influences. Though it was far from the only example of U.S. intervention to avert reforms that would redistribute Guatemalan wealth more equitably, one focal point of the rebels' outrage was the 1954 coup, engineered by the U.S. Central Intelligence Agency, which toppled the democratically elected government of the reformer Jacobo Arbenz. This dramatically antidemocratic act, today acknowledged by the CIA, was orchestrated partly in retaliation for Arbenz's programs to redistribute uncultivated lands—including those held by the powerful Boston-based United Fruit Company—to landless peasants (for a richly detailed and elaborately documented account, see Schlesinger and Kinzer 1982). Determined to create "a better Guatemala," yet barred from pursuing this through peaceful political channels by the U.S.-installed regimes that followed the coup, the rebellious officers eventually formed the first leftist guerrilla movements. Their activities were initially centered in the eastern provinces and the capital, and in response the first major waves of counterinsurgency violence gripped these areas in the late 1960s.

Survivors of these early campaigns regrouped and eventually shifted their guerrilla operations to the western highlands in the 1970s, in part in a strategic effort to incorporate the country's oppressed indigenous masses into the revolutionary struggle. Beginning in the late 1970s and early 1980s, the army responded with its notorious scorched-earth campaigns, a series of brutal counterinsurgency efforts aimed at undermining the insurgents' base of popular support by literally "draining the water from the fish." These campaigns were punctuated by brutal massacres—over six hundred in the course of the war—in which thousands of noncombatant Maya peasants were slaughtered; but they also included more subtle and sustained forms of military domination of daily life in highland communities. A U.N.-sponsored truth commission, known in Guatemala as the Historical Clarification

Commission (Comisión para el Esclarecimiento Histórico [CEH]), estimated in 1999 that some 200,000 Guatemalans had lost their lives in the
conflict, the vast majority of them civilian noncombatants; that 93 percent of the abuses were committed by agents of the state (the army and
its paramilitary associates); and that in four distinct areas of the highlands, acts of genocide had been carried out against the Mayan populations (CEH 1999).

In 1996, the government and guerrillas formally signed the last in a
series of peace accords that committed the state to initiate far-reaching
reforms to the country's political, economic, and military structures. As
Susanne Jonas (2000: 9–10) reports, and as I can attest from having been
there at the time, this was a moment of great optimism in Guatemala, as
it seemed for a moment that the enduring causes of so much violence
might be addressed as a matter of state policy. Yet ten years later, little
progress has been made toward implementation of the accords. Though
the guerrillas have demobilized and the country has "democratized,"
the socioeconomic inequities that fuelled the conflict have yet to be
systematically addressed.

The Contemporary Crime Wave

Perhaps as a result of the persistence of deep inequalities, the end of the
civil war has not marked an end to the violence. In fact, many of my respondents described to me a terrible double jeopardy: first, they told me
about the violence that wracked their communities during the war, especially the waves of terror in the 1970s and 1980s; then they explained
the crisis of postwar crime as a sort of contemporary insult heaped
upon injury. Some felt angry and betrayed by the broken promises of
peace; others reacted with grim resignation. One elderly Maya woman
summed it up with a wave of her wrinkled hand: "Violence is like the
rain," she said. "It comes down hard for a while, then it passes a little
bit, and you might think it's over but it always comes back."

The character of the violence, however, has changed: compared to
the darkest days of the 1980s, the number of politically motivated
killings has declined sharply; "disappearances" are now rare. Yet the
decline in state killing and the cessation of the armed conflict have been
accompanied by what, to many, would appear to be a flourishing of
new forms of violence. This new wave of terror is usually referred to
as *delincuencia* (delinquency) or common crime. And although the

government's human rights record has improved, there is still ample cause for concern: in 2003, reacting to a wave of office break-ins, death threats, and attacks on human rights defenders, Amnesty International declared that the country was experiencing a "human rights melt-down," the worst human rights crisis since the era of state-sponsored genocide. In 2005, the first six months of the year alone saw some seventy attacks on human rights defenders, according to the country's human rights procurator ("PDH registra 68 ataques" 2005). The government touts its improved human rights record, but observers should keep this in perspective: although the state's disavowal of tactics involving the mass slaughter of unarmed civilians does constitute a step up from past practices, there is still need for further improvement.

Many estimates place the country's homicide rate among the highest in Latin America—a continent that already boasts a regional homicide rate at least twice the world average (Buvinic, Morrison, and Shifter 1999: 2), and by some estimates as high as four times the world average (Inter-American Development Bank [IDB] 2003). Two 1999 studies by the Inter-American Development Bank found that Guatemala had the highest indices of violent crime in Latin America and concluded that Guatemala City was the region's most violent capital (Gaviria and Pages 1999; Londoño and Guerrero 1999). In 1997, the World Bank estimated Guatemala's homicide rate at 150 per 100,000; by way of comparison, the United States' rate for the same year was calculated at 10.1 per 100,000 (Ayres 1998). In Guatemala, official government statistics are largely unavailable, and problems in the system of data collection call into question the reliability of those numbers that can be obtained,[3] yet even the Guatemalan National Institute of Statistics' figures on violent deaths suggest a 1996 rate of 58.68 per 100,000 (Centro de Investigaciones Económicas Nacionales [CIEN], "Diagnóstico de la violencia en Guatemala": 2). This figure, though significantly below most estimates by international sources, nonetheless places Guatemala's homicide rate at an alarmingly high level.

Although precise statistics are lacking, citizen awareness of the problem is not. One recent study found that one out of every three Guatemalans reports having been a victim of violent crime in the past year, with robbery the most frequent cause; 42.5 percent of those surveyed considered crime to be worse than it had been in the past (Instituto Centroamericano de Estudios Políticos [INCEP] 1999: 39, n. 19). Another survey, conducted in the municipality of Villa Nueva, just outside Guatemala City, found that 34 percent of those questioned had been a victim of crime in the past year, and that 76.7 percent felt that the crime problem—nationally, not just in their local area—had become worse over the past few years (Rico and Quiñones 1998: 31–32). My own research corroborates these figures, finding that citizens around the country report a significant increase in levels of actual criminal victimization and a widespread perception of a crisis in crime control. People of all classes described a sort of collective psychosis that curtailed their ability to participate in social events, send their children on school field trips, use public transportation, travel away from home, and frequent public areas, including markets, shopping centers, and movie theaters. Many told me they lived in a state of more or less continual fear.

Kidnappings, in particular, have a strong grip on the national imaginary. Although official statistics are much lower, the neighborhood watch–like organization Guardianes del Vecindario reported almost two thousand kidnappings in 1997 (Palma Ramos 1999: 10). Kidnappings span the classes; ransoms extend from $1 million down to $100, depending on the means of the victim's family. I visited one woman who operated a tiny one-room *tienda* (convenience store) out of the front of her extremely modest home in a marginal settlement outside the capital city; she had received typewritten notes threatening to kidnap her children if she didn't pay 5,000 quetzales (roughly $670). Another woman, who shared with me the anguishing story of her son's kidnapping and later return, described among the negative outcomes of that experience the now-constant accompaniment of Israeli security guards hired by her husband, who, she said, even stood guard while she used the Stairmaster at her gym in Guatemala City's exclusive Zone 14.

Despite these developments, the justice system has failed to respond adequately, a fact that only exacerbates the problem. According to one recent study, out of 90,000 potential criminal cases brought to the attention of the system in a year, literally *zero* were predicted to reach sentencing (Hendrix 2002). These failures are well publicized—the continuous escape of prison inmates, at times through spectacularly staged breakouts, achieved with the obvious complicity of at least some guards; the courts' failure to dictate sentences against well-known assassins of the past, who openly flaunt their untouchability; the corruption of the system at all its levels, such that its officers are the subject of oft-repeated jokes; the apparently unstoppable public lynchings, graphic images of which frequently appear splayed across television screens and the front pages of the popular press; and the general state of siege under which criminal gangs maintain the population, without relief from the authorities. A 1997 study conducted by the private research company Aragón y Asociados found that nine of every ten people surveyed around the country considered the administration of justice in Guatemala "inadequate." Three-fourths of the one thousand respondents judged the problem to be "very grave," the most severe of possible responses to the question (cited in Pásara 1998). In late 2002, a survey by the government itself revealed that 86 percent of the population agreed with the statement that in Guatemala, "justice is corrupt" (Seijo 2003).

The roots of the contemporary crime wave undoubtedly lie, in part, in the country's socioeconomic problems. In a country with some 83 percent of the population living in poverty (U.S. Department of State 2002), confronted with a rising cost of living set against the decreasing value of the national currency, economic desperation fuels many crimes. In recent years, the economy has stagnated, thanks to the fall in international prices for coffee, a decline in exports, and the faltering U.S. economy. The shrinking legal economy, combined with the dire lack of social services (such as education) to facilitate the entry of Guatemalans from marginal areas into the legal labor market, makes illegal enterprises much more attractive. Furthermore, the same inequality that fuels political violence also contributes to everyday criminality: World Bank researchers have concluded that "countries with more unequal distributions of income tend to have higher crime rates than those with more egalitarian patterns of income distribution" and that "changes in income distribution, not changes in absolute levels of poverty, are associated with changes in violent crime rates" (Lederman and Loayza 1999: 8; see also Fajnzylber, Lederman and Loayza 1998, 2002).

There are cultural factors to consider as well: many people who spoke with me attributed increasing crime to the loss of traditional values, fueled by an ever-increasing penetration of U.S.- (and to a lesser extent Mexican-) made movies, television, and other forms of popular culture into Guatemalan homes. Some cited the U.S. Immigration and Naturalization Service's policy of deporting "criminal aliens" from the United States, thus flooding many Central American nations with newly returned citizens, now schooled in gang violence on the streets of Los Angeles or other major cities (Moser and McIlwaine 2001). Others bemoaned increasing drug traffic as a source of cultural corruption, as more and more young Guatemalans become accustomed to the consumption of intoxicants.

However, many aspects of the crime wave can be directly traced to the experience of internal armed conflict. In the next section I explore two of them: the war's effects on institutions charged with upholding order, and its psychosocial legacies.

Legacies of a Dirty War

As elsewhere in Latin America (Chevigny 1995; Huggins 1998; Ungar 2003), in Guatemala the rise of the national security state brought about an institutional deformation of the public security apparatus. As Steven Hendrix writes, "Regrettably, a sort of justice and rule of law existed for years in Guatemala under which suspects were rounded up and shot. The system was efficient and gave the illusion of security. There was no need to invest in the institutional development of courts, prosecutors, public defenders, or even civil society—the military could do it all" (2000: 866).

Indeed, the Guatemalan military's seizure of power was so complete that throughout the war, military and paramilitary authorities were officially charged with combating not only guerrillas, but also common criminals, and the two categories were often deliberately blurred as a means of both delegitimizing the political opposition (calling them *delincuentes* or common criminals) and broadening the scope of potential targets. The "crime-fighting" tactics used against them were those of death squads. A former paramilitary explained in the 1980s:

What is happening lately, above all in the countryside, is that the officers are ordering the military commissioners to assassinate all those who are considered common criminals, such that the officers give us lists of the victims. They have told us to kill them with machetes, because that way people get confused. The thing is that also, on those lists they put people who are suspicious of being part of whatever political organization. They, the officers, order us to act like death squads. It's because of that that now more cadavers are appearing with machete wounds. (Comité Pro Justicia y Paz, Situación de los Derechos Humanos en Guatemala, October 1988, cited in CEH 1999, vol. 1, chap. 2, para. 468)

Throughout the war, the army's social-cleansing sweeps eliminated street children, prostitutes, homosexuals, and members of other marginal groups, along with the armed opposition and virtually anyone involved in activities that could be construed as even remotely political. Testimonies indicate that these social-cleansing practices were sometimes incorporated into the training of soldiers for counterinsurgency war; as one former member of the military intelligence (G-2) confessed:

In order to commit [*comprometer*] the new officers who arrived, when there weren't any guerrillas to kill or bury, then they would say: "Today you're assigned to Operation Cleansing." What was that? For those from the G-2 it was to take a civilian truck and go to the bus terminal, where you can find people to pick up: bums [*charamileros*], drunks [*bolitos*], thieves, and take them to La Laguna del Pino and eliminate them. La Laguna del Pino is covered [*está sembrada*] with bones. I know that much. (Oficina de Derechos Humanos del Arzobispado de Guatemala [ODHAG] 1998: vol. 2, 165)

The militarization of social order was so complete that the National Police was entirely controlled by the G-2; for many years, the directors and subdirectors of the National Police were themselves military intelligence officers (CEH 1999: vol. 1, chap. 2, paras. 244–45). In addition, the military infiltrated many private security companies, such that these collaborated with the army not only in providing order, but in eliminating political opponents (CEH 1999: vol. 1, chap. 2, paras. 258–59). At the same time, the military intelligence units also frequently abused their powers in order to line their pockets with bribes or payoffs for moonlighting jobs, as one witness told the truth commission:

In those days [1981] the Treasury Police [*Guardia de Hacienda*] killed many people, and even killed for hire; if you wanted to get rid of someone, you just gave a few quetzales to the Treasury Police and they would kill whomever [you wanted]. (CEH 1999: vol. 1, chap. 2, para. 261)

As these examples illustrate, social order was maintained through a hyperrepressive authoritarian state, dominated by its military apparatus, which was able to justify any excesses—and there were many—on the grounds of the peculiar exigencies of counterinsurgency warfare. This led to the creation of an elaborate subterranean justice system; while a formal, aboveground legal system continued to function throughout the war, it was both overshadowed and undermined by the creation of a much larger and more powerful illegal system for the dispensation of summary justice, in which the military and its paramilitary associates functioned in roles parallel to those of police officers, judges, attorneys, wardens, and executioners. As this illegal system grew, the legal one shriveled; civilian police and courts were deliberately maintained in a state of professional incompetence and fiscal unsustainability by military authorities who preferred to oversee all matters relating to crime and security.

Admittedly, this bifurcated justice system may also have served as an effective deterrent to common criminal activity in some cases.

Although the formal legal system wielded little power, the swift and brutal "justice" meted out by its clandestine counterpart was enough to inspire fear and obedience in even the most hardened criminal—except, of course, for those criminals who were affiliated with the army, for the same system undeniably encouraged criminal activity among the armed forces by assuring them impunity.

The laws of this new social order were enforced by a violence that was illegal, extreme, and exemplary, in the sense that acts of terror were purposely public, intended not only to eliminate enemies but also to convey a message to survivors. This order-through-violence infused all aspects of social control: it was, of course, the archetypal way to discipline suspected guerrilla collaborators, but it also came to be the way to deal with a range of other issues. As the truth commission reported, "The militarization of social life brought as a consequence the exacerbated use of violence to resolve conflicts of all sorts among neighbors. The famous lists of guerrilla collaborators ended up being used to resolve private conflicts and personal jealousies, attempts to seize others' land, romantic conflicts, personal vengeance" (CEH 1999: chap. 3, para. 473).

This parallel power structure has not disappeared in the postwar period. Quite the contrary: it has been privatized. Today, it is an open secret that many ex-military men are now active in most forms of organized crime in the country, including drug trafficking, auto theft, bank heists, and kidnappings. The lengthy peace process and the reformist agenda that emerged in the accords had alienated many army hardliners and forced others into retirement. As Ana Arana explains, "This group [of retired hardliners] has transformed itself into a highly powerful criminal cartel, one that today combines a variety of lucrative illegal enterprises with a systematic campaign of political violence. To build their operations, these rogue officers have made new allies among drug traffickers and strengthened their connections to the current government, forging strong links to customs, immigration, judicial, police, and army officials" (2001: 89–90). The Myrna Mack Foundation, a prominent Guatemalan NGO active in justice reform efforts, describes a network of "illegal forces that have existed for entire decades and have always exercised real power in a parallel fashion, at times more forcefully and at times less, in the shadow of formal state power" (Myrna Mack Foundation, quoted in Peacock and Beltrán 2003: 5).

Many of these acts draw on wartime training: kidnappings, for example, were frequently used by the army and guerrillas alike during the civil war, and familiarity with clandestine movements and surveillance operations was the daily bread of fighting forces on both sides. Yet they have spun out of control in the postwar era, as many parlayed these skills into a lucrative private industry driven by profit, not politics. As such, anyone may fall victim to a kidnapping, not only politically prominent figures. Indeed, many respondents, particularly in the capital city, told me that while previous acts were aimed at those involved in politics, leaving one the option of staying out of politics to stay alive, today there is no safe quarter from the violence. As former president Vinicio Cerezo told me in 1999:

There are high criminals, who used to be politically controlled but who are now uncontrollable. There's criminal anarchy. Why? Because before, someone from the guerrillas kidnapped someone because his boss told him, "Kidnap him and we're going to get the money, and then don't do anything else." And the army, too: "Go kidnap so-and-so, and kill him." But now, each one of these people is doing whatever he can, whatever happens to strike his fancy [*ahora cada una de estas gentes está haciendo lo que pueda, y lo que les dé la gana*]. Nobody controls them, there is no centralized insecurity doctrine [*no hay una doctrina centralizada de la inseguridad*]. Instead, there's an anarchy of insecurity.

The executive director of the private sector organization CACIF told me:

Kidnappings, for example, kidnappings have been around a long time in Guatemalan society. What's new, Angelina, is the component behind the kidnapping. Because kidnappings were a political tool for a long time, a way that the armed subversives raised money. So, during the thirty-six years of armed conflict, we have records of more than 150 kidnappings where ransoms were paid . . . kidnappings of a political type. In this case, now, the component is totally different, it's a purely lucrative component. That is to say, here there are no political motivations, simply the motivation to make money. And what's more, this type of kidnapping is more dangerous because, if you permit me to describe it this way, it's not a kidnapping carried out by "professionals." That is to say, in the case of the political kidnappings, the people who did it were professionals at what they did, people who were at war, people who knew that you had to exchange and hand over the victim once you got paid. In this case, no. Here we have very cruel gangs, very unprofessional, nervous criminals, and they don't care for example if the victim dies on them—they keep negotiating. The problem has gotten worse. It's not new, but it's gotten worse. And in the case of bank robberies, no doubt about it, it's gotten more intense.

As a result, even powerful businesses and families have been affected. Throughout the war, in many ways the military had acted at the behest the country's landed oligarchy, eager to uphold the status quo and squash revolution; now that the war is over, some told me, some factions of former officers have turned against the very oligarchy that formerly maintained them in place. One upper-middle-class woman I interviewed explained this to me by saying, *Se les volvió la muchacha respondona*—"They [the army] turned into the maid who talks back." This "uppity maid" metaphor is an apt one, for like servants, these criminals were familiar with the homes, businesses, and modus operandi of the wealthy elite, making it easy for them to plan attacks against them in the postwar era. At the same time, other sources point to the involvement of some elite factions in these mafialike structures. In 2002, Amnesty International warned of an "unholy alliance" between traditional sectors of the oligarchy, some "new entrepreneurs," police and military, and common criminals (Amnesty International 2002).

This insecurity also permeates poor communities, even though many of their residents own almost nothing to steal. As one Maya K'iche' woman from a rural village in El Quiché told me,

From the '80s to today, the violence has not been calmed down in the community . . . from there, from the '80s, is where the robbery comes from. Because like the *compañero* [another respondent present] said, the civil patrollers and the soldiers stole—they weren't thieves [before the war] but then they learned to steal, they entered into the houses, grabbed what was there. They learned to steal like that and this generated more and more [theft]. Because there have even been robberies inside the communities, they have stolen from the houses and that's where the idea of doing that came from, because before it was unknown. But the patrollers stole, there were even ones who stole livestock, and who took everything they could find inside the houses, so that's where the idea came from to be stealing in the villages, because there wasn't any [robbery] before. And to this day, well, people are stealing.

Today, numerous illegal industries flourish in Guatemala, many with far-flung tentacles reaching into the territories of other states: these include trafficking in drugs, migrants, stolen vehicles, pirated goods, small arms, and other illegal trades. And because these networks retain ties to well-placed individuals in government, they are sheltered from prosecution and also can be activated to serve political, as well as purely economic, ends. The result is a new hybrid structure in which death squads may no longer operate out of the presidential palace, but they have not closed up shop; indeed, some might argue that they have now encircled the palace, holding its very occupants hostage.[4] Even President Portillo sent his own relatives out of the country in June 2000 when he feared retribution after the state executed some members of a powerful kidnapping gang (Rogers 2000). Other civilian authorities occupy even more perilous positions, particularly when they strive to uphold the law: as the U.N. Special Rapporteur on the Independence of Judges and Lawyers reported following recent investigative trips to Guatemala, judges, prosecutors, and members of the judiciary are harassed, intimidated, and even killed with alarming frequency (see United Nations Economic and Social Council 2000, 2001). In 2002, the country's highest-ranking prosecutorial officer, Attorney General Carlos David de León, was the victim of an apparent assassination attempt following his announcement of the opening of investigations into five retired military officers with suspected ties to organized crime. Several were members of President Portillo's inner circle of advisers; most had enjoyed long careers in military intelligence. In 2003, as these investigations proceeded, threats against de León and his team of investigators continued apace; in April, for example, a device reportedly exploded outside public ministry offices in the capital, releasing pamphlets bearing crosses and the ominous slogan "Rest in Peace, Carlos de León."[5]

In contemporary parlance, the shadowy forces who carry out these acts are known as *cuerpos clandestinos* (clandestine forces); it might be more forthright to call them death squads. In 2002–3, many in the human rights community backed a proposal to form an international commission known as the Commission to Investigate Illegal Forces and Clandestine Security Apparatuses (Comisión para la Investigación de Cuerpos Ilegales y Aparatos Clandestinos de Seguridad [CICIACS]). This body would have investigated the clandestine forces and their connections to organized crime (including drug running), politically motivated attacks, and other forms of violence originating along this murky border between state and nonstate entities. It is significant that the commission's official name recognized these entities as "clandestine security apparatuses": more than merely private criminal gangs, they form part of a parallel power structure that exists alongside (and at times intertwined with) the state's security forces, carrying out violent acts to protect the political and economic interests of those involved and often deliberately blending the two. Not surprisingly, those associated with the formation of this commission were themselves targets of violence (Amnesty International 2003b).[6]

Some have called this the Colombianization of Guatemala,[7] alluding to the powerful role of narcotrafficking mafias in the Andean country's ongoing civil conflict and their propensity for acts of horrific violence against state officials and everyday citizens alike. Indeed, Guatemala's growing role as a transshipment point and storage area in the international drug trade has undoubtedly fueled the operations of the clandestine groups, and some of the country's leading figures in both government and crime have been linked to the Cali cartel.[8] In October 2002, the U.S. State Department's top diplomat for Latin America, Otto Reich, said that drug lords had "very close ties to the highest levels" of Guatemala's government and that retired military officers with links to drug trafficking were deeply influential in the Portillo administration (Kettmann 2003), and the United States revoked the visas of several former intelligence officers with links to the administration. In January 2003, the country was one of three in the world officially decertified by the U.S. government in recognition of its failure to collaborate with U.S. counternarcotics efforts (Johnson 2003). So drugs do constitute an important part of the problem. At the same time, the proliferation of well-financed organized criminal networks with shadowy links to weak states, the ability to permeate national borders, and the potential to carry out politically motivated acts of violence designed to sow fear and disrupt politics is characteristic of a new global reality that should be painfully clear after September 11, 2001. There is nothing inherently "Colombian"—or Guatemalan—about this; what we are witnessing is the globalization (and privatization) of political violence.

In this world of parallel structures, the state itself has been left largely on the sidelines of criminal justice, a second-string player that many perceive to be irrelevant, inept, or worse. The deliberate debilitation of the civilian justice system throughout the course of the war has left a dangerous legacy. Civilian police forces were widely acknowledged as too weak to assume responsibility for the country's internal security in the early postwar period, and as Douglas Kincaid has shown (2001), this weakness justified the ongoing involvement of the military in domestic policing despite specific prohibition in the peace accords of this use of the country's armed forces. Initially contemplated as an interim measure, joint military-police patrols were established under the Arzú administration (1996–2000); and despite the improvements in the new Civilian National Police and its increased coverage of the national territory, this arrangement was formalized into law by the FRG-dominated congress in 2000; the practice continues to this day. The military also plays primary roles in the U.S.-led wars on drugs and terrorism. Many citizens endorse these measures as necessary to stop crime;

indeed, many voted against the May 1999 constitutional reforms, which would have brought the constitution in line with the peace accords, specifically on the grounds that their prohibition of the army from internal security functions would effectively abandon the citizenry to criminal assault. (Another controversial aspect of the reforms, relevant to this discussion, was their endorsement of indigenous justice.) Many citizens clamor for military involvement in crime fighting, as experience has shown them that neither police, nor judges, nor courts, nor the law is able to effectively deter criminals—only fear. And that, of course, is the army's specialty. In this way, paradoxically, the army is perceived as protecting the populace against crime, even though it has contributed more than any other institution to the propagation of violence.

The courts, similarly, are woefully underequipped to handle their mounting caseloads; the public ministry, which is in charge of prosecuting crimes, is underfunded, and key prosecutors (*fiscales*), even those assigned to high-profile cases, are often unable to carry out their work because of scarce resources (office phones disconnected as bills go unpaid) or fear of violent reprisal. Although the 1990s brought a host of much-needed modernizing reforms to the Guatemalan justice system, including the change from written to oral procedures and the elimination of numerous outdated and inefficient practices, many employees have yet to receive adequate training in new techniques.

Of course, the years of war did not only affect state institutions; violence also permeated the population as a whole. The contemporary crime wave is also clearly a consequence of the psychosocial devastation caused by the brutal violence so many suffered, what Edelberto Torres-Rivas has called the "trivialization of horror" (Torres-Rivas 1999). Not only did the population become militarized, at times armed, and accustomed to the solution of conflicts through force; entire communities were displaced, families flung apart, and villages converted into enclaves of suspicion. Local authorities and elders, particularly in the indigenous areas, were supplanted by paramilitary figures, who in some areas still exert de facto control despite having been formally stripped of their charge in the era of purported peace. The social sanctions that communities normally exert upon their members have been drastically weakened in the face of such transformations. Among other things, this means there are fewer deterrents to criminal activity— World Bank studies in Guatemala have rightly cast this in terms of social capital—and fewer ways communities can curb such activity, once it happens, without resorting to drastic acts of desperation. In many ways, the same factors that make it more likely for criminal acts to occur in the first place also make it more likely for communities to respond with a kind of counter-criminality most commonly known as *la justicia a mano propia*.

Mano dura

Across Latin America, but perhaps most dramatically in Guatemala, these deliberate institutional distortions led to a functional inversion of legality in the authoritarian period. Public servants became private predators, the security forces enforced insecurity, and the law became illegal. It is possible to understand contemporary developments only against this stark and perhaps surreal backdrop.

In Guatemala, and indeed in much of Latin America today, a common maxim warns, "If you see a police officer coming, cross the street." The depth of its meaning may be difficult to appreciate without some consideration, particularly for those not accustomed to such attitudes. In my research, I asked people why this was a wise precaution. Whether or not *you* were doing anything illegal, respondents told me, it was often a good bet that the police officer would be; if you wanted to avoid being hit up for a bribe, hauled off or beaten for a crime you didn't commit, or somehow harassed, it was simply best to avoid contact. Not only are police officers not a resource to turn to in times of trouble; they themselves *are* trouble. In Guatemala, a new civilian police force was implemented in the postwar period, and a significant percentage of respondents did tell me they viewed this force more favorably than they had its predecessor; nonetheless, people warned me to cross the street when I saw the law. This cynicism is centered not only on law enforcement, but extends to the courts, the legislature, and the law itself; in fact, although the minor offenses of some police are sometimes assumed to be understandable transgressions in light of their notoriously low pay, poor training, and lack of education or advancement opportunities, a special wrath is reserved for the courts and "political class," whose duplicity and venal self-interest is often the source of great populist anger. It is this rejection of the law itself that finds expression in *mano dura* today.

The term *mano dura* evokes a tough, no-holds-barred approach to social control; it is sometimes compared to a Latin American version of zero tolerance, but as a direct allusion to authoritarian policies, it comes with more baggage. In the following pages, I highlight three manifestations of this trend in Guatemala and Latin America more broadly and then discuss why these present a unique challenge to human rights, drawing again on a close examination of the Guatemalan case.

First, one key component of *mano dura* across the region is *support for private acts of vigilantism,* locally known as *justicia a mano propia,* or "justice by one's own hand." These include lynchings, as well as the murky work of "social cleansing" squads, usually carried out under cover of darkness. As noted in chapter 1, in Guatemala, the United Nations documented some 482 lynchings, between 1996 and the end of 2002; one survey found that some 75 percent of the population expressed some support for such actions (Ferrigno 1998). Lynchings are not limited to Guatemala but have been frequently documented in Mexico, Venezuela, Bolivia, and other countries. Expressing a common view, a middle-aged *ladina* woman in the capital told me without a moment's hesitation:

Oh yes, I agree completely with [lynchings], if there's a criminal there they can and should do what they want with him, because if they don't, they [criminals] will do it to you. Oh, yes. If they can do it, they should do it [*Que si lo pueden hacer, que lo hagan*]. May God forgive me, but I agree completely with that.

But not all acts of *justicia a mano propia* take this form. In an interview, a *ladino* schoolteacher from the eastern Guatemalan province of Jutiapa explained his community's approach:

In Oriente we haven't had lynchings where they burn people, but yes, once I even had to participate in [an act of *justicia a mano propia*] because I tell you, I was desperate. What happened? In the rural sector and in the urban sector in Jutiapa, we organized ourselves in our neighborhoods, and the neighborhood itself took the necessary measures, for example, to figure out what to do. And if it wasn't possible to resolve things, then things got arranged another way. And in the rural areas, the ranchers [*finqueros*] also, since there was a lot of theft of livestock, and lots of killing, and robbery, they organized themselves and said, "Well, since the authorities don't do anything we're going to use certain groups of people so that they fix this, so that they punish the criminals, and that's how there were even killings combating crime" [*Bueno, ya que no actúan las autoridades entonces vamos a valiarnos de ciertos grupos de gentes para que vayan a componer, vayan a sancionar al pícaro y así incluso hasta hubo muertos combatiendo la criminalidad*]

So, in Oriente you don't see that they're burning people, but yes, it's just known that if a thief or a criminal comes along, everyone joins in to beat him up [*Así que por el sector de Oriente no mira usted que quemen a la gente, pero sí, ahora ya saben, que si viene un ladrón o un pícaro entre todos lo pencacean*]. They beat him and everything, and maybe even kill him. Burned, no. But that's because here people generally get their vengeance with guns. The criminal, well, since there are people who are available for that, pay them and they go do the killing, hired killers, they're cleaning things up, it's a cleansing I'd say [*matones a sueldo, ya están limpiando el lugar, es una limpieza digo yo*].

Q: Has it always been that way, or has this increased recently?

SCHOOLTEACHER: It's increased. It's increased. Since crime has increased, so has the fear, the danger, the distrust of the people, and that's made people take the law into their own hands. If the government were rigid, if it made sure the laws were followed, people wouldn't do this. There would be no need. . . . Look, you never used to see that the people would take measures of their own like burning people, no, that's only come since the end of the armed conflict. It's that before, somehow, before the level of crime was lower. But from some time to now, it went up. It went up incredibly. It's incredible, but ever since the armed conflict was solved, in some ways Guatemala has gotten better, but in that aspect it's gotten worse. And you can see it. The majority of the people are furious, . . . in our side of the country, on the side of Oriente, you won't see us burning people. But here, if there's a thief, a criminal, who people want to get rid of, and the authorities don't do it, the people know what to do.

Q: But is it a public event?

SCHOOLTEACHER: No, no, it's generally hidden. You know that there are organized groups of criminals, and that they have their way of getting by, charging a fee to get rid of criminals [*Usted sabe que hay grupos organizados de maleantes, de delincuentes, verdad, y que ellos hasta tienen su modus, su modus de vivir cobrando por ir a descartar al maleante*]. So these groups are organized, and they have certain rates. Say, for example, we want to get rid of Mr. So-and-So, a criminal and a kidnapper, and the authorities aren't doing anything. Well, then you go talk to these groups, and the groups know how to go kill the man, or go beat him up, or whatever you ask for. In other words, these are the ways that the people have to defend themselves since the authorities provide no response. The people find themselves obligated [to do it] [*O sea, que son formas que tiene que valerse la gente en vista que por parte de la autoridad no hay una respuesta buena. Se ven obligados*].

In 1995, the Sombra Negra ring of vigilante executioners was exposed in El Salvador—where more people have been killed by common crime in the postwar period than during the entire twelve years of civil war—provoking a public reaction divided between support of and rejection for the group's activities (Call 1997: 17); in more recent years, evidence of social cleansing surfaced in the capital and Soyapango, where "extermination groups" declared themselves the opponents of youth gangs (Comisión para la Defensa de los Derechos Humanos en

Centroamérica [CODEHUCA] 1998). In Venezuela, similarly, self-designated "extermination groups," composed of off-duty police officers and partially financed by some local businesses, have reportedly emerged in recent years in the states of Portuguesa, Falcón, Yaracuy, Anzoátegui, Bolívar, Miranda, Aragua, and Zulia. (Human Rights Watch 2003).

Second, *mano dura* encompasses *support for increased state violence against criminals*, whether through a tightening of legal sanctions or support for extralegal forms of violence. In Brazil, for example, where increases in vigilante practices have also been recorded (Neild 1999), the anthropologist Teresa Caldeira has documented widespread public support for illegal, even lethal, acts of violence against purported criminals committed by death squads and the authorities alike (Caldeira 2000). In Honduras, more than 1,800 youths have been killed by unknown forces in the last five years; some may have been killed by rival gangs, but a number of the bodies bear telltale signs of death-squad "cleansing" activities: their hands tied behind the back, killed with a single gunshot wound to the head. President Ricardo Maduro, who took office promising zero tolerance for crime, has acknowledged the involvement of police officers in some of these death-squad deaths (Sullivan 2003).

In many countries, advocates of *mano dura* have pressed for an extension of the death penalty to new crimes and/or a reversal of its previous abolition; legislation to this effect has been proposed in El Salvador, Ecuador, Mexico, and Guatemala, and popular clamor for capital punishment has grown in Brazil and Venezuela. Protections for juvenile offenders have been rolled back in many countries: in Uruguay, the parliament approved a law permitting the jailing of juvenile offenders in adult prisons; in Bolivia, a law lowering the age at which criminal responsibility can be imputed to juvenile offenders was approved, and similar measures were debated in Chile, Mexico (Elizaldo 1997), and other countries (Albornoz Tinajero 1995); in Panama, maximum sentences for juvenile offenders were extended in 2003 ("Aprueban en Panamá" 2003). In Argentina, politicians have collaborated with family members of murder victims in prominent cases to call for crackdowns on criminality, and legislation has been passed to provide longer sentences for lesser offenses (Human Rights Watch 2005).

Sometimes these proposals take the form of suspending certain rights for the accused or provisions meant to protect against false accusations. In Venezuela, for example, the 1999 Código Orgánico Procesal Penal

(COPP), which included stricter regulations regarding the nature of evidence necessary to detain suspects, was widely denounced as making it impossible to detain anyone not caught *in flagrante*. Among other things, the adoption of COPP freed many Venezuelan prisoners who had been detained for more than half the probable sentence for the crime of which they had been accused, despite never having been convicted (Poleo Zerpa 1999). Venezuela's attorney general, Javier Elechiguerra, claimed in 2000 that lynchings were a direct result of these protections (Efe News Service, February 17, 2000), and political figures of various stripes blamed rising crime rates on the COPP and its various due-process protections. Concern about crime led the governor of Caracas to propose that parks and public plazas be used as sites for the administration of punishment ("Pena máxima" 1999).

In Guatemala, according to a survey by the national newspaper *Prensa libre*, some 86 percent of the population was found to support the death penalty ("Fuerte SI" 1998).[9] This has proved a controversial topic: Guatemala's 1986 constitution provides for capital punishment in certain cases of aggravated homicide, such as those where the victim is extremely young or old, or in cases where murder is committed as part of a kidnapping, but recent legislation has moved to extend the use of the death penalty to a broader range of crimes, especially kidnappings of all sorts—even those that do not result in death. As a signatory of the American Convention on Human Rights (Pacto de San José), Guatemala is precluded from expanding the use of the death penalty to crimes for which it was not previously contemplated.[10] Guatemala's new death penalty legislation, therefore, directly contravenes its responsibilities under international law and even violates article 46 of the Guatemalan constitution, which recognizes the preeminence of international humanitarian law and human rights treaties. This contradiction has created confusion: some judges recognize the primacy of national legislation and therefore dictate capital sentences in such cases, while others refuse to do so, complying instead with international norms (and the provisions of article 46).

As a "solution" to this problem, some have suggested that Guatemala withdraw entirely from the inter-American system, specifically as a measure to allow the free execution of criminals. A 1998 survey found that 65 percent of the population favored annulment of the Pacto de San José ("Fuerte SI" 1998), and the question of whether or not to remain beholden to the terms of the pact became a campaign issue in 1999, when Alfonso Portillo and other candidates promised to with-

draw from the pact during the presidential campaign.[11] A *ladino* salesman from Guatemala City told me:

I think that Guatemala should renounce the Pacto de San José, apply the death
penalty right and left, knock off half the population, but not for political reasons,
but for crime, for questions purely of civil jurisprudence [*Yo opino que Guatemala
debería de renunciar al Pacto de San José, aplicar la pena de muerte en dos pencazos,
tronarse a medio mundo, pero no por cuestiones políticas, sino por delincuencia, por cuestiones puramente de jurisprudencia civil*]. Disgracefully, the more democracy there
is, the more opportunity there is for trickery, in some aspects. When there's a dictatorship, like [Anastasio] Somoza's in Nicaragua, only he and his people could
make money, right; but now, in democracy, more people have made money. And
the more democracy there is, the more consciousness there is about civil rights,
so the more opportunity there is for lawyers and transgressors of the law to take
advantage, where they catch [a criminal] and "Hey! Where are my human rights,
you're hurting my human rights, man!" [*Entonces entre mas democracia haya, mas
conciencia hay de los derechos civiles, entonces mas se pueden aprovechar tanto abogados
como transgresores de la ley, en que le agarran y "Qué? Dónde están mis derechos humanos, me los está lastimando hombre!"*] So I think that in Guatemala, democracy
and security don't go hand in hand. I was telling you a little bit ago, that if the government makes itself firm [*si el gobierno se pone firme*], OK, but then there's less democracy. The thing is, we Guatemalans are not prepared for democracy. Maybe
if right now they initiated an educational process, in fifteen, twenty years we
could talk about democracy, but for us to manage a democracy like the *ticos*
[Costa Ricans], the *ticos* don't have an army, and I don't even think their police
carry weapons. But we don't have the culture for that yet [*Pero nosotros no tenemos
la cultura para eso todavía*].

And lastly, inasmuch as human rights and the influence of the international community are often seen as obstacles to this increased violence, some proponents of *mano dura* favor a *return to strongman leadership
in express disregard for human rights*. Concern about crime thus provides
the platform for a new generation of *caudillos* promising swift, strong action against crime—sometimes even if this violates the terms of international agreements, and even if it reverses important, hard-won progress
toward demilitarization (Kincaid 2001). In Guatemala, for example, Alfonso Portillo (2000–2004) was elected on a populist law-and-order platform, and his administration has responded to the population's concern
about crime by stepping up the role of the military in domestic policing
and repeatedly suspending constitutional guarantees to allow the
authorities greater latitude in detaining criminal suspects.

In Argentina, throughout his years as president (1989–99), Carlos
Menem frequently emphasized anticrime measures, explicitly denying

the notion that the sources of crime might lie in social conditions such as unemployment or poverty (Smulovitz 1998, cited in Chevigny 2003). He backed such measures as stiffer penalties and longer prison terms. In a series of interviews with the Argentine daily *Clarín*, Menem declared in 1999, "Human rights organizations can scream to the sky, but I think that here the criminal is more protected than the police, or the people"; though he acknowledged that critics compared *mano dura* policies with a "trigger-happy" (*gatillo fácil*) approach to crime, he said, "We can't let the *criminals* be trigger happy" (cited in Human Rights Watch 1999). In the lead-up to the 1999 elections, the Peronist Eduardo Duhalde made a pilgrimage to New York City to show his support for zero-tolerance policies and advocated the reinstatement of the death penalty, and Menem assigned the military to patrol the streets of Buenos Aires, recalling for many the days of the dictatorship (Chevigny 2003: 85). By 2003 the rhetoric had become even more inflamed, and among those vying for the nation's highest offices were several leaders of the military uprisings that rocked the country's fragile democracy in 1987, all of them proposing *mano dura* against crime: Enrique Venturino, in particular, called for "triple-zero tolerance of criminals" (*tolerancia triple cero con los delincuentes*) and paired himself with a hardline running mate, Federico Pinto Kramer, former defense attorney of the Paraguayan dictator Lino Oviedo ("Los carapintada" 2003).

In Mexico, similarly, Ernesto Zedillo called in 1996 for sweeping changes to penal procedure, including the introduction of such measures as faceless judges, anonymous witnesses, autonomous intelligence agencies within the police with an increased ability to carry out surveillance such as wiretapping, and a lowered age of criminal responsibility (Chevigny 2003: 89). He argued that human rights guarantees and strict evidence standards hampered the authorities' ability to enforce the law (Human Rights Watch 1999). Although not all the proposed measures were adopted, the role of the military in crime fighting has been expanded (Human Rights Watch 1999), the habeas corpus rights of defendants were restricted, and the discretion of the police to arrest without a court order was extended (Chevigny 2003).

In Peru, Alberto Fujimori's heavy-handed policies against crime were, by most accounts, popular despite being characterized by Human Rights Watch as violating the most basic due-process guarantees, reducing such provisions as habeas corpus protections against arbitrary detentions and subjecting those accused of organized criminal activity to trial by military courts (Human Rights Watch 1999). Yet they led to the arrest and imprisonment of thousands on ambiguous charges (Amnesty International 2003a).

Even in countries such as Chile, widely regarded as the "safest" country in Latin America, fear of crime has increased in recent years (Dammert and Malone 2003). Crime emerged as the central issue in the presidential campaigns of fall 2005, despite the fact that Chile's crime rates are far lower than regional averages; one candidate, Joaquín Lavín, called for a "three strikes and you're out" law (Dammert 2005), to which his opponent, Michelle Bachelet, responded by calling for a "one strike and you're out" law (Toro 2005).

Even in peaceful Costa Rica, concern about crime has led more citizens to purchase weapons for personal protection (Rogers 2000) and a 1999 survey found that 64.2 percent of those questioned indicated that they wanted "a *mano dura* leader, a strong and decided man who would impose order," echoing the results of an earlier study by the University of Costa Rica, which found that 84.6 percent of those surveyed wanted "a strong man who imposes order" (Efe News Services, October 22, 1999). This desire for strongmen has revived the careers of some military figures who previously headed dictatorships, such as General Efraín Ríos Montt in Guatemala or General Hugo Bánzer in Bolivia, or for past coup plotters such as Lucio Gutiérrez in Ecuador or Hugo Chávez in Venezuela.

In Guatemala, neither the term *mano dura* nor the practices it connotes are new: both were invoked (and implemented) by right-wing military hardliners during the war. During the regime of Ríos Montt (1982–83), for example, petty criminals were regularly rounded up and executed by state forces, through both clandestine practices and the official use of the death penalty following trials that failed dramatically to conform to international standards of criminal justice.[12] Perhaps unsurprisingly, rising concern about crime served as a springboard for the general's return to the national political stage in the late 1990s. Undeterred by widespread acknowledgment of his responsibility for genocide and war crimes (it is well known in Guatemala that the state's counterinsurgency machine cranked into its most murderous overdrive during his eighteen months in office), or perhaps in some ways capitalizing upon it, Ríos Montt claimed for himself the mantle of *mano dura,* recalling his earlier "success" at imposing order in times of great social turbulence.

A surprising number of Guatemalans appeared to accept this characterization of his leadership. A baker from the central department of Sacatepéquez, for example, told me in 1999:

There's a saying, here in Guatemala, that the only one who can get rid of all this crime is Ríos Montt. Because in those days, in Ríos Montt's days, a criminal caught was a criminal killed. You know, at night, they didn't make any noise or anything, they just disappeared them and then the next day, a corpse appeared, like that, and that's the only way . . . that's how people started to be afraid of him. But now, today, with democracy and these parties . . . it's hard. It's hard, because today they're caught, and tomorrow they're free again. You know, even in jail there are privileges, they have microwaves, they have cocaine, marijuana, they have alcohol.

In a lower-middle-class neighborhood of Guatemala City, a focus group discussion recalled the figure of El General in similar terms:

RESPONDENT NO. 1: Remember that in the regime of Ríos Montt, everything was in order. Order. And I liked that.

RESPONDENT NO. 2: It was a death for a death.

Q: So in your opinion, he governed well?

RESPONDENT NO. 1: For me, yes. He governed well.

The Guatemalan political scientist Dinorah Azpuru (2000) has found a significant correlation between fear of crime and support for the FRG. During the 1999 campaign, Ríos's party, the Frente Republicano Guatemalteco (FRG), made crime and security issues central to their broad populist appeal, identifying its candidates as the defenders of law and order (an ironic characterization, given that Portillo admitted to killing two men and evading justice for the crime, and Ríos Montt was facing charges of genocide). The FRG's symbol—in a country with many illiterate voters, party symbols are eponymous—is a hand holding up three fingers representing security, justice, and well-being, the three pillars of the FRG's platform. Several of the people I interviewed even volunteered their opinion that the symbol of *la manita* represents *mano dura*; both, after all, are allusions to hands. (This is not the meaning ascribed to the symbol by its creators, but it is still worth noting that in the minds of at least some voters, this is the meaning the party's emblem has taken on.)[13]

Crime, *mano dura*, and Human Rights

Widespread citizen concern about crime presents a number of deep challenges to advocates of human rights in the region. In many ways, human rights groups' reluctance to embrace this area of paramount concern to citizens has led their path to diverge from mainstream public opinion. For although the majority of my respondents expressed support for what might be considered human rights groups' core message—the condemnation of genocidal excesses committed by state forces in the context of civil war—many perceived such groups as primarily focused on past problems and offering little in terms of solutions to today's most pressing issues, especially crime. Though human rights groups and supporters were at the forefront of the pro-democracy movement, now that democracy is in place they have been somewhat sidelined—in part because their reluctance to address such issues as crime plays into the hands of their adversaries, who are only too eager to label human rights advocates as "soft on crime." Charges that human rights groups are "on the side of criminals" have delegitimized the human rights discourse to the point where many of my respondents expressed passionate outrage at the mere mention of human rights in the context of a discussion about crime.

At the same time, there are a number of reasons human rights groups are ill-positioned to address issues of crime. First, the human rights movement has historically been premised on the assumption that states are the primary, or, according to some formulations, the *only* actors capable of violating human rights on a significant scale. Though such an approach made perfect sense in Latin America during the authoritarian period, the reality has shifted: today, for most residents of the region, the most immediate threats to their well-being stem not from what the state does, but from what it does not do. Decades ago citizens clamored for freedom from state repression; today they clamor for liberation from crime, poverty, and lack of economic opportunity. Yet the historically state-centered human rights paradigm makes it difficult for these groups to respond to such concerns.

Of course, there are reasons the paradigm has focused on the state: not only did the modern human rights regime emerge as a response to state abuses committed in Nazi Germany, but it is grounded in international law, to which states, not individuals, are accountable.[14] States, not individuals, are signatories to the various human rights conventions and protocols and therefore are most readily held accountable for their failure to adhere to the norms inscribed therein. Furthermore, acts of common crime and other abuses by private individuals are simply too numerous for human rights groups to take on except through very indirect routes. (Even if this were somehow practically possible, it would almost certainly be strategically inadvisable for human rights advocacy groups to cast themselves in a role that might essentially parallel that of an attorney general, overseeing the prosecution of all crimes. It makes much more sense for them to target their energies by focusing on certain specific areas of concern and pressing states to attend to these.) Furthermore, adherence to human rights norms entails both positive and negative commitments on the part of states, so human rights advocates can target states even in cases where private individuals or groups are the primary culprits by holding the state accountable for its inaction.

Yet in practice, the movement has historically been more vocal and effective at defending negative rights (freedom from torture, for example) than positive rights (such as the right to housing)—in large part because, as Margaret Keck and Kathryn Sikkink explain (1998), certain types of cases are easier for advocacy networks to mobilize support around. As a result, not only common crime, but abuses by corporate actors and violence against women have historically received a weaker response from human rights groups, which are simply best situated to tackle abuses where the state can be shown to be *directly* involved in committing an act of violence, rather than simply remiss in fulfilling its many formal duties.

This is, of course, changing; smaller human rights NGOs have for years defined human rights in broader terms, recognizing the interdependence of rights and the multiplicity of rights abusers, and in recent years even giants such as Amnesty International have tackled abuses by nonstate actors and sought more flexible ways to work on issues outside the narrow spectrum that originally defined their work. As regards crime, Amnesty International's efforts to call attention to the murders of hundreds of women in Ciudad Juárez and Chihuahua, Mexico, and, in 2005, in Guatemala as well, represent important shifts in focus and policy. It is a difficult balance: though human rights organizations can insist that states fulfill their positive commitments to providing citizen security—and some, particularly organizations based in Latin America, do mention this in their reports—to campaign heavily on this issue places human rights advocates in the awkward and unprecedented position of asking states to strengthen what is at some level an in-evitably repressive function, carried out by the very security forces most organizations have spent decades denouncing. For many mem-bers of this movement, most of whom cut their teeth on protesting state violence during the authoritarian period, this would require something of an ideological about-face; and well-founded fears about postauthor-itarian security forces' propensity for abuse call into question the wis-dom of such a strategy.

It is not surprising, then, that rather than protesting governments' failure to protect the majority of citizens from common crime, tradi-tional human rights groups have focused largely on denouncing ex-cesses committed by the state in the context of fighting crime. Unques-tionably, such common abuses as the involvement of police in death squads, the torture and ill-treatment of criminal suspects, and the in-humane conditions of imprisonment prevalent in many Latin American countries constitute egregious affronts to human rights and merit force-ful criticism; clearly, such a critique is consistent with human rights or-ganizations' historical areas of expertise and furthers the ultimate goals of their work.

However reasonable the rationale behind such choices, however, their result has strained public relations for human rights groups in many Latin American contexts. Arguments about the historical trajec-tory of human rights work, the campaigning potential of negative rights, and the primary importance of states in international legal re-gimes mean little to anguished parents who have lost a child and are desperate for justice to be done. It may be difficult for them to under-stand that if their child was killed by a neighbor, virtually nothing will be done to investigate; if he or she was killed by a member of the secu-rity forces, however, international human rights groups may intervene on their behalf. This selectivity is sometimes seen as unfair, even un-conscionable, by citizens who feel threats from multiple quarters and may perceive human rights groups as claiming universality but in truth only concerned about certain politically motivated assaults on certain individuals' rights.[15]

In Guatemala, many of my respondents told me that on the topic of crime, human rights groups seemed out of touch and out of date. Most said human rights criticisms made sense in the era of state terror but to-day seemed to have been twisted in favor of criminals. In this regard, the following excerpt from my conversation with a middle-aged *ladino* bureaucrat at the University of San Carlos, who had recently completed

a course on human rights, is typical in sentiment, although more restrained in tone than many:

The question that I have, like I told you I've studied some of these things [human
rights] and my question is, how far and when are rights maintained for those
who violate the rights of others? I tell you, it's hard for me to be impartial, I try to
do it, and I've even had to free my mind from my religious principles sometimes
in order to do it, but the truth is, sometimes there are cases where you say, *why?*
Why for them, they who've done so much evil, without mercy, why at the time of
trying them is it so important to take care of their rights? . . . Sometimes the
people who defend those criminals really bother me, because it seems to me that
it's unfair, they shouldn't do that, in my opinion—forgive me if I offend you, but
for me, they should be condemned at once, that is to say, if they find them guilty,
they should apply the maximum punishment right away. For example, in cases
of children, why does anyone attack a child? . . . That's when I consider it unfair
for [human rights advocates] to defend criminals. Maybe when [criminals] touch
someone defenseless is when I feel the most indignant, and with the most desire
to see the law applied as it should be. About the human rights treaties, OK, that's
OK because we needed a bit of that because the military government was tremendous. . . . Those ingrates have committed many disasters, and it was very good
that some measures or laws be applied that could protect us, but I think that
should be for the citizen who works, not for those who transgress those very
norms [*esos ingratos han hecho muchos desastres, y estuvo muy bien de que aplicaran
ciertas medidas o normas o leyes que nos pudieran proteger, pero pienso que para el ciu-
dadano que se dedique a laborar, no para los transgresores de esas mismas normas*]. So
when I read the treaties, for example the Pacto de San José, which is one of the
most recent and is the one that they mostly protect themselves with now, I tell you
it bothers me, yes, it bothers me, that that happens.

As another *ladino* respondent told me:

And all this [crime] has come since they signed the peace accords. That brought
chaos. And there's another thing, that's called human rights, that really only
supports criminals, and not common citizens. They [criminals] have to kill you
first, before [human rights groups] say, "OK, it's true, he killed him."

Many express sincere amazement at why human rights "protect
criminals" and asked me to explain to them the reasoning behind a system whereby criminals are allowed to kill innocent people with impunity but human rights groups rise up in protest if criminal suspects
are abused in detention, sentenced to death, lynched, or otherwise
given "what they deserve." In one lower-class area of the capital I conducted a focus group with four *ladino* men:

Q: And what do you think of human rights?

RESPONDENT NO. 3: Oh, that's the worst. Because here the ones who have human rights are the criminals.

RESPONDENT NO. 1: The criminals are the only ones who benefit.

Q: And why don't human rights groups identify with the people?

RESPONDENT NO. 4 [LAUGHING]: Go ask the human rights procurator.

RESPONDENT NO. 5: The truth is, I don't know in whose eyes they work, I don't know what international organization, I don't know who the hell they act for when they always try to cover up or protect criminals. How can you think the people aren't going to feel outraged that they capture them, they take them to the courts, and because they don't have conclusive proofs, or decisive proofs, or whatever they want to call them [*pruebas contundentes, pruebas fehacientes, o lo que quieran llamarles*], they don't try them, they don't sentence them? What they do is, since there aren't proofs, they let them go. So the people feel outraged, they say, "With this one that the police caught, or that we saw what he was doing, if the police take him, they'll let him go again, so it's better to lynch him right here." And what do the human rights say? "What savage people, what. . . ." So there they are, the human rights.

RESPONDENT NO. 3: To give you an example, say they catch a criminal here on the corner. Because he stabbed a man, or something. And they take him prisoner. Tomorrow at three in the afternoon you see him outside. But what happens if they see me beating up a criminal? They take me prisoner, and I'm stuck in there a month while they investigate. Just while they investigate. And where are human rights then?

RESPONDENT NO. 5: And where are the human rights of the people the criminals killed? Since they're already dead, they don't have any human rights anymore. They didn't have them when they were alive either. So human rights, for me, are good, but if they're applied to good people. But if they're for the people who make harm, we're better off without human rights. And we're better off without the government if they can't even govern this country.

As this exchange suggests, the condemnation of acts of *justicia a mano propia* by human rights groups has also provoked resentment and anger. In the capital, I asked one family what they thought of social cleansing:

SON: Here people were doing that, social cleansing, but then afterward they stopped. They were even burning people, you know, did you hear about that? But then they said not to do that, because it was a violation of human rights. The same thing happens with the students—before the Huelga de Dolores,[16] in the [University of] San Carlos, when the students saw a thief or a criminal, they ran after him—

DAUGHTER: They stripped them naked.

SON: Yeah, they stripped them naked, in Central Park, so that everyone would see them—

DAUGHTER: They put them in the fountain naked, where everyone could see.

SON: And they beat them up.

Q: But they don't do that anymore?

SON: No, they still do, but only during the Huelga.

DAUGHTER: And the police go after the students, too.

Q: What's your opinion of that?

MOTHER: It's a contradiction. Because for [the police], they say they're fighting for human rights, right? But in reality, they don't have any consideration for the rights of the people, because people want to see criminals punished. So, they enter into a contradiction there. They should really find another way.

DAUGHTER: And it's a way for people to vent [their anger]. Since they see that the police don't do anything, well, they have to do it, they have to take justice into their own hands. Isn't justice a human right too?

Others maintain that "the human rights" have acted to reinforce rather than reduce impunity:[17] the state, by limiting the repressive actions of the state and providing certain legal protections for accused criminals, constrains its own ability to fight crime.[18] Rather than a source of support for embattled communities, the human rights movement has been recast as their enemy, in a turn of events that to many seems inexplicably cruel.

Another middle-aged *ladina* woman explained to me:

The criminals, when they are poorly treated, then there are human rights for them. But they don't stop to think about their victims, about the people they've killed, raped, and everything; for those people there were no human rights. So we come to the conclusion that human rights are for criminals. They are the ones who benefit from that human rights stuff. I have an acquaintance who's a policeman, and he tells me that sometimes when they see a criminal they can't do anything to him, although sometimes criminals have even killed police officers. But they say that because of human rights, the police can't do anything to the criminals.

In the municipality of Sololá, a Kakchiquel Mayan man who worked as a Bombero Voluntario told me:[19]

What happens is that the police many times can't get involved [when there's a conflict], because if they are treated with violence, they have to respond with violence, but now [if they respond with violence] they are condemned. In other words, one factor here that's twisted everything around is the human rights, what they call human rights, because the criminal seizes onto that more than anything to defend himself, to favor himself, and so then the policeman can't get involved because he knows he'll have problems later if he interferes. They're afraid of being tried too, because the criminals . . . what happens is that the National Civilian Police was born after the signing [of the peace], and like I tell you, ever since they started to talk about human rights it's only come to spoil [*perjudicar*] a bunch of things, a bunch of factors here.

In many cases, the presence and prominence of international organizations charged with human rights tasks, such as MINUGUA, have been vehemently, at times violently, protested. This is particularly true in cases where the mission has criticized illegal actions taken to combat crime, such as lynchings, extrajudicial executions, or the creation of semiclandestine state crime-fighting agencies. From the rural peasants who arm themselves with sticks and stones to prevent the mission from interrupting a lynching, to the wealthy Botrán family, who filed legal charges against MINUGUA following the mission's criticism of a clandestine military intelligence unit's illegal intervention in a kidnapping case on the family's behalf, many Guatemalans express their displeasure at the United Nations' intervention in such cases.

Although elements of xenophobia may underscore some of these reactions, there is more to this critique of human rights than mere mistrust of foreigners. Many citizens perceive human rights as an imported concept, out of step with the everyday reality of a country like Guatemala. Some respondents told me that human rights sounded very well and good but didn't make sense for the crude realities of impoverished nations like Guatemala. "It must be nice to live in a country where everyone can be treated like that, with human rights and everything," a university student told me. "But I don't think those ideas make sense in Guatemala. They try to implement them here, but of course they don't work, we're too underdeveloped."

Others expressed similar views in response to the Catholic church's condemnation of the death penalty. "I'm Catholic," one man told me,

and I know the pope is against the death penalty. And I think if the world was better, I think if things in this country were better, that I should be against it too. Maybe if we lived in Europe, we could all be against the death penalty, because it wouldn't be necessary. But here, here it is necessary, here things are really bad, and there is no law, so we really need it. We need a punishment like that, to orient people toward morality.

In other words, some people recognize that human rights or other moral imperatives do represent some ideal form of regulating interaction in society, but express a sort of resignation to the notion that these ideals are too lofty for a place like Guatemala. The influence of international organizations and foreign governments may be well intentioned, but it is misguided; as a result, their pro–human rights policy prescriptions are meddlesome and unhelpful.

Still others charge international human rights promoters with cultural imperialism or reject the influence of human rights organizations and norms as a violation of Guatemala's sovereignty. Sitting in his newly constructed house in Guatemala City, digital phone by his side, a businessman and former congressional representative from the ultraright-wing Movimiento de Liberación Nacional (MLN) questioned the legitimacy of human rights conditions imposed by countries such as the United States that themselves violate the rights of others on a grand scale:

I think that in order to break out of our problem, it has to begin from the developed countries, the countries that provide security for the world. Everyone has to do what they want. And they talk about human rights. I laugh when many international organizations talk about human rights, but they can block out the sun with one finger [*tapar al sol con un dedo*] if they want to, and change any country. . . . How do you call a country that demands that human rights be respected in whatever place in the world, but then, it happens to strike the fancy of some politician in office and he gives the order for three hundred planes to go bomb someplace?

Later, becoming ever more animated, he thundered:

Our government sells out to an international protocol, and at a table just like this one, in an official banquet, over drinks, we sign the papers. We are selling our people a life that isn't true. It's a fantasy. And as long as the countries of the world keep believing in signing papers, it will be a failure. Papers put up with everything, but the tolerance of the human being has limits. It has limits. Here the criminals come, they kill entire families, they catch them—if the authorities *can* catch them—and you don't catch a criminal with the Bible in your hand. You catch him with weapons in your hand, because they carry weapons in their hands. And they shoot to kill. You don't catch them kneeling. You catch them when they're defeated, when they've run out of grenades and munitions. So someone's going to come out injured or beaten. MINUGUA comes running. The gringos come running, the Spaniards come running, to lock up the police who injured him, to defend criminals. *Those* are the human rights that they come to give us! So then we, we who are losing our lives and our belongings, we who are like pigs to them, what are we, less than human! So it shouldn't come as a surprise, to any embassy in the world, that . . . one of these days, things are going to explode! And they are going to burn people! Because the people are getting tired. We're getting tired. We're very respectful of international protocols, and very respectful of visitors to our country, we are the noble Indian, but *we get tired.*

At this point his wife, who had apparently overheard from an adjacent room, intervened abruptly: "Honey, you're going to frighten her! That's enough talk about burning people!" Turning to me, she smiled very sweetly, shook her head, and offered me *cafecito.*

A brief examination of the case of one proposed piece of human rights legislation, the ill-fated Children's Code (Código del Niño),[20] illustrates the antagonism often sparked by human rights interventions in domestic policy debates. Designed to provide improved protection for the rights of children in Guatemala, the Children's Code was first proposed as a preliminary bill in 1995 and debated intensely in both public and private circles in the ensuing years, attracting considerable media attention and provoking unusually passionate opposition from many sectors. The content of the bill was not radical—it merely aimed to institute a framework in national law for the enforcement of the International Convention on the Rights of the Child, which Guatemala had already ratified. Following repeated postponements of its debate and implementation, it was conclusively defeated in early 2000.

LaRue, Taylor, and Salazar-Volkmann's case study (1998) of the polemic generated by this legislation documents its opponents' accusations that foreign agencies were using the code to subvert Guatemalan family values. The authors cite excerpts from several newspaper editorials. "The code, in its entirety, is a great mistake. In the first place because it disregards the social and cultural ethos of the Guatemalan family, that has nothing in common with the situation of the institution of the family in Scandinavia," one editorial reported, alluding to the bill's backing by several European NGOs.[21] Another article stated, "A good part of the content of the code was imposed—although hidden in diplomacy—by international organizations that had their own agenda and pushed their own objectives, as is the case with UNICEF."[22] A third went even further: "Engraved in the most diabolical minds of UNICEF and associates, the Code for Children is a frontal attack on biblical and Christian principles, 'Honor thy father and thy mother, that your days may be long on the earth that God has given you.' . . . Those in UNICEF know perfectly well that undermining this principle by means of the generalization of exception is to break up the family and open the field to the URNG."[23]

This assault on human rights has important implications for progressive politics more generally. To the proponents of this legislation, which was far from radical in its aims, the sharp opposition it generated came as something of a surprise. Yet, as LaRue, Taylor, and Salazar-Volkmann argue:

We think that what is being discussed is not really a new legal framework for Children and Youth. The debate so far is a reflection of the political struggle for the direction that will be taken in the peace process and the democratization of the country. Thus the defenders of the Code found themselves involved in a discussion that transcends "child issues" but pointed into the heart of the contemporary political debate of the country. And this meant that suddenly the organizations working on behalf of children and adolescents had to confront powerful social and economic forces in the country. (LaRue, Taylor, and Salazar-Volkmann 1998: 2)

Similar issues are at stake in the effort to elucidate a meaningful state response to crime. In some ways, that debate is even more polarized: in the case of children, human rights organizations and some opinion leaders mounted a vigorous defense of the code, despite the opposition's effort to demonize them as blasphemous fanatics. In the case of crime, however, speaking out against the right's *mano dura* machinations has proven extraordinarily unpopular. No one wants to be depicted as defending criminals. The current situation places Guatemalan human rights organizations in the unenviable position of either choosing to call for repressive action (in the form of law enforcement) from the state they have spent decades condemning, or standing idly by while the crime rate climbs. Although many mention the need for social policies to address economic exclusion as a means of reducing crime, emphasizing a preventative approach, the absolute absence of serious alternatives to the *mano dura* approach to crime is striking.

Today, the momentum behind implementation of the peace accords has greatly slowed. Crises and pressing problems—among them, crime—have sidetracked efforts at lasting social reform. Yet although some might argue that the crime wave—at least that portion of it that is driven by economic desperation—might be addressed precisely by implementing the peace accords, the issue has been addressed in a manner that seeks short-term symbolic results at the expense of long-term social transformations. *Mano dura* has not only delegitimized the groups calling for government implementation of the peace accords; it has also reinforced the existing structures of state repression that the accords themselves sought to dismantle. In this way, ironically, the forces that promised a strong hand against violence may be those least equipped to deliver it—and those most likely to curtail the very rights citizens considered most fundamental to democracy in the process. In seeking to restrain crime, Guatemala's citizens have unwittingly empowered institutions antagonistic to democratic rule and rolled back the very rights in which they reveled on the eve of the peace. But why?

What is the appeal of *mano dura?* In the following chapters, I seek to explore this question from the bottom up. I turn first to the matter of lynchings, in chapters 3 and 4, and then return to some broader considerations about *mano dura* more generally, in chapters 5 and 6.

CHAPTER 3

Militarization and Lynchings

AS A MEANS OF INVESTIGATING *mano dura* from the bottom up, I conducted extensive (and intensive) research on the phenomenon of lynchings. In Guatemala, this research took me to the highlands department of El Quiché, where the war had raged most fiercely and where the phenomenon of postwar lynchings has been most prevalent. And despite my dogged pursuit of information about *today's* violence, this research also took me to the past.

In El Quiché, my careful attempts to craft politically neutral first questions fell flat. I didn't have to ask about *la violencia*: usually sometime between the turning on of the tape recorder and the phrasing of my delicately scripted introductory question, my respondents would simply start spilling their stories. And they always began with the war. This was as true of the elderly, some of whom could still remember how things had been before the conflict, as it was of the young—those who had grown up after the cessation of formal hostilities but who nonetheless felt the need to explain up front why they had no father, or no land, or no money for school. For the Mayan campesino communities of Guatemala's western highlands, the scorched earth campaigns of the late 1970s and early 1980s were a defining experience. And despite the fact that the war ended in 1996, its legacies linger in unexpected ways. So although I aimed to understand present-day violence in Guatemala, I learned quickly that in a country ravaged by decades of brutal state violence, there can be no explaining the present without exploring the past.

After some time in the field, of course, this seemed obvious. It wasn't a coincidence that most highland Mayans tie their life histories so intimately to the war, just as it isn't a coincidence that their communities, besieged by criminal lawlessness, sometimes seek to uphold order today through acts of counter-criminal terror strikingly similar to those used by the army—and to a lesser extent, by the guerrillas as well—against those who were its enemies during the conflict period. As MINUGUA notes, the departments where most lynchings have occurred are also the departments where the CEH documented the largest number of human rights violations during the war; this is also true at the municipal level, within departments. A large number of lynchings are also evident in three of the four areas where the CEH concluded that genocide had been committed (MINUGUA 2002: 5–6). Despite this, however, the connections between state terror and lynchings are not as simple as one might expect.

Some observers have argued that lynchings constitute evidence of the continued domination of highland communities by the army. One nationally prominent Mayan leader, for example, told me that lynchings were instigated in Mayan communities by pro-military outsiders who even brought their own gasoline. More often, observers point to the influence of individuals within the communities with ties to the armed forces—especially former civil patrollers (also known as PACs [*patrullas de autodefensa civil*]) and military commissioners (Amnesty International 2000; Molina Mejía 2001). MINUGUA, particularly in its 2000 report on the topic, stresses the participation of former patrollers and the use of tactics at times identical to those implemented by the army and patrollers during the war (MINUGUA 2000b, 2002). In a context in which the phenomenon has been cited as evidence of indigenous backwardness and barbarism (see chapter 1), these sources rightly strive to disarticulate lynchings from Mayan traditional justice and trace the responsibility for such acts to past practices of state repression. Yet in doing so without discussing the willing, even at times enthusiastic, participation of many Mayan communities in lynchings—or in reducing such participation to yet another reflection of their victimization—they may unwittingly perpetuate simplistic understandings of Mayan communities as insular collectivities of victims manipulated by outside forces, rather than as agents actively struggling to better their situation. These communities may be deeply divided and disempowered in the wake of decades of repression, but they are still able to contemplate collective action without coercion.[1]

In this chapter, I trace the lynchings' roots in state terror. In the Guatemalan highlands, the destruction of the social fabric in Mayan communities was a deliberate objective of the state's counterinsurgency war; following campaigns of selective assassination of leaders and the destruction of repositories of cultural meaning, the army sought to replace preexisting structures and practices with new, militarized forms of authority and governance. This process did more than traumatize individual survivors; it altered the institutions of justice, collective decision making, and community authority, and it decimated intangible undergirdings of institutional health such as trust, shared traditions, and collective memory. In the wake of the war, it is not surprising that many communities have chosen to reenact violent rituals performed by the occupying army after their own practices were systematically eradicated. In some cases, Mayan villagers told me they were forced to collaborate with lynchings led by ex-patrollers. But in other cases, they told me they were willing participants, even organizers, of this contemporary vigilantism. This is not a story of villains and victims; it is a story of the complex, confounding effects of violence on communities and the challenge of negotiating justice in a postgenocidal world where fear and repression persist. In this chapter, I first explore the ways state terror unraveled the social fabric of Mayan communities, and then I examine two ways in which lynchings flow from this process: first, through the forced imposition of lynchings in some communities by former military or paramilitary leaders, and second, through the willing participation of some communities themselves in these acts.

Genocide and Community

Although violence and terror are always devastating to individuals, and by extension to the communities they inhabit, genocide is more than the sum of its parts. Defined by the United Nations Genocide Convention as "acts committed with intent to destroy, in whole or in part, a national, ethnic, racial or religious group," whether by killing its members, causing them serious bodily or mental harm, forcing them to live under conditions calculated to cause their destruction, or other means,[2] genocide is the destruction of collective life itself. Yet we seldom examine exactly what this means in concrete terms, often assuming the definition hinges on the mere massiveness of the killing campaign. The case of contemporary lynchings in Guatemala provides a specific window into the uniquely sociological effects of genocide.

Though it is often tempting to view acts of state terror as the work of madmen, loose cannons, or rogue officers out of control—and indeed, this has generally been the defense of commanders when called to account for abuses that happened on their watch—the systematic and deliberate nature of the abuses committed by the army in the highlands has been well documented by a series of sources. Scholarly analyses include those of Gabriel Aguilera Peralta (1979), Robert Carmack (1988), Carol Smith (1990), Susanne Jonas (1991, 2000), Jennifer Schirmer (1998), Linda Green (1999), Ricardo Falla (1998), Beatriz Manz (2004), Victoria Sanford (2003), and many others. Human rights reports include periodic releases by large organizations such as Amnesty International and Americas Watch/Human Rights Watch, as well as documents variously published by U.S.-based groups such as the Washington Office on Latin America, the International Human Rights Law Group, Human Rights First (formerly the Lawyers Committee for Human Rights), and the Robert F. Kennedy Memorial Center for Human Rights; and Guatemalan NGOs such as GAM, FAMDEGUA, and CALDH; and finally, broader truth-seeking initiatives including the Catholic church's Interdiocesan Recovery of Historical Memory (REMHI) report, *Guatemala: Never Again!* (1998), and the CEH's monumental *Memory of Silence* (1999). All these sources provide ample evidence that such abuses occurred in the context of a campaign of terror systematically orchestrated from the highest levels of state authority. It is not my intention here to provide a new or unique analysis of this period in Guatemalan history; rather, I will sum up some of the most salient conclusions expressed in this rich literature and use them to inform my analysis of postwar lynchings.

Both the guerrillas and government forces committed atrocities against the civilian population of Guatemala's highland communities. But the army's efforts were uniquely aimed at eliminating an entire social world. By the early 1980s it had become clear that the army could not defeat the guerrillas on the battlefield; its sporadic and brutal attacks, including massacres and selective killings, had served only to radicalize much of the population, bolstering support for the armed insurgency. A secret CIA cable from April 1981, declassified in 1998, provides a telling glimpse of the army's encounter with one community where many reportedly sympathized with the rebels. Upon the arrival of an army patrol in the village of Cocob, the document explains, villagers greeted the soldiers by pelting them with rocks. A house-by-house search turned up automatic weapons, literature from the

Guerrilla Army of the Poor (Ejército Guerrillero de los Pobres [EGP]), uniforms, and other signs of support for the armed insurgency. The CIA's source reported: "The local population appeared to fully support the guerrillas. . . . It was impossible to differentiate between the actual guerrillas and innocent civilians, and according to [name excised] the soldiers were forced to fire at anything that moved. The Guatemalan authorities admitted that 'many civilians' were killed in Cocob, many of them undoubtedly were non-combatants."

According to some estimates, by 1982 the guerrilla forces boasted as many as 500,000 supporters among the civilian population (Schirmer 1998: 61). The guerrillas had shown themselves to be effective at acts of sabotage and the selective assassination of troops, officers, and military commissioners, contributing to an overall impression that the army, for the first time, found itself in foreign territory and was losing badly. A turning point came in March 1982, with the coup that brought Ríos Montt to power. Ríos presided over a new military effort that aimed, in the words of Jennifer Schirmer, "first to exterminate thousands upon thousands of indigenous noncombatants in waves of terror and then [to] recoup any refugee-prisoners left over in order to ensure the permanent destruction of the combatants' infrastructure" (1998: 45).

A 1982 CIA cable (declassified in February 1998), in describing the army's sweeps into Ixil territory in February 1982, illuminates the logic behind the killings:

The commanding officers of the units involved have been instructed to destroy all towns and villages which are collaborating with the Guerrilla Army of the Poor (EGP) and eliminate all sources of resistance. . . . Comment: When an Army patrol meets resistance and takes fire from a town or village it is assumed that the entire town is hostile and it is subsequently destroyed. The Army found that most of the villages have been abandoned before the military forces arrive. An empty village is assumed to have been supporting the EGP, and it is destroyed. . . . *The well-documented belief by the Army that the entire Ixil Indian population is pro-EGP has created a situation in which the Army can be expected to give no quarter to combatants and non-combatants alike.* (Emphasis mine)

The declassification of these lines merely confirmed something many had long suspected: that centuries of entrenched racism against the country's indigenous populations, combined with the model of all-out internal war embraced under the National Security Doctrine promoted by the United States, had led to a decision by the army high command to equate indigenous identity with armed insurgency. It was on the basis of this assumption that the army turned from selective sweeps

aimed at routing out rebels to the massive and total reengineering of social life in Mayan communities; it was through this logic that state terror became genocide.

The army's imposition of a new social order took place through a
multi-step process. In her recent book *Buried Secrets: Truth and Human
Rights in Guatemala* (2003), Victoria Sanford offers a painstakingly detailed account of what she calls a "phenomenology of terror," tracing
the multiple stages of state violence and repression experienced by
Mayan communities, before, during, and after the massacres; here, for
the sake of simplicity, I condense these processes into two phases. The
first was the decimation of the preexisting institutions of civil society in
Mayan communities; the second was their replacement with new, perverse forms of social organization that have endured into the postwar
period.

Phase 1: Rupture

To begin with, the army sought to destroy highland Mayan communities as social units. During its early incursions into the area, it systematically eliminated an entire generation of leftists and political activists:
organizers of such entities as trade unions, Catholic Action groups, student activist committees, and other organizations with anything that re-
sembled a social justice agenda were assassinated. Eventually, however,
the army's failure to draw a distinction between the Mayan population
and the guerrillas meant that *any* community leader—not only those
involved in overtly political activities—came to be viewed as a representative of the internal enemy. This led to the widespread elimination
of Mayan priests, mayors, village elders, traditional authorities, and
others. Because they were the people charged with carrying out important tasks in local government, passing on religious and cultural
traditions to future generations, and guiding their communities
through times of trouble, the loss of these leaders had inevitable and
far-reaching effects on collective life in the region. As the truth commission reports:

Between 1980 and 1983 the military strategy caused the dismantling of the
Mayan communities as social collectivities. It oriented its activities toward the
destruction of order based on authority and the organization and abolition of
the symbols of cultural identity. In its extreme form, the army carried out the total elimination of communities, as in the scorched earth operations, massacres,
executions, torture, and mass rapes.

Between 1980 and 1983 the army assassinated ancients, *principales, k'amal b'e,* municipal and auxiliary mayors or other municipal authorities, indigenous spiritual guides or *ajq'ojab,* directors of committees, *cofrades,* leaders. The persecution, death, torture or disappearance of these leaders left the communities without "guides," and was aimed to terrorize them, disperse them, or reduce their capacity for resistance, or as a phase prior to a massacre or massive action. (CEH 1999: chap. 3, paras. 459–60)

In addition to leaders, entire communities were eliminated: the truth commission estimates a total of 626 massacres during the war, and according to the Catholic church's report, in the department of El Quiché alone some 344 villages were razed (CEH 1999: vol. 2, chap. 2, para. 97). More than merely collective assassinations, these massacres were attempts to destroy society itself. Even when all human inhabitants of targeted villages had been killed or forced to flee, homes and crops were set afire, household implements were systematically destroyed, and livestock and animals—horses, dogs, pigs—were killed. At times, when the army abandoned a community following a massacre, it left bags of poisoned foodstuffs at the site of its encampment or attempted to poison the well (REMHI 1998: vol. 1, 106); fleeing refugees were systematically hunted, bombed, and raided in the mountains where they sought shelter; every effort was made to ensure that no survivors could reestablish an independent settlement. The effects of these tactics, then, have a permanence that extends beyond the numbers of dead or disappeared; for those who survived the killing campaigns, there was literally nothing left to return to; not only the destruction of life, but the elimination of conditions which could enable *future* life, was a deliberate and unambiguous goal.

Furthermore, the army targeted Mayan culture itself. Sacred sites were profaned,[3] the wearing of indigenous dress and the speaking of languages other than Spanish effectively criminalized,[4] and the practice of Mayan religion and cosmology, with its links to the earth, the harvest, and the ancestors, was made nearly impossible by the burning of cornfields, the deliberate display of corpses without the performance of proper burial rites, the forced displacement of entire communities, and other forms of transgression. The effects of such a holocaust cannot be measured merely in individual lives lost. As the REMHI project explains:

Many of these material and social losses . . . take on the character of symbolic wounds, that is to say that they wounded the sentiments, the dignity, hope, and the . . . elements which form a basis for . . . culture, for social life, for politics and history. The normative system was destroyed when the force of arms was imposed, when traditional leaders and authorities were killed; and in destroying basic social organization, the community's ethical and moral principles were also transgressed. Confusion among the inhabitants was generated, because it was precisely the most respected and valued people, those considered guides of the community, who were first killed by the army, since it considered them . . . guerrillas and communists. The sacred was profaned; the land was taken; the harvests, the hills, nature in general was cut and burned; the houses were burned, and within them the home altars; the water was poisoned; the church was burned; their loved ones were killed in the places where ancestral ceremonies were performed; the spaces in which the dead had been buried were profaned; dignity was stepped upon; struggle, hope, life, were all attacked. (ODHAG 1998: vol. 1, 107)

Phase 2: Replacement

Among survivors, the second and perhaps more insidious feature of the transformation of highland community life was the army's effort to replace the previously existing institutions of civil society and traditions of collective life with new, militarized substitutes. Traditional leaders were supplanted by a network of army informants and collaborators, including military commissioners, civil patrollers, and individuals known as *orejas* (literally, "ears") who conducted surveillance, provided information, and carried out orders issued by the army.

The most pervasive of these structures was the civil patrols (PACs), in which the army obligated male residents of highland communities to serve as paramilitary forces—informing on community members' behavior, assisting the army in counterinsurgency operations, patrolling the community to "protect" it from guerrilla infiltrators, and at times, participating in executions and massacres of community members. In 1986, an estimated one million citizens were involved in the patrols— by some estimates, one of every two men in the entire country (CEH 1999: chap. 2, para. 1376), and up to 80 percent of the male population aged fifteen to sixty in the rural zones of the indigenous highlands (REMHI 1998: vol. 2, 119). At their height, the patrols were described by Americas Watch as "the most extensive counterinsurgency model of its kind in the world."[5] In many communities, militarized authority came to be so pervasive that military commissioners, patrollers, or the army governed everyday decisions about the distribution of aid, the granting of permission for cultural events, and the resolution of daily conflicts, including marital disputes and quarrels between neighbors. The army thus controlled social life so completely that other, nonmilitary forms of organization were not only illegal, but unthinkable.

By supplanting local authorities with paramilitary figures chosen from within the communities themselves, the army was able to effectively divide and conquer the civilian population, neutralizing resistance at its root—at the very sense of belonging to a community. This disruption of social bonds between neighbors and kin was further heightened by forcing some to participate in atrocities against members of their own community. In some 13 percent of the massacres documented by REMHI, the army used people from the target communities themselves to identify others for execution, frequently assembling all members of the community and obligating a collaborator to point out the guerrilla sympathizers among them (REMHI 1998: vol. 2, 34). One out of every four mass killings included the participation of civil patrollers or military commissioners (REMHI 1998: vol. 2, 122). These practices replaced community cohesion based on shared traditions with submission to the military based on fear.

In the wake of the war, these forms of authority remain embedded in local practices, not only because many ex-paramilitary leaders retain de facto control over some communities, but, more significantly, because community life itself—people's ways of coming together and relating to one another, their interactions and expectations—have been deeply infused with violence. The war's most lasting legacy in Guatemala, then, may lie not in the long lists of victims nor the hundreds of unmarked gravesites. It may reside in something that left no visible remains: these violated networks of community cohesion, trust, and meaning. Although new generations of Guatemalans now inhabit the places left vacant by the massacres, the social space that binds them is still haunted by this history of terror.

Lynchings and Community

How does the loss of community translate into today's lynchings?

First, in the wake of the fighting, many highland communities remain fragmented. In some cases, victims of violence live side by side with army collaborators; returned refugees inhabit the same areas as former residents of army hamlets; and human rights groups and widows organize alongside ex-patrollers. In this atmosphere of fragile coexistence, collective decision making is fraught with difficulty, particularly around topics—such as crime—that ignite passionate re-actions. The elimination of traditional Mayan leaders and their replace-ment with militarized forms of authority has left these collectivities profoundly vulnerable, forced to confront contemporary problems without leadership structures that transcend wartime differences.

Civil Patrols and Lynchings

In many cases, lynchings are instigated by former paramilitary leaders (MINUGUA 2002; Amnesty International 2000; personal interviews). Today, former patrollers and military commissioners continue to exer-cise de facto authority in many communities, despite the peace accords' mandated dissolution of these structures. Former patrollers have orga-nized to stage jailbreaks for their convicted comrades,[6] to demand com-pensation for their years of unpaid service to the state, and to carry out attacks and acts of intimidation against human rights organizations throughout the highlands (Amnesty International 2002). Some have been organized by a national group called AVEMILGUA, founded in 1995 to promote the interests of former military and civil patrollers (Lawyers Committee for Human Rights [LCHR] 2003). Beginning in 2002, former patrollers, at least some of them under AVEMILGUA lead-ership, staged a series of collective demonstrations demanding com-pensation from the government; mobilizations of at times up to twenty thousand ex-PACs took place in Mazatenango, Alta Verapaz, Quetzal-tenango, Sololá, San Marcos, El Quiché, Chimaltenango, Jutiapa, Toto-nicapán, and Huehuetenango, their size and scope pointing to the presence of a significant national organization. In June 2002, former pa-trollers held foreign tourists hostage for days at the Mayan ruins at Tikal as part of their strategy of demanding government attention to their concerns. Yet while a teachers' strike for increased wages dragged on for months that same year, President Portillo moved quickly to con-versations with the ex-patrollers (Amnesty International 2002), and plans were soon announced to buy European bonds to finance com-pensation to the former patrollers—despite the fact that many pa-trollers participated in egregious violations of human rights and most victims of this violence have yet to receive any reparations whatsoever.

In light of these developments, many highland residents told me that far from waning, the influence of the former patrols has grown in recent years. This has palpable effects at the local level. Contemporary ethno-graphic research in highland communities documents the climate of ongoing fear that exists in some areas where ex-patrollers or commissioners still wield considerable power (González 2000; Remijnse 2000). In many cases, these men have now assumed leadership roles as auxiliary mayors or members of local municipal councils, often though not always affiliated with the right-wing FRG; in others, they function under the guise of local development committees; and in yet others, they form part of influential personal networks, without any formal organization.

Some organized structures of former military collaborators have remained active, although semiclandestine. In the region surrounding Chichicastenango, El Quiché, for example, many residents report the existence of a paramilitary organization known as La Cadena (The Chain). La Cadena was formed during the war and served as a way for civil patrol commanders to coordinate their actions between communities and with the army. Today, the formal dissolution of the civil patrols has forced the organization underground, but it remains powerful, and many of its members play key roles in local politics. The following is an excerpt from a discussion I had with several area residents on this topic:

RESPONDENT NO. 1: La Cadena is a chain they've made. The ex-patrollers are all . . . in the organization, and they linked up with some others. They have their bosses in each village, and they have their meetings whenever there's a problem, to decide if they want to lynch or what they're going to do, all those questions, then they gather together all the villages and they decide to do away with someone.

RESPONDENT NO. 2: What I understand is that La Cadena is a kind of a union between the community leaders, and many times they receive orientations or instructions from the army. But sometimes they go beyond what the army says, they act more brusquely than what the army tells them. I don't think that they only do what they're told, but that they now feel that they have the freedom to do things as they please.

Q: But is it a clandestine organization, or is it publicly known?

RESPONDENT NO. 2: It's clandestine, now, after the signing of the peace. But it's been around for years. They legalized it in some communities by putting another name on it, like calling it a development committee or something, but it's the same thing always. They don't say anymore that they're from the civil patrols, they say that they're an institution that has projects for the community.

For some of these organizations and individuals, the widely acknowledged crime wave constitutes an unprecedented call to action. Former patrol leaders, schooled in the use of weapons and reputed to be tough, often view themselves (and/or are viewed by others) as "naturals" to assume leadership roles in policing the community against crime. In some parts of the highlands, local security committees now patrol for criminals—sometimes at the insistence of former military collaborators, and sometimes with popular support—in much the same way as the civil patrollers formerly did for guerrillas. In some areas, the integration of these committees has been voluntary, in others it has been described as coercive, and in many cases it appears to be a murky blend of both. In any case, the formation of such groups at the hands of those who formerly wielded military or paramilitary power in the region can only invite ongoing abuses, as the human rights groups Comunidades Etnicas Runujel Junam (CERJ [Council of Ethnic Communities—"We Are All Equal"]) and CONAVIGUA have warned (López Ovando 2000).

One community organizer from a village near Chichicastenango told me:

There are two opposite situations [in the community]. One is that the structure of the PAC continues. It's latent. And two is that the *compañeros* who are organized, who are members of some organization, they also are receiving training, so there are two latent currents in the communities and these could lead to a confrontation one day. Why? Because those who are organized aren't going to let their rights be violated, they aren't going to allow the people to act like they acted before. And also the PAC are also strong, they have not been disarticulated—formally, yes, but they still exist. Formally, in the eyes of the government and the international community, the PAC were disarticulated, they turned in their weapons, everything, but in the communities they maintain a structure . . . and with the arrival of this government [the FRG government, 2000–2004], the paramilitary structures were strengthened, although formally the government can't reactivate the PAC, they can't give orders for them to act like they acted before, but they, morally, they feel strengthened because it's the FRG, it's Ríos Montt, even though they can't act legally.

The infiltration of former patrol leaders and military commanders into contemporary structures of formal authority complicates the divisions within communities:

There are local authorities but they have those ideas of the past stuck in their heads. So those people, now they're the authorities, but many of them have ideas, well, they were brainwashed by the army. They told them that the guerrillas were the ones who stole the chickens, who raped the women, all those things, but the people know, the guerrillas didn't have problems with the people because it wasn't true. The ones who did those things were the soldiers and the people knew it, although you couldn't say so. But it's known, it's known nowadays who were those who killed people, who were those who burned people, it's known who they were but you can't say anything to them about it. So that's the root of the problem, because since they organized the civil patrols, there those people that were in the patrols got accustomed to those things, to burning and all of that. Nowadays they don't burn with their houses and all, but they're still burning. Those people are trained [*viene orientada esa gente*], that's the problem. The people are trained but the rest don't know it, the rest allow themselves to be manipulated by the fear that exists in the communities. That's the problem. There are some who are naive, who get involved with things without really knowing what they're doing. Since the 1980s we've known that this type of thing was going to happen, these lynchings, because those were the ideas that they gave to the heads of the patrols, because our people, people from our own community were patrollers, and they heard the . . . orientations that they gave them in those days. They said don't back down [*no se dejen*], when we go another time will come [*cuando nos vamos habrá otra época*], and for a long time you will have to be like this with the people [*y durante tiempo ustedes tienen que ser así con la gente*]. They already knew that things were going to change and they were preparing the people. Since then. So we know, because many of our people were part of the patrols and received that training, and there was information since that time that things like lynchings were going to happen.

In many cases, paramilitary leaders have not only promoted lynchings, but even forced area residents to participate in them, threatening those who have resisted. These acts of intimidation have been denounced by MINUGUA, local human rights groups, and international organizations such as Amnesty International (MINUGUA 1999a, 1999b, 1999c; Amnesty International 2000, 2002).

In one community, residents told me that a former PAC commander and member of La Cadena, who currently forms part of a local municipal council, had taken up a collection among the villagers. Each family was charged one *quetzal* to pay for gasoline, which he would purchase and keep "should the need for action arise." Some reported that they were afraid of him because of the atrocities he had committed in the past but felt forced to contribute to the collection.

One young K'iche' woman told me that her community had trouble surmounting the legacies of past violence because of the ongoing presence of one man:

In the case of Anastasio Choc,[7] who was a military commissioner, that is the one thing he never forgot, and now he thinks he's great because of it. [*Impersonating a male voice*] "Ah, I was in the service, I was a military commissioner, so if this doesn't straighten out, it's pure war" [*Ah, yo presté servicio, yo fui comisionado militar, así que esto si no se compone, a pura guerra*]. I know another [man] who was the head of the patrols. They think they're better because they were in the service.

In those days, if someone was in the service, careful—he's an authority. You couldn't say to them "listen here" ... no. "I'm the authority, and I'm the authority" [*En aquel entonces, si prestaba servicio, cuidado. Es una autoridad. Y nada que uno les dice "mire usted." ... No. Soy autoridad, y soy autoridad*]. And now they're the ones who, when we had our last [community] meeting ... the people said, "Ay, it's that Anastasio Choc, he's the one that kills people, that scares people."[8] He can't motivate people because they people have been traumatized by him, because he's a man that really destroyed the community [*El no puede motivar la gente porque ya la gente se ha quedado traumada con él, porque es un señor que de verdad, destruía la comunidad*]. Before, during the armed conflict, the commander came, grabbed people, killed many people ... and so Anastasio Choc and his men, since they thought they were the most manly, people respected what they said to do. "Look, go form a patrol." And if they didn't patrol, he caught them and beat them [*a puros cuentazos les agarraba*]. So people had to respect them, because if they didn't respect them, then in the morning they wouldn't exist anymore [*Tenían que respetarlos, porque si uno no los respetaba, ya al amanecer ya no existía*].

... And those men, when they drink, when they get drunk, how they yell! Sometimes Anastasio used to yell, "I was in the service, I had a position ..." [*yo presté servicio, yo ocupé un lugar ...*] and he'd say a bunch of names then of the people he'd served with, and all that, and he'd throw rocks, really, like to show how strong he was, and sometimes he'd pass by, since we live at the edge of a path he'd pass by yelling, "I'm not afraid of anyone, not students, not *licenciados*,[9] I'm not afraid of anyone!" [*A veces gritaba, que "yo no tengo miedo a nadie, que ni que estudiantes, ni que licenciados, no tengo miedo a nadie," decía*]. "The police are coming, we're going to denounce you!" I yelled back once. "What do I care? What do you think? I'm a sergeant"—or something like that—he made up many things. And it was always like that. ... That's what happened. But really, the majority of the people there in my village don't have any education, they've only been educated by the military, that's where they went to get educated. They'd barely turn eighteen and they [the army] would grab them [by forcible recruitment], you were lucky then if you were already too old [to be recruited], although sometimes even up to thirty-five they'd take them too, because they tried to grab my father too, to make him serve, but he was always hiding. Sometimes he wouldn't sleep at home, since at night was when they'd come and grab them, so sometimes my father slept in the wheat cane,[10] and we piled the trash around him so that you couldn't see, and he'd sleep in there. And when they'd come to knock on the door, my mother would say, "Look, my husband's not here." That's how they used to do. And now, the people who did give [military] service, well, people say, "Careful with him because he did [military] service, and you didn't do any service so don't you say anything" [*Y ahora, las personas que han prestado servicio, pues dice la gente, "O, él prestó servicio, cuidadito con él porque prestó servicio, y ustedes no prestaron servicio así que no digan nada"*].

... But thank God some of that is calming down now.[11] In the case of Anastasio Choc, oh God, he made life impossible for the people. Sometimes he would charge [a fee] at the market, where people were selling in their little spots, he would charge, and if you said you couldn't pay, [imitating his voice] "Well, I was in the service, and the soldiers are right there" [pointing]. And just seeing a soldier standing there in the market, the people—especially since some don't speak Spanish—would be quiet. Even me, there was a time when I was scared if I saw soldiers. Worse, in the old days, when they painted their faces, and they wore those costumes, well, I was afraid of them. But now by the grace of God, slowly that's being forgotten, because like I said in that meeting when we were all there, "Be careful gentlemen, we want peace, so why do we want to stoke the fires again? Things are calm now, we are starting a new life. We have to support young people today, and look for a way to forget those traumas, those things that are really nightmares and terrible but that happen in life. So that they don't exist anymore" [*Cuidadito señores, que nosotros queremos la paz, entonces ¿por qué nosotros queremos juntar otra vez el fuego? Ya calmados, ahora empezamos una nueva vida. Hay que apoyar a los jóvenes el día de hoy, y buscar cómo olvidar esas traumas, esas cosas que de verdad son pesadillas y son tremendas pero pasan en la vida. Para que ya no existan más*].

Although most lynchings appear to target common criminals, the summary nature of the executions makes it easy for influential individuals to promote the lynching of their political adversaries by accusing them of petty crimes. As one man, a member of a local human rights group, told me:

They say that the organization [of the PACs] was destroyed, but it hasn't been destroyed. They're organized, they're coordinated, and they're united clandestinely. Only they know, but whatever thing that happens, there they take advantage of the popular organizations to eliminate the leaders [*descabezar*, literally "to decapitate"] again, just like in the past it's happening today. Before they didn't burn people, they kidnapped them, and who knows where they threw their bodies. So now they can't do that, since they signed the peace. Now they're blaming the government authorities, because they say that the judges don't make justice, that [it's the fault of] the Public Ministry, that [it's the fault of] the courts, that's what they say, but that's purely a strategy of those people [*es pura estrategia de esa gente*]. So nowadays I think, from what I've lived and what I've heard in San Pablo, I'm talking about San Pablo here, that they know the relatives of the organized people, or the people who were involved in the war, and they take advantage to get rid of those people, so now they're accusing them of being thieves, of being criminals, of other things. Today they're taking advantage of the situation to burn people in these areas. I don't know if you've noticed, but only in the areas where there was conflict during the war, that's where these things are happening now, and in other areas nothing has happened. Why? Because in other areas there are no heads of patrol, or there are but they're not organized, so there isn't any structure. For me that's the root of the problem, the first root of the problem that we're seeing. We're seeing that they're people who have struggled since the beginning, the ones they're burning now, they're eliminating them for being thieves, like in the case of Santa Ana recently. . . . Now they're burning people, they're burning, but they're trained by certain people, and that's the real root of the problem, I think, it's not the people's fault because they were trained, they filled their heads with many things.

. . . Now there aren't any [kidnappings], but there have been rumors. Just rumors and like that, because like they say, the peace has been signed and the people have already seen how the war was, and all of those things. What's happening now is that they're in La Cadena, and they're orienting people, telling them that they shouldn't let those people make fools of them, that it's better to shut them up so they stop bothering others, and so that's when they come up with the idea of burning them, to get rid of those people. That's what's happening, but they're all rumors. They're the men who were the leaders of the PACs, who manipulate the people in the communities, who say these things.

A number of cases lend credence to this man's accusations. The most notorious is the July 8, 2000, lynching of eight people at Xalbaquiej, near Chichicastenango (Amnesty International 2002). A crowd of approximately two hundred residents created roadblocks and waited—apparently for hours—for the arrival of their victims, whom they dragged from their trucks, doused in gasoline, and set afire. The clearly planned nature of the attack and the identity of the victims and alleged victimizers suggest that there was more at stake here than inflamed passions over crime. Five of the victims were the surviving relatives of a single family massacred by the civil patrols of Xalbaquiej in 1993; a ninth intended victim, who managed to escape, had testified before the truth commission about the massacre, providing information that was later featured as a case study in the commission's final report. The family had also denounced the massacre of their relatives in court, leading to the detention of two former patrollers for two months (Llorca 2000). Those implicated in organizing the lynching, on the other hand, shared links not only to the civil patrols and paramilitary associations of the past, but also to the staff of the then-mayor of Chichicastenango. The clear political antecedents that mark the victimizers' relationship to their victims and the complete lack of evidence to substantiate the accusations of thievery that drove the lynch mob to kill suggest that the victims' "criminal record" may have been fabricated by locally powerful paramilitary leaders in order to eliminate their personal and political rivals. Indeed, a local priest, Rigoberto Pérez, has insisted this incident should be considered not a lynching, but a postwar massacre committed by former civil patrollers.

The incidents that followed the lynching also suggest a coordinated effort by locally powerful forces. The incident at Xalbaquiej remains the largest lynching—in terms of the number of victims—to date, and perhaps for this reason it received an unusual amount of public and media attention within Guatemala. Days after the event, according to local news reports, approximately seven thousand people from some twenty-nine nearby villages returned to the scene of the lynching to declare their support for such actions, challenging the authorities to either administer justice or allow the communities to do so themselves. President Alfonso Portillo visited the area in a response to this gathering, purportedly to discuss area residents' concerns about crime; he was greeted by a defiant crowd of several thousand who insisted that if a single arrest were made following the incident at Xalbaquiej, "there would be consequences" ("Linchamientos" 2000).

When I spoke with residents of the region three months later, all confirmed that members of the notorious Cadena had been involved in the incident at Xalbaquiej and in the public gatherings that followed it. This organization called leaders in each community to mobilize their followers to appear at the lynching and at the subsequent meetings, although these leaders were not told what was going to happen. Many went because they were afraid of the consequences if they failed to appear. Furthermore, those who returned from the meetings returned with a message: anyone who spoke about what had happened would also be lynched. Residents of one village told me that they had declined to participate and that weeks later, members of La Cadena had issued a warning that those from that village would no longer be "protected" by the organization should they fall victim to unspecified acts of crime.

Although the case of Xalbaquiej is perhaps the most widely recognized, further investigation reveals that many other lynchings bear similar characteristics. In a number of cases, former paramilitary leaders who now occupy local political office have taken an active role in instigating these incidents, and the extent to which the collaboration of the crowd has been voluntary is difficult to establish. Ex-patrollers and others who occupied positions of power during the war may use these acts as a way to maintain their power in the postwar era, relying on the same tactics of terror and intimidation used during the war to preserve their sense of authority. Some see an even more sinister subtext to these acts, suggesting that they may be evidence of a larger plan to use lingering paramilitary structures to destabilize postwar democracy, prompting calls for greater military intervention in daily governance. The frequent involvement of local political leaders in the lynchings is clear; what remains uncertain is the extent to which they choose to act independently, and the extent to which they have been instructed to do so as part of a coordinated political strategy.

Popular Lynchings

At the same time, not all lynchings are instigated by ex-military or para-military figures. Indeed, though their protagonism in many lynchings constitutes a troubling pattern, there is a danger in overstating the par-ticipation of ex-military in these events, particularly when they appear (in some cases) to enjoy such broad support. To anyone who has spent time talking with the residents of highland communities about their current problems, it is clear that large numbers of local residents view the lynchings as an unfortunate but necessary form of self-defense against crime.

I discussed the topic with a group of four Mayan men and one woman from a village near Santa Cruz del Quiché:

Q: Would you say that a majority of the people in your community supports the lynchings as a response to all of this [the crime problem]?

ALL RESPONDENTS: Yes.

RESPONDENT NO. 1: Yes, the majority. They support the lynchings now. In earlier times, no. When they used to burn people during the armed conflict, they didn't support it. But what they're doing now, yes, they support it.

RESPONDENT NO. 2: Since they saw that nothing else can be done, they sup-port it now. I don't remember when the first lynching around here was—was it the one in Joyabaj?—I think so, but anyway that was when they found out that only in this way could this [crime] be detained a bit. Only in this way. That's how it was, and we've heard that in many places the same thing has happened, until finally it hit close to home, right close to where we live.

Q: And did you see it?

ALL RESPONDENTS: Yes.

Q: What was it like? What happened?

RESPONDENT NO. 3: Terrible. It was terrible! Imagine, let's say, to see an ani-mal be burned, alive, not even talking about a human being. You don't even kill animals like that!

RESPONDENT NO. 4: Yes, even with animals, you look for the least cruel way to kill them, it's true. And with a person! . . . But we have seen what they've done, the criminals, and they do horrible things. So we can't have pity on them.

RESPONDENT NO. 1: But it's all due to the poor administration of the law. They say that earlier, when you did something wrong, the same community corrected you, told you to do this or that, gave you a punishment. And if you did it again, again there would be another justice, but it never reached the point of taking away your life, because [the communities] didn't live that way before the violence came. But like many said, since the violence came and disrupted everything, now there is no system, now there is no justice.

Q: And when the lynching happened, did many people attend?

RESPONDENT NO. 3: Oh, yes, lots.

RESPONDENT NO. 2: Almost the whole village.

Q: I've heard that in some other places, sometimes people attend lynchings, but because someone obligates them to . . . but it seems like, from what you're saying, that wasn't the case in your community.

RESPONDENT NO. 2: Oh, no, there it's voluntary.

RESPONDENT NO. 1: And the people were right. Because in these regions, almost 90 percent of us work on the coast, and [to do that is] only to suffer, to be counting the days until we can go home, and if you come back with your hands empty because they robbed you along the way, the pain is really intolerable. So, knowing that those people live by stealing money from honest people who come from working on the plantations, knowing that, the people couldn't put up with so much abuse. And after the lynching, everyone saw that the violence calmed down. Not all of it, but it calmed down. There are still problems, but less.

RESPONDENT NO. 5: More or less it served as a lesson, an experience, because there they saw that the communities made justice, and that they couldn't go on like that. So giving that example is providing a lesson.

Q: So do you think that lynchings could be a solution?

RESPONDENT NO. 5: Yes.

RESPONDENT NO. 1: Yes, because we had nothing else left. I don't know what else we could have done.

The combination of support for lynchings and lamentation of their necessity was common. Indeed, many expressed great reluctance to lynch and repugnance at the act itself. Another woman was a witness to a lynching in her community:

We went to watch when they were setting them on fire. *Ay*, you should've seen how that stank, even my head hurt from the stench, and to see them melting like that. . . . I felt pity [*me daba lástima*], and I cried. But on the one hand I give thanks to God that they burned them. May God forgive me, but it's good that they finished them off. Also, that way things get more peaceful around here. It's that . . . it was no kind of life [*Es que ya no era vida*]. We couldn't go out to do an errand because we were afraid, all of us were afraid, we didn't know when from one minute to the next they were going to come and finish us off, and since we live in the mountains, we were scared to go out. Even more so at night. And worse with the girls. Sometimes when there was an errand to do, I would say to them, "It's better if I go, you stay here, because I don't want anything to happen to you on the way." Then after that [the lynching] happened, then things calmed down a bit."

Most underscored a sense that few, if any, other options existed. A young K'iche' Mayan woman who had recently witnessed a lynching described to me the following:

"What are human rights good for," the people said. "We're going to make justice with our own hands. If we let [the criminals] go, they're not going to solve anything, since there's no evidence, they're just going to let them go free, so why are we going to hand them over?" And so they burned them. And there, the people saw. They saw that it's true that you can make justice with your own hands. Since then, things have calmed down. And we live better.

A K'iche' Mayan man explained the sentiment in his village:

The people have talked about this, and the people make a deep analysis that there is no justice, and they know that if they [the police] catch the thief he'll just pay those who are responsible for the so-called justice [*sólo paga a los responsables de la supuesta justicia*], so money is what talks and since the thieves always have more money than honest people, they're the ones who always come out ahead, so for this reason the people have arrived at this determination [to lynch]. . . . The people are tired of the lack of application of justice . . . and in the end they take justice into their own hands [*la gente está cansada por la no aplicación de la justicia . . . y pues al final toman la justicia por las manos*].

Significantly, when I asked villagers where the practice of lynchings came from, most were unequivocal in connecting such behaviors with army practices during the war. Not only the structures of authority but the very methods employed are reminiscent of past acts. In my initial inquiries, I was struck by the frequency with which suspects were burned to death before the eyes of the assembled community. Why, I asked, was public burning so popular? The answer, to locals, was obvious: for many survivors of the violence in the Guatemalan highlands, fire had become familiar as a method of execution. Indeed, in more than half (some 56 percent) of the eyewitness accounts from wartime massacres collected by REMHI, the incineration of houses and/or bodies was reported (ODHAG 1998: vol. 2,15); after gunshot wounds, burning was the second most common cause of death documented in the massacres (ODHAG 1998: vol. 2, 56). Even the original name of the 1982 offensive that launched the massacre campaign in the highlands—Operación Ceniza, or Operation Ashes (Schirmer 1998: 44–45)—alludes to the importance of this strategy.

Of course, not all lynchings involve burning. Other methods include stoning, shooting, and beating victims to death; at least one case was documented in which a victim was thrown from a bridge at the urging of the assembled crowd (from a 1999 MINUGUA internal document given to me), and one interviewee told me his community had dragged a man behind a vehicle until he died. Furthermore, the extensive media attention received by lynchings predisposes later cases to mimic the methods of execution noted in earlier attempts, so every incident of burning does not reflect a community's independent invention of the technique. Clearly, the phenomenon is more complex than a mechanistic repetition of wartime practices in new contemporary settings; yet the prevalence of such accounts suggests the lasting legacy of state terror may be its transformation into a means of enforcing social order long after the fighting has ceased.

In many cases, even as they connect such practices to the very painful past, villagers have solicited the return of militarized structures to resolve the contemporary crime problem. Ironically, in many cases, these communities voted for the party of the former dictator who had presided over the scorched-earth strategy that cost their own loved ones their lives. And all too often, these same communities support, advocate, and participate in lynchings, whether or not these acts may occasionally be instigated by ex-patrollers.

As one woman, visibly upset, explained:

One the one hand, those who are in La Cadena, on the one hand I think they do something useful, because now there are laws which are not being kept, what the law demands is not being met [*por una parte, pienso que esa gente que está encadenada, por una parte pienso que cumplen, porque ahorita hay una ley que no se está cumpliendo*], and therefore other initiatives are born. Since there is no law which is being respected, well, they take the law into their hands, and there are times when they find the guilty parties in the act of committing a robbery, and if they put them in jail, in two or three days they're out again. On the streets. So in that sense, the people become furious, they don't like it that the thieves get out of jail just like that. . . . What are we going to do? Because, when we talk about the past, well, I think we're old, those of us who suffered the violence of the past, but those who are young now, those who are in gangs aren't ex-patrollers, they are sometimes even the children of members of organizations, and the people know them, the people know that many of those who are in gangs now are children of very organized parents, human rights defenders and everything, and that's what makes me feel, well, it makes me feel ashamed and worried. . . . What solution can we come up with? My concern is that of the present, because of the past, that's past, well, the *compañeros* have already died, may God keep them in his glory, but what worries me the most now, right now, is what we're living now. I'm very worried. What are we going to do?

. . . Because the people who are active now in the violence, when they find you, they don't take any pity on your life. They rape a girl in front of her parents. And that's the problem that we have. Because not long ago, when those people who did the lynching not long ago in Xepocol, I know why they were so angry, because I always take people from here to the hospital and that's why I know all about what happened. The people who lynched the criminals, they were very, very wounded, because one day, one Sunday they [the criminals] took all the people from the community, and they raped the young women, minors [*menores de edad*], like from [age] fourteen and up! Fourteen and up! So that girl, the young girl, I saw her with my own eyes, she was injured from the abuse, sexually, and she was taken to the hospital. Still today she is in a wheelchair, and she's a minor. That's why, like Efraín Ríos said in his political campaign, the rats, we're going to kill them all! In other words, we're going to finish off the lives of the criminals. And that mentality stayed inside people. The same people, our people from here. So with those things that the terrible people do, well they have to make their own justice with their own hands. . . . For that, on the one hand the people are right. On the other hand, the people themselves turn into criminals. Criminals fighting criminals, on both sides they're criminals. That's what worries me. That young girl, I saw her myself, I know that she is still in a wheelchair, she was left really wounded because they opened her little body. . . . She was left injured like that because so many men went with her, and for me, it caused me great pity, I cried in front of her when I saw her like that, all twisted. That's why the people get angry. . . . It's not that I'm in favor of [lynching] or I'm opposed to it, I'm just trying to speak about the reality.

How do we understand support for renewed violence among communities that have struggled to survive state terror? Certainly, military domination of these communities was extensive and powerful; the attitudes of some survivors may be reflections of the ideological indoctrination they received. The psychological effects of having witnessed—and participated in—acts of extraordinary brutality clearly play a part. And the current climate in these areas is still infused with danger; political expression is freer than it has been, but it is still laced with fear, so it may also be that in some cases, residents of the region are coerced into expressing opinions not their own. Yet to assume that ongoing repression of peasants' "true" sentiments is the only way to explain popular support for militarized authority in the region is to fail to acknowledge the deeper roots of these phenomena.

Today, many communities lack traditions of peaceful conflict resolution. Before the war, Mayan communities generally resolved local conflicts through traditional systems of justice known as *derecho consuetudinario, derecho Maya,* or customary law. Yet the armed conflict hastened the abandonment of such practices, replacing them with militarized patterns of local governance—and practices such as public tortures and executions as punishment for criminal offenses. Although the imposition of militarized authority came at a terrible human cost, it did provide a system of order and stability for highland communities during the war, providing a means, however brutal, for resolving disputes. In the wake of the war, the army's retreat has left these areas newly vulnerable to criminal violence and suddenly stripped not only of their traditional means of self-government, but also of the militarized substitute to which they had been subjugated. Crime is common; citizens live in fear; and the authorities and legal system lack the legitimacy, capacity, and perhaps even the will to provide justice and order for area residents. As a result, even where communities have come together across political differences to seek solutions to the crime problem, they often reenact the violent practices of the recent past.

At the same time, there are signs of hope. I witnessed many debates about lynchings among community members, and I also met community leaders who had taken a personal stand against lynchings. In one community, an elderly man who headed a human rights group told me he had been instructed to preside over a lynching—"because the human rights committee talks about justice, and the community wanted to 'make justice' so they said we would be the ones who should do it"— but had refused, telling others that justice and violence were fundamentally incompatible. Although in this case the community lynched the suspect anyway, I heard about other cases where the resolute opposition of respected members of the community had shattered the resolve of lynch mobs, turning near-tragedies into occasions for a broader discussion of justice and reconstruction in the wake of violence. In chapter 5, I discuss some of these community-based alternatives to popular injustice.

The Sociological Legacy of Terror

Lynchings in contemporary Guatemala can be grouped into two broad categories. First, there are those lynchings imposed through force and fear by former paramilitaries or military supporters, many of whom continue to exercise de facto authority in the postwar period. These lynchings reveal the ongoing protagonism of forces linked to the country's bloody past in acts of contemporary violence, and they are important reminders of the fragility of the country's postwar peace. Second, however, there are also many lynchings carried out without coercion, by communities in which majorities often support such practices. These acts are testament to a more troubling and complex sociological legacy of violence: not only to the persistence of dark forces, but to the seductive promise of order through violence that was imposed by the state during wartime but today may be carried out at the behest of new and emerging forces in civil society. Ultimately, it is the perplexing tragedy of these "popular" lynchings that concerns me most, for they reveal in many ways the full extent of the transformation of social life under the practices of state terror.

Today, there exists a profound ambivalence in the highlands—and in Guatemalan society as a whole—around the question of violent justice, of governance by force, of human rights and their place in postwar democracy. Though most Guatemalans embrace the political rights associated with democracy, and virtually all told me they condemned extrajudicial executions, acts of torture, and other egregious violations of human rights when targeted against political opponents, the lynchings reveal a high tolerance for such abuses against purported criminals. The logic of governance through fear infuses much of Guatemalan society and is nowhere more palpable than in the highlands. More than evidence of individual human rights abusers' ongoing influence, the lynchings attest to a profound transformation of society itself.

On the one hand, lynchings underscore the ongoing relevance of the conventional human rights approach: focusing on holding the state accountable for its complicity in acts of politically motivated violence. They show that the failure to redress past acts of state violence by prosecuting those individuals and structures responsible for abuses leads to further human rights abuses in the postwar period. At the same time, however, such an approach cannot explain the apparent popularity of lynchings in some communities. Indeed, by blaming the lynchings almost exclusively on the army or its agents and thus continuing to view these communities primarily as victims of state violence rather than as agents pressing for social change, scholars and activists alike drastically underestimate the complexity of communities' reactions to lived violence. They also unwittingly deny what may be ambivalent and potentially contradictory but nonetheless important expressions of local agency.

In Guatemala, the postwar wave of lynchings tells us as much about the present as it does the past. Though these acts bear witness to the lingering legacies of state terror, including the ongoing influence of its protagonists in postwar politics, they also reveal that genocide's effects linger long after the killing subsides. In viewing the Guatemalan killing campaigns as a collection of atrocities suffered by individual victims, we miss the ways that fear infuses not only people but the social space between them—their institutions, customs, and ways of relating to one another. In this way, the residue of state terror may outlive its survivors and even its perpetrators, replicating itself in new settings and circumstances.

CHAPTER 4

Modernization, Crime, and Communities in Crisis

IN HUEJUTLA, HIDALGO, MEXICO, TWO suspected members of a kidnapping ring were detained by police on March 24, 1998; the following day, in sixteen separate broadcasts, a local radio station announced that the men would soon be set free and called on the local population to "impede" their liberation. In a span of hours, some one thousand residents descended on the courthouse, trapping the judge and his staff inside while they destroyed two police cars and ransacked municipal buildings, dousing some in gasoline. They forcibly removed the two suspects from the jail, dragged them to the main plaza, and beat them to death. The inert and bloodied body of one man was then strung up in the plaza's central gazebo.[1]

In Mariara, Venezuela, residents enraged by the recent murder of a six-year-old boy seized upon forty-one-year-old Omar Pérez Gallardo on April 16, 2001. After dragging him to the boy's house, where the grieving mother claimed to recognize him, the crowd attacked him and would likely have killed him had the police not arrived to save his life. Later that same night, a crowd of some four hundred to five hundred residents—among them the local mayor—converged on the small hospital where he lay recovering from his wounds and threatened to set fire to the entire establishment if Pérez was not released. He was subsequently beaten to death in the Plaza Bolívar; one arm was severed and hung in a tree, and the remainder of his corpse was set afire in the plaza amid a passionate protest against rampant criminal activity in the region. As part of this protest, locals occupied and temporarily closed the regional highway. It was later revealed that Pérez was innocent of all charges; he had apparently been mistaken for a legendary serial killer known as the "Monster of Mariara" ("Apresado" 2001; "Comunidad de Mariara" 2001; "Mariara" 2001).

As these examples illustrate, lynchings are not limited to Guatemala, nor are they found only in postgenocidal settings: throughout the 1990s, related incidents have been reported in Ecuador, Peru, Brazil, and other countries of Latin America. Although precise statistics are unavailable, many indications suggest they are on the rise (Castillo Claudett 2000). Clearly, then, there is more to this story than the postwar mimicry of state violence. In this chapter, I step outside the particularities of postconflict Guatemala and explore some reasons this phenomenon appears to be growing across the Americas. I argue that although most literature on the region tends to regard contemporary violence as a predominantly "top-down" phenomenon (carried out by state against citizen, by landowner against peasant, and by mestizo against Indian), these incidents reveal a new sort of violence originating at the bottom, which is purposeful, powerful, and political. In these pages, I focus on lynchings as indications of an "agentive moment" (Daniel 1996: 189–92), an attempt by embattled communities to reassert their autonomy and agency after decades of repeated assault by state armies, locally powerful elites, a shifting rural economy, criminal bandits, and other adversaries. I contend that by enacting these highly ritualized, unequivocally public displays of justice, communities seek not only to punish and deter criminal activity, but, perhaps more important, to collectively reassert themselves as agents rather than victims.

This is, to be sure, a dangerous argument. My intention here is most decidedly *not* to celebrate lynchings or to imbue these incidents with a democratic spirit that is not their due. On the contrary, I believe that lynchings suggest a dark side of what passes for democracy in contemporary Latin America, one too frequently overlooked in contemporary scholarship. In continuing to assume these incidents are isolated eruptions, we fail to understand what may be their most important, if unsettling, message: *this is what "democracy" looks like from here.* Or, more precisely, this is the unsurprising result of the juxtaposition of an ostensibly democratic legal order with the widespread denial of justice and the daily reality of mass exclusion and marginalization.

This exclusion, of course, is not new, but in recent years the changes associated with globalization have made many communities increasingly aware of their position in the global hierarchy of power; today, many perceive that their destinies are dictated by forces beyond their control. In this context, lynchings constitute angry attempts to reconstitute community and empower the excluded through violence. As John Comaroff writes, "When they begin to find a voice, peoples who see themselves as disadvantaged often do so either by speaking back in the language of the law or by disrupting its means and ends" (1994: xii).

Lynchings often occur in rural hamlets without paved roads, electricity, or potable water, or on the outskirts of urban settlements, where migrants cluster in shantytowns largely constructed of recovered materials such as cardboard boxes and corrugated aluminum siding, on land often occupied without title and lacking basic services. It is tempting, therefore, to view lynchings as evidence of underdevelopment. But the contrary is true: lynchings should be seen as a commentary on the character of the development that has occurred—specifically, its erosion of locally bound notions of community and the deepening awareness it has occasioned of vast global disparities of wealth and power. The impoverishment and marginality of highland villages or urban slums are a consequence of the coupling of economic growth and abject misery that is built into the modernizing project in peripheral nations such as Guatemala. There is no reason to believe these are fleeting moments of incomplete transition: after all, for nations that have staked their economic future on low-skill, high-volume export processing in which international competitiveness is contingent on low wages, the success of the system depends on the availability of a labor pool impoverished enough to staff the sweatshops.[2]

In Guatemala, the story of modernization and maldevelopment is inevitably intertwined with the brutal wartime violence that racked highland communities in the 1970s and 1980s,[3] as discussed in chapter 3. But the cataclysmic nature of that violence sometimes obscures other transformations that occurred during the same period, many of which are analogous to processes occurring across the region. In this chapter, I focus on these processes in the hopes of charting an argument more broadly applicable to other areas of the so-called developing world. First, the long-term modernization of rural life in Guatemala, accelerated if not fundamentally altered by the globalizing processes of recent decades, has produced social and economic changes that provoke anxiety about change and community and a growing perception of powerlessness in poor communities. Second, this broader anxiety is often expressed as fear of crime; in this way, even in areas where real crime rates are low or stable, criminality becomes the focus of great collective attention as a metaphor through which the community makes sense of its own multiple vulnerabilities. Lynchings, in this context, are acts taken in defense of collective norms, carried out by communities in a profound state of crisis.

This, ultimately, is not new: numerous studies of crime, dating all the way back to Durkheim, argue that deviance is socially constructed to affirm collective boundaries. But in a departure from Durkheim, I argue that these communities channel such acts into violent acts of public vigilantism not because of their "primitive" nature (and hence, *qua* Durkheim, the strength of the collective sentiments offended) but because of a profound lack of social capital—in Durkheimian terms, solidarity—in these collectivities. Though we often assume that acts of collective violence reflect strong solidarity within communities (Gould 1999), I suggest that in this case the opposite is true: lynchings reflect desperate acts taken when other attempts at social control founder amid mistrust and divisiveness, leaving violence alone as a sort of lowest common denominator for social control.

Modernization and Change at the Community Level

In the Guatemalan highlands, as throughout most of the country (and indeed, the continent), modernization and development have always been at best a mixed blessing for rural peasant communities. Though such processes have sometimes brought valuable social services to the countryside for the first time, national development strategies have historically regarded Mayan traditions as an obstacle to modernization and have therefore encouraged the abandonment of communal lands and ways of life as a precondition to economic development.

Early attempts to liberalize the country's economy and open it to international capitalism came at the end of the 1800s, resulting in the seizure of Mayan communal lands and the legalized enslavement of thousands of Mayan peasants under so-called vagrancy laws, which provided forced labor to the large plantations (Lovell 1988; Grandin 2000, 2004). Throughout the 1900s, successive administrations' strategies for development targeted rural communities for modernization, attributing the nation's underdevelopment either explicitly or implicitly to the isolation and cultural backwardness of its indigenous communities (Fischer 1996). Beginning in the 1940s, the state began promoting the modernization of agriculture through tax credits and other programs, most of which privileged *ladino* landowners or merchant middlemen at the expense of Mayan smallholders, relegating these to an ever more peripheral position even on their own ancestral lands.[4]

Contemporary neoliberalism's advocacy of market-oriented development strategies has thus marked a continuation and intensification of, rather than a departure from, past practices. This has transformed life within peasant communities. As William Robinson (1996, 2001) has shown, market-oriented development disentwines traditional peasant populations from subsistence agriculture in order to make them available as a large, mobile, and eminently replaceable pool of inexpensive labor to be utilized in the burgeoning economic sectors that drive growth in these nations—chiefly export processing (*maquiladoras*) and commercial agriculture for export. These changes have collectively contributed to the weakening of the social fabric, as solidary ties of kinship, tradition, ethnic identity, social trust, and shared values weather the onslaught of rapid social change. These are extremely complex processes, worthy of a more sustained and sophisticated study than I can offer here (see, for example, Smith 1990; Green 1998); but for purposes of this discussion, I group them in three rough and overlapping categories: occupational shifts, migration, and cultural changes. Here and throughout the chapter I draw on data gathered in Guatemala, but analogous changes are underway across the Americas, and I therefore intend my argument to be more broadly applicable.

Occupational Shifts

In recent decades many peasant communities have experienced what Alain de Janvry and colleagues have called the "double (under-)development squeeze": forced to abandon subsistence agriculture and seek sources of cash income even as the opportunities for off-farm employment dwindle (de Janvry, Sadoulet, and Young 1989). Today, many Mayan peasants participate in new commercialized activities in or near their communities of origin: some have become involved in contract farming, using their subsistence plots to cultivate snow peas, broccoli, or cauliflower for export rather than traditional corn and squash for local consumption. Others work as field laborers on larger farms producing export crops (Green 1998). And still others have become active in nonagricultural employment, particularly in the expanding *maquiladora* sector and in piecemeal assembly work (Goldin 1999).

The abandonment of traditional agricultural activities that play an integral role in Mayan cosmology—a system of beliefs and practices deeply tied to corn, land, and relations with nature and the ancestors (Green 1998)—has altered the fabric of community life in rural villages. It has also occasioned feelings of resentment at a perceived surrender of autonomy to broader forces. Though many prefer growing export crops to surrendering their land, many told me of frustrating and alienating experiences with "foreign" crops. In order to grow crops suitable for export, small farmers were forced to invest heavily at the outset, and sometimes the promised payoff never came; dips in the global market, the often rapacious practices of intermediaries, and a steep learning curve cut into profits. "We grow it, but then, if they don't buy it, what can we do?" one farmer explained, his callused palms turned upward in a gesture of futility. In past generations, subsistence farming had meant a simpler life.

Others told me that they welcomed the arrival of *maquiladoras*, particularly because they provided employment opportunities for women and young girls, but these, too, were unstable sources of income. Tales of abusive employers, factory closings, and unpaid wages abounded. On the outskirts of Guatemala City, a manager of a *maquila* that attracted young women from rural areas told me, "They don't last. They come here to work but they get sick, they get pregnant, they miss their village. As they get older they all quit. That's why [the employees in the plant] are all young." The high turnover is in part attributable to the difficult working conditions: long hours with very limited breaks; repetitive, even at times dangerous work; and low pay. It is also, as this manager suggests, a reflection of the social uprooting that often accompanies such employment, as workers often migrate to take the jobs but find it difficult to establish ties in new communities, especially while simultaneously working long, exhausting shifts in the plants.

Migration

Migration is a second factor that is transforming life in highland communities. Many peasants undertake seasonal migrations to work on the large coastal plantations to the south, such that in many villages sizable sectors of the economically active population are absent from the community for long stretches during key harvest periods. In other cases, migrations involve permanent or semipermanent relocations to other areas of the Guatemalan national territory—most particularly to the capital city, where entire neighborhoods of migrants have sprung up in recent decades, in many cases under extremely precarious living conditions; but also, to a lesser extent, to newly settled "frontier" areas carved out of the rainforest.[5] Still others have relocated to Mexico, the United States, or other destinations.

Of those who shared their stories with me, few described these relocations as choices. Many spoke of seasonal migration to the Pacific coast as a form of servitude, even invoking the word "slavery." Others spoke of moving to Guatemala City as a desperate attempt to feed their children. In most cases, these changes also separated families, as men often migrated alone, leaving women and children behind to receive remittances. Many told me they worried about migration hastening marital infidelity or otherwise rupturing family relations, but felt there was no other choice. At the community level, the increasing mobility of the population contributes to instability in local institutions.[6]

The seasonal or semipermanent absence of men in the community also affects authority structures. "There aren't *principales* anymore because there aren't any men left. Either they killed them, or they're working [elsewhere]," another K'iche' woman told me. The word *principal* refers to traditional leadership roles in Mayan communities; although specific practices vary by locality, in general *principales* are male village elders who have ascended to a position of authority based on their prior performance of community service in lesser roles, through *cofradías* (religious brotherhoods) and other local leadership institutions, over the course of many years. Men's ability to gain experience and legitimacy as community leaders is based on long-term service and visibility in the community, something made difficult when many men are absent from the community for prolonged periods. "What community is left," one middle-aged K'iche' woman said, "when all the men are gone?" (*¿Qué comunidad va a haber cuando todos los varones están fuera?*).

Migration also exposes many to the world beyond the village, often for the first time. This leads to a growing awareness of global and local disparities and to a cascade of new cultural influences. For example, one young K'iche' woman told me:

It was when I started to work in the *maquila* that I noticed certain things that seem unjust, for example, the Koreans. They are the bosses there, and you ask yourself, why? It's not like on the coast—there there's always a boss too, but it's because his family has had that land a long time. But in the *maquila* it's just Chinese [*es puro chinito*], even the names [of the factories] are in Chinese, and for them we're just machines that work, not humans.

At this point she was interrupted by an older woman who was present and who said that on the coastal plantations the work was equally harsh and that workers were ill-treated by bosses. The first woman agreed, but added, "It's true. But I still don't understand why the Chinese are in charge of everything." Other respondents shared similar concerns about foreigners' apparent power (although this was more frequently commented upon by *ladinos* than by indigenous respondents).

Cultural Changes

Lastly, improvements in communications have led to what many Mayan leaders describe as a virtual assault of Western culture through television, movies, and other media. Sometimes migrants return home, bringing new customs, clothes, and habits. Highland communities remain geographically remote but today are increasingly enmeshed in a transnational network of relations that facilitates the transmission not only of resources (remittances from abroad have become the nation's number 1 source of revenue and a vital support for highland families struggling to scrape by), but also information, ideas, and culture (Popkin 1999; Portes 2001). In many cases, contact with other cultures and lifestyles has opened a generation gap within Mayan families (Green 1998; Goldin 1999). For the first time, countless respondents told me, their communities are dealing with drugs, gangs, and teenagers who may not want to follow in the footsteps of their ancestors.

The problem of youth gangs (*maras*) was mentioned more frequently than any other in these conversations. A World Bank study of urban violence in Guatemala concluded that the explosion of youth gang activity was a direct result of "the post-conflict return-migration of many individuals and their families from other Central American countries such as El Salvador and Honduras, as well as from the United States. In addition, it was one of a number of consequences of globalization, in terms of the transnational transfer of influence of violent movies, designer and sport clothing, and popular rap and rock music" (Moser and McIlwaine 2001: 97) A large number of these *maras* share names with gangs in Los Angeles, San Salvador, and other cities; some of this may be due to imitation, but much is undoubtedly due to the existence of a transnational structure of organized crime, facilitated in part by the United States' deportation of not only "criminal aliens" but of permanent residents convicted of "aggravated felonies" (a category that, its dire-sounding name notwithstanding, includes relatively minor crimes such as check fraud and drug offenses) under the U.S. Antiterrorism and Effective Death Penalty Act and Illegal Immigration Reform and Immigrant Responsibility Act, both of which became law in 1996. Most of Moser and McIlwaine's respondents indicated that young people joined gangs for support and solidarity, because they liked the fashions, and because they became addicted to drugs. In my prior research with street children (Godoy 1999) some of whom expressed an affinity for certain elements of gang activity, many said such organizations provided them a much-needed feeling of belonging and a support structure.

Of course, not all of these changes are bad; globalization is neither an absolute evil, nor its antecedent an absolute good. Long ignored by state policy, highland Mayan villages have historically suffered interethnic conflicts over land, endemic illnesses, illiteracy, and a host of other problems; contemporary ills must not be attributed to modernity's pollution of some imagined romantic past. In many ways, contemporary changes have created openings for Mayans to redefine their cultures and identities in new contexts, to explore opportunities for education, employment, and self-advancement through avenues not available to older generations (see, for example, Nelson 1999). Recent years have seen a revitalization of Mayan culture (Fischer 1996; Hendrickson 1996; Warren 1998), including a revival of some traditional mechanisms for dispute resolution (see chapter 5). Though many customary practices exclude women from decision-making roles, today many women have taken up positions of new-found leadership, spurred by opportunity and necessity but also aided by the networks of international cooperation and assistance made possible through globalization. Human rights networks, similarly, have brought changes welcomed by many Mayans: I will always remember one elderly K'iche' man in particular, who told me in broken Spanish and a voice quavering with emotion about how his grandfather had been treated as a beast of burden, forced to transport his *patrón* (the owner of the land on which he worked) seated in a chair strapped to his back. Today, this man said, human rights groups could and would protest such abuse: "We hear for the first time that the Indian has rights, has value, that we are people." Although many of those rights are still violated, for this man at least, the formal recognition of his dignity as a person represented an important gain in and of itself.

For this and other reasons, my intention here is not to present glob-alization as a purely destructive force; after all, it has also opened new opportunities for Mayans and other populations who have historically experienced poverty and exclusion. Whatever positive opportunities recent changes have created, however, they have also indisputably weak-ened the hold of traditional institutions, norms, and practices, some of which had formed the basis for semiautonomous self-governance by Mayan communities for centuries. My point here is not to weight the comparative merits of "traditional" versus contemporary forms of so-cial cohesion, but merely to articulate the profound sense many of my respondents expressed that their community's way of life, and by ex-tension its very existence, was under assault.

"Globalization Anxiety," Insecurity, and Crime

Expressions of what might be diffusely termed "globalization anxiety" have emerged in diverse settings around the globe and have been found by numerous researchers, using quantitative and qualitative method-ologies alike, to be linked to rising attention to crime, even in the ab-sence of a "real" increase in criminality. For, as Richard Sparks and col-leagues note, "In speaking of crime, people routinely register its entanglement with other aspects of economic, social and moral life; at-tribute responsibility and blame; demand accountability and justice; and draw lines of affiliation and distance between 'us' and various cat-egories of 'them'" (Sparks, Girling, and Loader 2001: 896). These re-searchers found that "crime-talk" among residents of Macclesfield, an "ordinary" English town near Manchester, revealed broader insecuri-ties about their community and its shifting boundaries. Their concerns were often centered on the conduct of young people and the changing composition of their community. They were not reactions to discrete criminal incidents; rather, they tapped into widely held feelings of un-easiness about social and economic change.

In quite a different setting, Tom Tyler and Robert Boeckmann (1997) examined attitudes toward California's "Three Strikes and You're Out" ballot initiative, finding that support for this punitive legislation corre-lated with a perceived decline in social cohesion in the wake of recent changes in the state's population. These authors claim that rather than the instrumental fear of crime itself, the punitive turn was driven by concerns about the family and ethnic or cultural diversity. In particular, they argue, "people are troubled because they feel that important insti-tutions within society (for example, the family) are declining. . . . People are concerned about the symbolic harms that develop from the lack of a clear, shared set of moral values as well as from declining social ties among people" (256). In this context, people favor punitive solutions because they fear that shaming punishments or other forms of social de-terrence to rule breaking are insufficient when society lacks a reliable bedrock of shared values: "Without moral values or social ties to use as a basis for changing lawbreakers, as in the use of shaming, there seem to be few alternatives to simply incarcerating criminals for the rest of their lives ('warehousing')" (257).

In Chile, too, Lucia Dammert and Mary Fran T. Malone documented a growing climate of public insecurity expressed through the language of concern about crime, despite crime rates that remain very low by re-gional and global standards. The authors created an "insecurity scale" measuring poverty and economic instability and found it far more closely related to fear of crime than to other commonly tested variables (including identity characteristics, actual victimization, urbanization, and others). Confronted with rapid change and a growing sense of eco-nomic vulnerability, Chileans express a mounting fear of crime—ac-cording to the authors, largely because "it allows the public to name the potential enemy: the fearsome stranger, the excluded. However, the criminalization of the other (Garland 1996) obscures the real nature of fear of crime and diminishes the importance of other insecurities in cit-izens' lives. In that sense, crime becomes a tangible scapegoat for all types of insecurities" (Dammert and Malone 2003: 80).

Something very similar is happening in the Guatemalan highlands communities I visited. In my conversations with residents of these villages, I found that their concerns, though nominally about crime, often radiated out into a broader sense of insecurity. Forced to confront so many rapid social transformations even as they were stripped of their traditional means for doing so, residents of these communities told me not only about crime, but about a diffuse lack of control and autonomy:

You see, I'm from Aguacatán [Huehuetenango], and there we see the increase in crime with great concern. And just now, about a week ago, they buried a young man who was killed in a village, and it caused a kind of scandal, an ex-perience that had not been lived before in that area, and that, well, it led the community to reflect about what's going wrong. This kind of thing creates instability within the communities. And it also creates disintegration within the family. The young people that are living in the communities, it's like they don't have . . . they don't value the principles that their families have, so they don't listen to their parents, and they've learned other principles that don't go with the principles of the community. So this creates instability within the family, and also within the community. And the indigenous communities, like I say, maybe we haven't lived through things like this before, but now we're living it.

Q: How is this related to the end of the war?

RESPONDENT: . . . Well, it's related, but the war isn't the only factor. There are many other factors that also have to do with the crime wave. For example, in the communities, they also see it in the sense that many have gone to other countries, for example to the United States, to work, and they've brought with them ways, customs of life that were unknown in the communities, and this, according to the communities, has had a great deal of influence. On the other hand, the media; if you go to one of these communities in the interior they will tell you that the media has too much influence. And although it sounds, well, maybe not so acceptable, but there's also the idea that it's education that has caused our children to be this way. . . . But I see it more related to the fact that many young people have to move to the urban areas, to the municipal centers, to study for example at middle school [*el nivel básico*], and there they live with young people from that area, and it's like these attitudes are contagious, so then later they return to the communities with different attitudes than they had before.

. . . I'm talking about what I've seen in Aguacatán. Even in the case of this last experience that we had, and another one where they killed a young man with such cruelty [*saña*] that it seemed so incredible. The body turned up in a river, but it appeared with the head destroyed as if someone had pounded it with a rock, and there were remains of the scalp on a nearby rock, and . . . and . . . and they had stabbed him, they had opened his mouth and stabbed him in the mouth. . . . [*Grimacing, shaking his head*] It's a kind of thing that until now we could never imagine, we had never known. Later it was discovered that there was a group of young people who did drugs, they were drug addicts, and that this had been a vengeance between them.

That's why I tell you, many of those who have gone to other countries have brought these customs and have influenced other youths. So, what they say now is that there has to be some kind of training, or some kind of activity of consciousness-raising [*concientización*] for young people, but also for their parents, so that they exercise more control over their children, because, for example, what's a young person doing outside on the street at 11:00 at night? Many people are asking themselves this. Why don't the parents impose more rigid discipline on their children? Maybe in the cities it was common to see that sort of thing, but in the municipalities it wasn't common at all, but now you see it more every day, you see young people in groups, or standing on street corners together, at 11:00 at night. So nowadays we're realizing that the parents have to assume their responsibilities.

Here the speaker traces the origins of the crime wave to the social transformations affecting his community. Other interviewees echoed this sentiment, often bemoaning young people's purported wayward-ness more than the violence or danger implicit in crime itself.

A Mayan woman from Chichicastenango told me:

In our community we have many problems with drugs, with violence, with crime, [that's] the situation we're in now. . . . Sometimes I hear noises at night and I go out and look in the street, I want to see what kind of people it is, and they're young people, youngsters, fifteen years old. Who's teaching them? Who has led them into this? And where does it come from? Where?

When I asked one man in Sololá why he thought there was so much crime today, he responded:

It's also important to emphasize [the influence of] television programs. For ex-ample, here in Sololá, there's a group called Los Cholos, and for us it was, well, strange, to see a kid from Sololá mixed up in that, and also to hear that there are other groups also called Los Cholos in various municipalities, how strange. But then, watching the cable programs, we saw that there are groups called Cholos in the United States. The media have a large influence on the mentality of teenagers, not in a favorable way but in a negative way, because in general, we have a culture, but many young people try to acculturate, and appropriate ac-tions that aren't of our people [*porque generalmente nosotros tenemos una cultura, pero mucha juventud trata de aculturizarse, apropiarse de algunas acciones que no son propias de nuestro pueblo*].

Some older Mayans also told me that it disturbed them to see young people increasingly adopting Western dress in place of traditional Mayan *traje*. During the conflict, many Mayans refrained from using such outward markers of their indigenous identity because the army of-ten assumed anyone in *traje* was a guerrilla sympathizer. In the postwar period, although several young people told me they were proud of their traditional clothes, others explained that it was too expensive to wear the elaborately handwoven garments, that they encountered discrimi-nation when they did so, or that they simply liked newer fashions. But one older man seemed to sum up the sentiment of many in his genera-tion when he told me that the young people in baggy jeans looked "like criminals." "We're losing our culture," he lamented.

Not only crime itself, but the specific criminal practices, often per-ceived as targeting that which communities held most sacred, also evoked a particular horror. For example, many spoke of the widespread practice of stealing items of cultural importance—religious icons passed down for centuries, for example, or elaborate weavings by local Mayan women—for resale on the black market. This caused special concern because it seemed to indicate the failure to respect even the most revered traditions, underscoring the sense of a society gone astray:

> Recently what I've noticed is that the young people of today, they don't dedicate themselves to study, they don't dedicate themselves to work, but what they most get into is drug addiction, and it's something shameful. But that also has to do with the parents, right, because maybe there are some parents who are irresponsible and don't correct their children. They don't notice, maybe, because they send them off to school, but maybe they never arrive, and they just pass time wandering the streets. So that's why the gangs have increased. We've had lots of people who have been raped, or also mugged or robbed, and even in the *cofradías* too.[7] We've noticed that our community has a great wealth in *cofradías*, and in these *cofradías* there are some images that are very important for our culture, but the ingrates that are thieves have even gotten into the houses to steal these images. For example, the *cofradía* of Santa María de la Asunción, who is the patron saint of this town, from that *cofradía* two silver images were stolen, and they were antiques. They stole them. They didn't hold back [*no se quedaron con las ganas*], and last Friday [the thieves] broke in again to that same *cofradía*. Two images had been left, those of the Baby Jesus that we use to celebrate an activity every January 6. And they took those two too, which are also very, very old. Because they know that in foreign countries people pay a lot of money for those things that are antiques.

Among my respondents, concern about crime was urgent and poignant and real—but as our conversations deepened it became clear that criminal activity alarmed them because it represented a symbolic threat to something larger. Lynchings sanction chicken thieves with such crushing violence not because the poverty of these communities means that minor thefts have major economic significance, as some have argued (Handy 2002), but because in its apparent inability to stop even offenses as ordinary as the theft of a chicken, the community sees its powerlessness cast in a new and desperate light. As many peasants told me in no uncertain terms, at stake here is not the item stolen, but the very meaning of right and wrong.

Rituals of Death: Lynchings as Attempts to Rebuild Solidarity through Violence

Ultimately, the idea of lynchings as attempts to rebuild solidarity is in many ways a return to Emile Durkheim. Durkheim, of course, argues that all punishment is an exercise in the collective reaffirmation of shared norms; crime, therefore, is functional in that it provides an opportunity for the community to redefine the sentiments which hold it together:

Since, therefore, the sentiments which crime offends are, in any given society, the most universally collective that there are; since they are, indeed, particularly strong states of the common conscience, it is impossible for them to tolerate contradiction. Particularly if this contradiction is not purely theoretical, if it affirms itself not only by words, but by acts—when it is thus carried to its maximum, we cannot avoid rising against it passionately. A simple restitution of the troubled order would not suffice for us; we must have a more violent satisfaction. The force against which the crime comes is too intense to react with very much moderation. Moreover, it cannot do so without enfeebling itself, for it is thanks to the intensity of the reaction that it keeps alive and maintains itself with the same degree of energy.

We can thus explain a character of this reaction that has often seemed irrational. It is certain that at the bottom of the notion of expiation there is the idea of a satisfaction accorded to some power, real or ideal, which is superior to us. When we desire the repression of crime, it is not that we desire to avenge personally, but to avenge something sacred which we feel more or less confusedly outside and above us. . . . That is why penal law is not alone essentially religious in origin, but indeed always retains a certain religious stamp. It is because the acts that it punishes appear to be attacks upon something transcendent. (Durkheim 1947: 99–100)

Thus, although residents may conceive of lynchings as forms of criminal punishment, the acts themselves are more important in affirming community than they are in punishing offenders. This, too, is clear from eyewitness testimony; there is often a sense that *something had to be done* in defense of the community, in defense of morality itself. Many invoked the law of talion ("an eye for an eye"). Others expressed indifference as to whether the state or its citizens carried out the punishment, as long as it was deadly. One small businessman told me:

Here what's needed is punishment. Punishment. If there's no punishment, of course there is no justice, and the morality of society is destroyed. There are tons of people waiting for lethal injection, but they don't kill them.[8] The day they start killing them, is the day that at least we know punishment exists. Justice exists. . . . I don't know if that will stop other murderers from committing crimes. But I know that it's correct to kill them, because they've killed others. If what's correct isn't done, then there is no justice.

Residents of lynching communities often said that the lynchings "worked," that after a lynching everything was calm. When I asked why, people usually referred to the lynching as a deterrent to further criminality. But one man's response was telling:

I think we feel calm [*tranquilos*] because we saw that we as a community were able to do something, because with so much evil that happens and no justice, well, you begin to question a bit, if there is a God, if everything's been ruined or what, it's a really bad feeling. And it was also a bad feeling to see a man die [in the lynching] but from there we started to recover, we started to see that there are certain things that are worth defending, it's like something very basic.

In other words, this man said, the lynching was effective not because of what it communicated to criminals but because it reaffirmed something sacred to the community itself—a classically Durkheimian insight. In many ways, the specific practices embedded in lynchings also resemble Durkheim's classic description of repressive justice in "primitive" societies: they are administered by very nearly the whole society (1947: 76) through violent, passionate acts (99), and they exhibit certain quasi-religious characteristics (100). Although press accounts of lynchings often focus on the uncontrollable exaltation of enraged crowds, underscoring the frequent assumption that such acts occur spontaneously, many lynchings, when examined, reveal this violence to be both methodical and meaningful, even quasi-religious. In Guatemala, as MINUGUA (2000b) has shown, would-be lynchers frequently detain victims for days prior to their execution, using this time to assemble the community, hold "trials" or popular votes, administer physical punishments sometimes aimed at producing confessions, and summon crowds for the execution itself.[9]

Furthermore, in many cases the process is clearly premeditated: residents in a number of communities told me security committees had been constituted to handle crime, and in some cases collections had been taken up among all residents to purchase gasoline in advance, as mentioned in chapter 3. The methods of execution, too, suggest a deliberate attempt to invoke religious symbolism: in Guatemala victims are generally burned alive or their bodies are set on fire after death; other methods include stoning and hanging, although less visually symbolic forms such as shooting or beating also occur. Corpses are sometimes displayed for some time after the execution. Furthermore, the moment of death is often accompanied by further ritual, including symbolic tortures and forced confessions on the pyre. Vilas (2001) notes that in Mexico victims were sometimes forced to participate in a so-called *paseo*, walking (or in some cases being dragged by a vehicle) through the village while community members spit on them, insulted them, hit them, and otherwise abused them, before finally facing their death.

Rather than spontaneous eruptions of expiatory fury, lynchings constitute a deliberate attempt by embattled communities to reaffirm values they see as threatened. As Durkheim's analysis insists, these acts of public punishment are only peripherally about the crime that precedes them; at their heart lies the goal of repairing ruptured solidarities and reinforcing bonds among the noncriminal members of the community. In this sense, lynchings may constitute a form of generative violence, recalling René Girard's discussion of acts of "violent unanimity" aimed "to restore harmony to the community, to reinforce the social fabric" (1972: 8). By overlaying violence with ritual, communities affirm that these—unlike the savage acts of criminals—are acts of *meaningful*, legitimate violence. Although at first blush they may seem to be spontaneous acts of collective outrage about crime, on a deeper level lynchings are purposeful, deliberate acts that reassert community values in response to widespread anomie stemming from a broad set of social transformations, of which the rising incidence of criminality is but a single symptom.

At the same time, however, contemporary lynchings depart in at least two significant ways from the "primitive" practices described by Durkheim and Girard. First, Durkheim described passionate, public displays of punishment as occurring in communities characterized by a high degree of solidarity, yet today's lynchings erupt in settings where solidarity has been largely shattered.[10] And second, Durkheim suggested that punishment of this sort was a precursor to the modern justice system, but today's lynchings emerge as a reaction to that system— indeed, as evidence of its failure to perform in the way Durkheim, in his functionalist understanding of the world, imagined it would. In this sense, lynchings are highly political acts of resistance to the structures of power that operate through law.

Solidarity and Violence: Lynchings as Last Resort

Lynchings present a certain paradox: they are forms of collective action that emerge in settings of low solidarity. Contemporary lynchings recall Durkheimian descriptions of mechanical solidarity in "primitive" societies, where public displays of punishment serve to reaffirm ties between and among community members. Yet Durkheim understood these "primitive" communities to be characterized by high solidarity. And contemporary scholarship would appear to agree: in a recent article on lynchings as a global phenomenon, Roberta Senechal de la Roche emphasizes their occurrence in tribal societies, noting that "as the Western world urbanized and atomized, lynching declined" (2001: 139). Indeed, most theories of collective violence underscore the importance of strong social bonds among the participants in such actions (Gould 1999; Senechal de la Roche 2001). According to such logic, as Senechal de la Roche suggests, lynchings should decline as societies differentiate. Yet I found no evidence of this dynamic in my research; despite the existence of ethnic conflicts among different groups in Guatemala, for example, lynchings are seldom used to settle intraethnic feuds or penalize identifiable "outgroups." Rather, even in the most conflict-ridden communities, people told me lynchings were acts intended to bring the community together against crime—and those lynched were, surprisingly, often members of the same community, who did not differ from the lynchers along any readily identifiable lines (ethnicity, class, age, religion, or political affiliation, for example). *These* lynchings are borne of low solidarity.

As we have seen, today's lynchings are not spontaneous eruptions of mass rage in reaction to egregious offenses unsanctioned by the state; they are attempts to repair splintered solidarities through lethal violence. But why such violence? It may make sense if we understand it as a mimicry of state tactics, as in the case of Guatemalan highland villages that experienced similar forms of social control through extreme violence in the context of the country's brutal civil war; but it is much more difficult to explain in the slums of Caracas, the hamlets of rural Ecuador, or the marginal settlements of Cochabamba, where public torture-executions of suspected criminals have not been state policy in recent memory. Though many marginalized communities may struggle to resist what they perceive as assaults on their values and identity, there is no reason such resistance must be violent, no inherent propensity for the excluded to favor violent expressions. Rather, violence serves as a sort of "lowest common denominator" of social control for communities in crisis that lack the social capital to construct an alternate form of justice. It may be tempting to consider Guatemala's a "culture of violence," where the threshold for the use of legitimate violence has been effectively lowered by the experience of widespread victimization—or to put it more bluntly, where mass violence has cheapened the value placed on human life—but I suggest that lynchings and other forms of *mano dura* function not as a mirror of the past, but as a last resort that becomes appealing only in the context of deep institutional and interpersonal distrust. They are acts of visible, violent "justice" that attempt to rebuild community through violence precisely because in its immediacy and finality, this is the only form of collective action on criminal justice that does not rely on sustained trust to be successful.[11]

Another way to understand the relationship between lynching and low solidarity is in terms of social capital. The concept of social capital as "networks, norms, and social trust that facilitate coordination and cooperation for mutual benefit" (Putnam 1995: 67), and its importance in grounding successful democracies in a culture of civic participation, was popularized by Robert Putnam in his enormously influential *Making Democracy Work: Civic Traditions in Modern Italy* (1994) and subsequent publications. In this book, Putnam takes the sort of bottom-up approach that I have argued is so important to understanding democracies' functioning, or lack thereof. He maintains that social capital makes possible the dense networks of participation in civic associations (such as bowling leagues, in one oft-cited example), which in turn forms the foundation for effective governance; where social capital is lacking, by contrast, citizens behave as opportunistic, self-interested actors, and as a result, government is less democratic.

The residents of lynching communities often described to me either a leadership vacuum or a situation in which leadership roles were occupied by proponents of violence. Communities were fragmented, and it was difficult, they said, to know whom to trust. As a result, it was difficult to organize an adequate response to complex current events; oftentimes there was no response to criminal acts, leading to feelings of frustration and impotence. Unlike the primitive carnival of passion and rage that some commentators envision lynchings to be, most people who had direct knowledge of these incidents described something much more painful and sad—in some cases, almost plaintive. They described these acts as desperate measures taken only when other attempts at social control through both formal and informal law had failed. Lynchings, in other words, were a last resort.

For example, one K'iche' Mayan man described lynchings as necessary in a context where other mechanisms no longer worked:

They say that earlier, when you did something wrong, the community itself corrected you, told you to do this or that, gave you a punishment. And if you did it again, again there would be another justice, but it never reached the point of taking away your life, because [the communities] didn't live that way before the violence came. But like many said, since the violence came and disrupted every-thing, now there is no system, now there is no justice. . . . We had nothing else left. I don't know what else we could have done.

This sense of the futility of other measures—of "having nothing else left"—was echoed in the testimony of many respondents, who de-scribed efforts to organize communities where trust itself had been all but demolished. I later spoke to the same man.

Q: I understand that in many communities, during the armed conflict, the conflict itself sowed a great deal of mistrust, in the sense that the people could no longer trust other members of their same community. . . .

RESPONDENT NO. 1 [NODDING]: That's true. It's that, in some communities it's true, really, because the people were left with that feeling, you know, it's difficult to believe people anymore. . . . Sometimes some people come and say, "Look gentlemen, let's do X thing, let's make X plan [*hagamos tal cosa, hagamos tal plan*] and the people are suspicious, they look at them and say to themselves, "My God, is he doing this honestly, or is he doing it because he wants to take advantage of us?" [*Dios mio, será que lo está haciendo de corazón, o lo está haciendo porque quiere aprovecharse de nosotros?*] That thing, that lack of trust has remained. Let's say, to give an example, that I was walking down the street, and a gang came and they stole everything from me. Then, well, I might have the idea that if I walked down that street again, they could come get me again. That's how the people in the com-munities feel. Even I was like that, but as time has passed, it's gone away a little bit, I've participated in some meetings and at the beginning I didn't believe in anything, but little by little that's gone away. Because I, when I was patrolling, I saw war, I saw blood, I saw people die in the shooting, and I had that in my mind and even in my eyes. . . . That stuck in my mind, practically, to see my brothers like that, destroyed and all. How I regret it, but that stuck with me and that makes it a little difficult for me to accept any organization or group. You feel kind of scared, you know, after having lived through those things.

This sense of deep skepticism was echoed in other respondents from the same community. One young K'iche' woman told me:

In my case, I like to work in the community, I like to support my community and help people get ahead, especially women, because many women suffered so much in the war, and I like to help them get beyond that, forget those trau-mas that they were left with. But how? When I say, let's have a meeting, they don't come, they're scared. Or they're too poor, they lost too much in the war and they can't afford to stop working to attend meetings. . . . In the communi-ties, in rural areas, women suffer a lot because they have no education, and they don't speak Spanish, and they're easily scared. . . . Well, if someone, someone of a certain category, comes along they get scared off, and they don't want to par-ticipate in anything. I'm the one that tries to persuade them sometimes—let's do this, let's do that—but they are intimidated.

In many cases communities struggle to organize, but postwar committees created to deal with crime are unable to fulfill expectations. In part this happens when their leadership fails to inspire confidence (a common problem given the war's erosion of trust and solidarity):

The community had formed a security committee [*comité de vigilancia*], above all to combat crime. But as it turns out, this committee was created by representatives of the community, community leaders, and it was a little strange, you know, because the committee itself caught a thief, and they started to interrogate him. Who are your other *compañeros*, your accomplices? And as it turns out, this criminal started to name his *compañeros*, and among the *compañeros* of this thief were the sons of some of the members of the committee. So what can the council do to punish? The solution they came up with was for each of them to grab their children—because for two of those who were on the council, it was pointed out that their children were criminals—so each of them grabbed their children, pulled their hair, punched them, like that you know, sort of beat them up [in public], in order to satisfy the community, because the community was very worried and expected the council to do something to combat crime. But they really just sort of pulled their hair, and then shortly after that the council disappeared, it disintegrated, because the people didn't like it that supposedly this council was a security committee, above all against crime . . . but how could they explain that it was their own family members who were stealing. So now there is no security committee, no nothing. . . .

This committee was elected by the whole community, because they are important men, experienced men, trustworthy men above all, because the people said, we're going to form a committee, but let's make it a committee that's very specialized in order to stop crime. But since this problem happened, the people stopped trusting them. Many even said, what example do they set for the rest of us if in their own families crimes are being committed? As he [another respondent present] said, the trust, the hope that they had after that committee was formed, it just disappeared.

Residents of another K'iche' community, for example, told me about their struggles to apply Mayan justice to one young man who had stolen repeatedly from others. At first, the community held a meeting to decide what to do about the teenager's repeated infractions, and those present voted to administer a public flogging "according to Mayan law." A group of respected elders was selected to administer the punishment, and the community gathered to watch. Yet the robberies continued. Another flogging was held. Days before my arrival, it was discovered that the young man had stolen a neighbor's cow, cut it up, and tried to sell the meat at the market in another town. The theft of something as valuable as a cow represented a significantly more serious offense than those committed previously, suggesting that past punishments had been entirely ineffective, and several people spoke about this with great frustration. As one told me:

The community has said that at first, they'll resolve it with the council of elders. But there's a warning from the community, that if the problem doesn't get resolved by the council of elders, then they'll look for another exit—they haven't said if they'll take him to the judge, if they'll tie him up, what they'll do specifically. They just say that if this criminal doesn't understand, and doesn't change—they haven't only given him several lashings, they've also assigned him to work some days for the benefit of the community, and he never repents—so there it's up in the air what stronger actions they're going to take. It's not said, but understood [*nos da de entender*] that he has to be burned in this case.

In response to the above speaker, another man explained: "It's that you try to do things the decent way [*Es que uno trata por las buenas*] . . . but the results are disappointing. And then you say, if we can't detain this [crime] with the traditions that we have, if that's not respected any more, the only [option] is to simply eliminate it once and for all [*si eso ya no se respeta, lo único es eliminarlo de una vez*]." And a younger man chimed in, "Yes, because when [the criminal is] supposedly being punished, [he] can still commit crimes. But once [he's] dead, [he] can't [*Sí, porque supuestamente castigado puede volver a delinquir. Ya muerto, no*]."

Many emphasized the difficulty of organizing in settings where even the forms of collective politics that were effective during the war seem out of step with contemporary realities. Some members of human rights groups told me with grave regret that the children of their human rights colleagues are sometimes gang members alongside the children of former paramilitaries, making it difficult to discern anymore who the "good guys" are. It is this sense of profound anomie, of communities without moral guideposts, of decay, doubt, and desperation, that gives rise to lynchings. Collective action, therefore, is born not only of solidarity, but also at times of mistrust. Although some aspects of contemporary lynchings may resonate with Durkheim's vision of public punishment, they emerge in settings characterized not by strong solidarities, but by their absence. Lynchings are not a reversion to past practices or an atavistic attempt to hold back the tide of globalization, but a new form of governance based on mistrust. For, as one woman asked me, meeting my gaze straight on with tired, tear-filled eyes, "What else do we have left? [¿*Qué más nos queda?*]"

For many residents of lynching communities, then, the absence of norms, rules, and institutions to detain future criminality means there can be no effort at rehabilitation. It is easier to kill criminals ("eliminate evil") than to negotiate complex notions of justice, because the latter requires sustained trust and collaboration—and because, given these communities' inability to influence state decisions on criminal justice and the evident weakness (in some settings) of their own indigenous justice systems, such attempts seem destined to fail. In this way, the lynchers echo the findings of Tyler and Boeckmann (1997), who suggest that Californians supported punitive solutions to crime because of a concern that, in a society they perceived as lacking shared norms that deter criminality, extreme punitiveness—in the California context, terminal incarceration; in the Guatemalan case, where even prisons are permeable, execution—is perceived as the only option. Punitiveness is thus not an inherent preference of the respondent but the result of his or her assessment of the viability of other options in settings of low solidarity.

Lynchings as Acts of (Perverse) Political Empowerment

More than sheer acts of desperation, lynchings are also articulations of resistance. Rather than the predecessors to a modern justice system— as Durkheim and Girard describe acts of collective violence—today's lynchings are explicit indictments of this system. The overtly "judicial" nature of many lynchings suggests that the state, courts, and legal procedures are clear reference points for lynch mobs. Lynchings often follow certain steps that crudely parallel formal legal procedures: suspects are detained and held while investigations are carried out; any evidence is brought before the decision-making body; suspects are questioned and confessions sought (often under torture); a sentence is decided upon; and sometimes proceedings are recorded for future reference. There is a deliberate attempt to mimic the functioning of the official justice system—in effect, to construct an alternate system subject to the controls of the community. This suggests that lynchings reveal a conflict not only between community members and criminals, but also between communities and the state—a conflict over whose authority prevails in matters of life and death.[12] In this way, communities who lynch struggle to regain control not just over crime, but over decision-making authority in matters of vital import to their day-to-day lives. Lynchings are, seen in this light, defiant expressions of local autonomy. They therefore aim at communicating a message not only to their own members (in a Durkheimian sense), but also to a broader audience, including especially the state.

This intention is underscored in the actions that often accompany these executions. First, participants often seek to project news of the proceedings far and wide, using the mass media and even human rights groups to carry their message. I spoke to one U.N. worker in Guatemala City who told me he had been present at various lynchings, invited by the community as a witness and forced, once there, to videotape the acts. A similar eagerness of lynch mobs to be filmed is discussed in the case of Peru by Eduardo Castillo Claudett (2000). And as Carlos Vilas (2001) notes, in August 1996 a videotape of a lynching in Tatahuicapa, Playa Vicente, Veracruz, Mexico, was sent to a human rights group in the state capital. Rather than shrinking from the spotlight, the communities engaged in these acts often actively seek the attention of outsiders and the mass media.

In calling attention to these acts, communities are careful, in order to avoid potential prosecution, to legitimate their participation on the basis of unanimity and popular support. In some cases, lynch mobs have signed documents affirming their unanimous intention to lynch, as if to preempt charges that a single person or group was responsible; these documents are presented to the authorities as evidence that the actions taken were legitimated by the popular will. Indeed, this willingness and even eagerness to be heard contrasts sharply with the nearly universal reluctance of individual respondents to speak on the record about lynchings. Although communities often want their collective determination to be known, individuals are understandably reluctant to talk about lynchings and particularly to be recorded doing so. Several told me this was because they feared that the "so-called law" or "supposed justice" would come after *them* for imposing "real" justice, further emphasizing their view of the law as not only untrustworthy but twisted against reason.

Furthermore, lynchings are often accompanied by public protests against the authorities, including the destruction of municipal property, the occupation of buildings and highways, and occasionally the taking as hostages of local authorities who oppose the mob. In Guatemala, judges and policemen themselves have been lynched. In Venezuela, as part of the lynching described at the beginning of this chapter, residents of Mariara took over the Central Regional Highway as part of their reported "rebellion against insecurity" ("Comunidad de Mariara" 2001) and pronounced their intention to carry out further protests as long as the intolerable levels of crime continued. These acts underscore communities' intention to force authorities to take their concerns seriously. As one interviewee told me, "I don't know with what intentions [lynchings] are done. Possibly to demonstrate to the authorities that they have to do something."

If lynchings are in part a collective rite aimed at fostering cohesion among community members, they are also in part a politically charged expression of popular will through violence, aimed squarely at outsiders and the state. In Durkheimian terms, they do constitute messages aimed within, at the "healthy consciences" of the noncriminal members of the community, affirming shared values and repairing the damages to solidarity occasioned by the offending act; but they also, in an important departure from Durkheim, constitute unequivocal reactions to the state's legal system.

Conclusion

Writing about the effects of authoritarianism in the Southern Cone, some Latin American social scientists have suggested that these societies were transformed into "cultures of fear" (Corradi 1992; Lechner 1992). Fear was an inevitable result of the widespread experience of arbitrary state violence as people saw neighbors, loved ones, and co-workers disappear overnight; but it was also instigated and strategically augmented by authoritarian regimes' use of propaganda to justify the ongoing "state of exception." Although the appeal of militarized rule lay in its promise of order in times of heightened insecurity, the military regimes themselves fed—rather than fought—the cycle of fear. These practices decimated citizens' faith in government institutions and even their interpersonal trust, leaving a legacy of challenging terrain on which to rebuild democracy.

In her analysis of public-opinion data from across the region, Marta Lagos (1997, 2001, 2003) has emphasized the historically low levels of interpersonal and institutional trust as a key factor inhibiting the consolidation of democracy in the region. Indeed, Lagos argues that the inefficiency of institutions is in part a reflection of this "regional heritage of mistrust": because institutions operate on the assumption of dishonesty, not only endless documentation, but also personal connections and influences, become necessary to navigate bureaucratic mazes when citizens need to perform even the simplest task. "The most fundamental challenge for Latin American democracies in the years ahead," Lagos writes, "is how, amid the fragmenting pressures of globalization and economic liberalization, to generate social trust and to widen and reconstruct networks of social capital" (2001: 144).

Lynchings are the ultimate expression of a lack of faith in institutions—not only state institutions, but also the informal practices that have long stood in their stead. In some ways, lynchings reaffirm Durkheimian insights about social life: shared identities are important, and their destruction by processes of rapid social change fosters feelings of insecurity that are often expressed as concern about crime. Yet they also reveal the weaknesses in functionalist approaches that characteristically ignore conflict and power. Lynchings are not acts that close doors on corporate communities, shutting out the polluting influence of crime; they are acts of resistance and struggle, within communities but also between them and the broader world, of which they form—and claim—a part. They are, above all, a reflection of communities in crisis, settings in which strong passions are stirred yet the social building blocks of a long-term, effective response to challenging circumstances have been systematically weakened by violence that is physical, structural, and symbolic. In this world, democracy is difficult. Solidarity has been shattered, customs pulled up and tossed askew; institutions for sustained collaboration have been gutted, and violence, all too often, lurks in the hollow.

CHAPTER 5

Civil Society and the Contradictions
of Neoliberal Democracy

ACROSS THE AMERICAS, POSTAUTHORITARIAN TRANSITIONS to democracy were frequently the product of fragile alliances forged over time, rather than a triumphant overthrow of tyranny. The pacted nature of these transitions is important: concerned about an authoritarian backslide, many democratization theorists (and practitioners) argued for moderate routes to democracy that guaranteed civil and political rights but stopped short of the more fundamental social and economic transformations that many on the Left had fought for. For theorists such as O'Donnell and Schmitter (1986), Rueschemeyer, Stephens, and Stephens (1992), Przeworski (1991), and others, as well as for political actors in many countries, this was an acceptable, indeed a necessary, compromise because more aggressive reforms might so threaten the Far Right as to provoke a coup. Furthermore, many considered it paramount to guarantee the integrity of political (primarily electoral) contests, not to prejudge specific policy outcomes. Democracy was understood as, at its core, a question of process rather than results;[1] it was to be the responsibility of civic actors within the country to make what they would of the political opportunities the system afforded. In this context, civil society was assumed to be the primary vector for the "deepening" of democracy from purely formal structures of rights to more substantive measures of social reform.

A similar progression from the granting of strictly political rights to the securing of social and economic rights was imagined by human rights scholars and advocates. Following T. H. Marshall's classic (1950) formulation, rights were assumed to progress from political to social, through a series of ever-expanding concentric circles; in a similar formulation, the United Nations adopted the terminology of "generations of rights," and human rights groups such as Amnesty International built this premise into their very purpose, placing civil and political rights explicitly at the core of their concerns in the presumption that other rights could be built on this foundation.[2]

Today, however, there is growing awareness that things didn't quite work out as planned. Although formal democracy is indeed the law of the land (everywhere in the hemisphere except Cuba) and there appears to be little risk of a return to military dictatorship, optimistic expectations of inexorable progress have been dashed. Indeed, scholars note a decline in the level of democracy in the region (Diamond 1996: 61). And although many citizens have mobilized to expand the rights formally conceded them by law (see especially Eckstein and Wickham-Crowley 2003, and the numerous contributors to that volume),[3] the historic structures of mass social and economic exclusion have remained largely intact, even becoming further entrenched in some cases. In fact, thanks to the debt crisis of the 1980s and the implementation of structural adjustment policies in its wake, most Latin Americans are economically worse off today than they were under authoritarianism; in many countries real food prices have quintupled in the last two decades, while real wages have yet to rebound to their pre-1980s levels (Eckstein and Wickham-Crowley 2003: 13). The widespread implementation of neoliberal reforms has further marginalized the majority of the region's populations from the institutions of political power, both by plunging an ever greater number into poverty and by expressly prohibiting state bureaucracies from attending to distributive concerns. So although many Latin Americans envisioned the transition to democracy as an *apertura* or opening of possibilities, structural adjustment policies and the dictates of multinational lending institutions have come to place sharp limits on the nature and breadth of possible transformations. This is, in short and simple terms, the neoliberal juggernaut:[4] formal political inclusion coupled with socioeconomic exclusion and a paring down of possibilities for social policy.[5]

Growing awareness of this has produced a volatile cocktail: though one generalized response has been the disengagement from democratic politics known as *desencanto* (disenchantment, expressed in low voter turnout, low citizen participation, the "atomization" of O'Donnell's

[1993] vision, or what Corradi [1992] calls "social inertia"), in states with weak public security regimes an equally viable—and increasingly visible—response is violence, which emerges around issues that have immediate and personally tangible effects such as crime, the privatization of essential services (such as the reactions to the privatization of water in Bolivia), the freezing of bank accounts (as was done in Argentina), or cutbacks in food subsidies (as in Venezuela).[6]

In these cases, citizen engagement is impossible to miss. But it is not engagement through the institutions of representative government— these have been so discredited among the poor that many regard them as objects of ridicule rather than realistic organizing targets—but through violent upheaval in the street. In reference to Venezuela, Naomi Daremblum has called this "hyper-democracy, a state in which political passions rule and neither side seems capable of offering responsible solutions . . . [and] this sense of frustration drives many Venezuelans toward non-institutional, non-democratic alternatives" (2003: 36). It prompts short-term "solutions" to crises, patched together under duress, and reduces policy making to a cycle of antagonism punctuated by moments of forced concession—each iteration of which only encourages future ones by reinforcing mistrust in political leaders and demonstrating the effectiveness of emergencies. Although some Latin American political leaders have expressed their desire to see democracy as a "rolling boil" of popular participation,[7] the metaphor may be all too apt: lynchings, mass riots, and outbreaks of popular violence suggest that in some settings the democratic pot may be boiling over. Could it be that participation by civil society, once assumed to be the force that would redeem the region's democracies, might scald them instead?

Of course, it might reasonably be objected that lynch mobs, vandals who attack foreign banks, and coca growers in revolt are not properly considered "civil society." Certainly they do not constitute the civil society that proponents of Anglo-American liberal democratic theory have in mind; if anything, they are its very opposite. If civil society is defined as a network of voluntary associations and institutions grounded in the exercise of and respect for liberal rights and the rule of law, then lynchings, organized food riots, and many popular movements on the periphery are disqualified from the outset.[8] Although often conflated in common parlance, "civil society" and "popular participation" are not the same thing.

Yet some have suggested that such a concept of civil society is inherently bound up with specific visions of social ordering that translate poorly to the postcolonial world (Mamdani 1996); the expectation of bowling leagues or their equivalent may be a tall order in the societies of the global south, where forms of associational life may not much resemble the European or North American model. Many Mayan peasants, for example, told me they did not have the luxury of debating political decisions when there were so many hungry mouths to feed; this does not mean they lack political consciousness, only that the forms in which they articulate political demands are likely to differ greatly from those favored by white male landowners in nineteenth-century Europe. (Ultimately, this point strikes me as somewhat unsurprising.) A more sociological approach might understand civil society as an intermediate realm between the state and the market, an arena in which citizens come together in autonomous, voluntary association for mutual benefit, without placing limits on the type of activities they undertake toward this end. The way in which they come together, of course, has profound implications for the character of democracy. But if we exclude violent, disorganized, and illegal groups from consideration in our theories about civic behavior, from the definitional get-go we undercut our ability to understand a world in which increasing numbers have embraced such tactics. This is a world particularly evident in postcolonial societies, but not only there: the 1999 World Trade Organization riots in Seattle revealed the emergence of some similar sentiments in a U.S. context. As the connections between private economic power and public authority, and the contradictions they imply, become clearer, uncivil societies erupt even in more established democracies. This shows that if the vitality of democratic institutions depends on the vibrancy of associational life, the perceived legitimacy and efficacy of these institutions also affect the way citizens choose to organize.

Nor are the distinctions between civic groups and uncivil actions as hard-and-fast as these conceptual categories might imply. As Alison Brysk points out, "The same local communities that are charged by shrinking states with taking on more responsibility for development and local governance are lynching suspected criminals in Latin America (and burning alleged witches in southern Africa). Supporters of social movements that unquestionably contribute new issues and voices to the wider arena (such as ethnic-rights organizations) seldom query these movements' relationships to their own constituencies" (2000:154). Clearly, not all forms of citizen organizing for mutual benefit promote the expansion of rights, or even the enjoyment of basic ones. Writing about Brazil's "disjunctive democracy," James Holston and Teresa P. R. Caldeira suggest (1998) that although political citizenship has indeed been consolidated in contemporary Brazil, the civil components of citizenship are lacking, and in fact there is widespread tolerance of that fact—tolerance that becomes particularly salient with respect to crime and insecurity. Indeed, examining civil society organizing around this issue in particular may illuminate some of its broader limitations.

Chapters 3 and 4 focused on problems stemming in part from the lack of social capital *within* communities. In this chapter I examine the effects of a lack of state legitimacy on the effectiveness of organizing efforts, even those among groups with relatively high levels of internal (or horizontal) social capital.[9] The suitability of civil society as a vector for the deepening of democracy is to some extent determined by the legitimacy of the state itself. In the context of an illegitimate state, civil society actors are disinclined to advance long-term goals requiring broad social reforms—in particular because these would require state collaboration. There are at least two alternatives: to advocate solutions entirely outside the state, or to propose that state involvement be circumscribed to simple, unambiguous tasks—in the case of crime, often to purely repressive ones. In the pages that follow, I examine examples of each alternative.

First, I look at the movement to revitalize traditional forms of customary or Mayan justice, spearheaded by groups such as Guatemala's Defensoría Maya, that work to defend the rights of indigenous peoples. Although a return to these community-bound practices may help repair the ruptured social fabric at a local level, such a strategy cannot substitute for a push for broader social and political reforms and an engagement with the formal legal system.

Second, I explore anticrime initiatives promoted by urban middle-class *ladino* organizations, primarily those dedicated to business interests. Rather than embracing private solutions to the problem of public security, these approaches place the responsibility for crime fighting squarely on the shoulders of the state; however, they advocate a purely punitive response to this complex social problem. It is a response that, because of its sheer simplicity, resonates with many citizens, but for the same reason its ability to tackle a problem with deep social and political roots is limited.

Both responses are deliberately and unequivocally opposed to violence and vigilantism, and both are rooted in respect for rights, democracy, and the rule of law. Yet both reveal a profound suspicion of the state. Their limitations expose some of the inherent problems in organizing in postauthoritarian democracies, where even if the challenge of weakened interpersonal trust can be surmounted, the authorities remain largely illegitimate in the eyes of virtually everyone.

Indigenous Justice and Other Informal Alternatives

Across the highlands, Mayan community organizers are striving to avoid lynchings. The most common, and probably the most promising, efforts are those which seek to revive traditional forms of indigenous justice often referred to as *justicia consuetudinaria* (customary justice) or *justicia Maya* (Mayan justice). Though local practices vary greatly, generally speaking these forms of informal dispute resolution seek to address conflicts through consensus building and restitution, in sharp contrast to the Western style of justice achieved through winner-take-all decisions. Justice is seen as flowing not from the punishment of the guilty, but from the restoration of disrupted community harmony. The process of making justice is therefore often more important than its specific outcome: eliciting a public confession and arriving at a shared understanding of what went wrong and how to move forward is usually identified by participants as more important than punishment. Decisions are often made in a public meeting, usually presided over by a council of elders selected for their years of service to the collectivity; there are no set precedents or preexisting code to adhere to. In the case of crime, the offending individual is generally ordered to repair the damage caused by his or her action; because many do not have cash available to replace losses, a "sentence" might require the performance of certain services over time for the benefit of victims or the community. In this way, rather than excising offenders from the community, sanctions often bind them more closely to it (see Defensoría Maya 1999; Yrigoyen Fajardo 1999).

Like other community institutions, these practices were decimated by the war. The application of Mayan law was effectively criminalized during the decades of counterinsurgency war as widespread repression clouded collective memory and selective execution of community leaders eliminated the living repositories of community traditions as discussed in chapter 3. And even where such practices were not uprooted by state repression, the changing reality of peasant communities deeply transformed by shifting economic and political conditions places new strains on traditional mechanisms for governance, as discussed in chapter 4.

Yet today, a number of indigenous rights organizations, including Defensoría Maya, CERJ, and others, are laboring to recuperate lost traditions of Mayan justice, to reconstruct devastated communities and make possible the peaceful resolution of local conflicts. Bolstered by Guatemala's "Mayan Renaissance"—a renewed appreciation for Mayan cultures and an efflorescence of civil society organizing around indigenous identity and culture—this movement seeks recognition for indigenous law as a legitimate system of justice and strives to facilitate and expand the practice of Mayan law. Defensoría Maya, for example, trains community mediators, who staff Justice Centers where local residents can go to seek resolution to their conflicts. Though the model they offer may differ from the way Mayan justice was historically practiced in specific localities (in that the mediator is not necessarily a community elder, nor are proceedings necessarily held in public, for example), it aims to adhere to the spirit of past practices. The participation of extended family, neighbors, witnesses, and other community members, in addition to the disputants, is encouraged in both the retelling of the events in question and the crafting of a solution suitable to all; restitution, not determination of guilt or innocence, is the ultimate goal; deliberations are held in the indigenous language of the affected parties; and no charge is assessed for the service. It is clear that as regards intracommunity conflict resolution, such practices meet the needs of the local population much better than the state courts do.

Beyond Guatemala, a resurgence in support for indigenous justice and semiautonomous governance characterized many postcolonial societies in the late twentieth and early twenty-first centuries. Around the world, and particularly in Latin America, recent decades have seen an upsurge in indigenous organizing (Yashar 1998), and new legal and political frameworks now recognize indigenous rights as human rights. The most important of these is the International Labor Organization (ILO) Convention 169, which has now been ratified into law by the majority of Latin American states (Sieder 2002). Although effective implementation lags behind formal recognition, constitutional reforms in Bolivia (1994), Colombia (1991), Ecuador (1998), Mexico (1992), Nicaragua (1986), Paraguay (1992), Peru (1993), and Venezuela (1999) recognized these societies as multiethnic and pluricultural (Van Cott 2000, cited in Sieder 2002), and specifically indigenous NGOs, political parties, and cultural initiatives have cropped up across the continent. A common element among their demands is recognition for indigenous forms of law—referred to as *justicia indígena, usos y costumbres,* or by other equivalent terms—as mandated in ILO 169.

The increased legitimacy afforded such practices has sparked a growing area of debate among both scholars and practitioners grappling with the challenge of integrating measures of indigenous legal autonomy into formal legal systems premised on Western conceptions of universal rights. Because they place a premium on community harmony rather than individual rights, indigenous legal systems may occasionally detain suspects for prolonged periods without bringing formal charges against them or sentence them to physical punishments, such as floggings, that can be interpreted as due-process violations in Western legal frameworks. At times, as Speed and Collier illustrate in an insightful and thought-provoking examination of these issues in Chiapas, Mexico (2000), state authorities may invoke human rights claims to undercut indigenous autonomy, legitimating the arrest and imprisonment of community leaders on grounds that they had "exceeded their functions" and violated due-process rights. (For an account of similar problems in Peru, see Yrigoyen Fajardo 2002.) This leads us to some important questions: What are the limits to indigenous autonomy? Are there outcomes and processes acceptable to indigenous communities yet incompatible with universal human rights standards? To what extent should autonomous institutions or spheres of civil society construct their own law?

These debates are not limited to specifically indigenous issues. John Gitlitz's descriptions of the *justicia rondera* practiced by nonindigenous Peruvian peasants in the Andean department of Cajamarca recall a similar system of informal, community-based justice, created in response to cattle rustling and widespread thievery. In an area where state justice is viewed as distant at best, and more often as both corrupt and ineffective, peasants construct their own system for dispute resolution. Like Mayan law, the justice of Peru's *rondas campesinas* strives to restore disputed community harmony rather than assign specific blame. Gitlitz argues that although *ronda* justice is not without flaws, by and large it succeeds at fulfilling its stated purpose and certainly is more effective than state justice; but the *rondas*, too, have been criticized for failing to respect due-process rights (Correa Sutil 1998: 101). Moreover, informalization extends beyond the so-called developing world. In the United States and Europe, many of the same justifications are offered as civil and criminal laws alike undergo reforms to encourage alternative forms of dispute resolution and facilitate community corrections, restorative justice, and other approaches to the law that rely on increased community involvement in resolving conflicts (Abel 1982).

Across the board, the selling point of such practices is their flexibility and appropriateness in the local context. As the coordinator of a Mayan justice center in the highland province of Sololá told me:

[We decided] to raise the profile of our indigenous authorities, our mayors, our auxiliary mayors, spiritual guides, elders [*principales*], in our communities . . . because for us the courts, the police, the Public Ministry, they aren't our authorities. They are the authorities of the other sector of the population. We have our own authorities and we have our own forms, our indigenous justice. Because most of the cases here don't make it to court. Many are resolved in the communities. And we also had a problem because we saw that in the courts of justice, those aren't our people who are there, rather they're our *ladino* brothers, who don't really understand our situation the way it is in our communities. And in the courts corruption prevails, incompetence prevails, impunity prevails, et cetera. And that system of justice is expensive. It's expensive, it's competitive, it's a racist, exclusionary court, it's a court where money prevails, and it's also for the long term. The problem is that the indigenous population, the Mayans, we're screwed [*estamos jodidos*]. Because to take a case to court, the judge always asks for lawyers. For example, with that guy [*gesturing*], he has a land dispute, what's the judge going to say? "Ah, you have a land dispute, well, what you have to do then is get yourselves lawyers." So he goes to get a lawyer and the other side goes to get another lawyer. Here in Sololá, there are cases where just to go see the file number on the case, the lawyer charges 150 to 200 quetzales [approximately US$21–$28]. Just to go see the number of the file, I'm not talking about the whole legal process here, say for example that the process takes a year. OK. And our salary? Here they're paying 20 quetzales [approximately $2.85], the salary for one person for one day. And with those 20 quetzales, the majority of the indigenous families have five, six children to maintain, so in a family that's seven or eight [people], so we have to divide the 20 quetzales for all eight, and on top of that pay a lawyer—well, for us it simply isn't possible. So what our people do is, they have to sell their land, have to sell their animals, and in one week, a lawyer from here, in one week—to give a low estimate—for one case, in one week a lawyer earns about 500, 600 quetzales. And sometimes the case takes a year, two years, three years in court. So there are cases that cost 10,000, 15,000, even 25,000 [quetzales]. We just can't do it. . . . In other words, it's a disaster in the courts of justice. So we here in Sololá, we said, if there are courts that are not indigenous, that don't agree with our worldview [*cosmovisión*], our culture, then why don't we make our own court?

. . . Also, we're against lynchings. Because many people say, they associate customary justice [*derecho consuetudinario*] with the lynchings. But the lynchings are the product, the result of all the war that happened. Many brothers were in the army, many were in the paramilitary groups, they learned what it was like to kill people, and that stuck in their minds, that only by killing people does one get to be a leader in the community. That's why they're provoking the lynchings [now]. But that's why we have always rejected, we have always said that the lynchings are not customary justice. We, as indigenous people who handle customary justice, indigenous justice, well, we reject that sort of thing.

Also, we reject what the system in Guatemala does with the death penalty. In Guatemala the authorities make a lot of noise. Right. They say they caught one, that he's headed for lethal injection, but it's never the people who [commit] big crimes, but just something to scare people and cover their eyes so they think that justice is being made [*sólo es para asustar a la población y para tapar el ojo de la población que sí se está haciendo justicia*]. But we as indigenous people have seen that all those who have died by lethal injection were poor people. They didn't have the right to a defense because they didn't have money. And for us, the one who has to be first in line for lethal injection, that's [former dictators, responsible for atrocities] Lucas García. Ríos Montt. Mejía Víctores. Why not them? Well, because they have justice in their hands, power. For the poor man, there's lethal injection. But what we say is, the people are there, right there [*ahi está la gente, ahi no más*], [*gesturing out the door toward the street*] we know a bunch of people who collaborated with the army in wartime, and who killed many, many people, and they're free now.

I spoke to some of the disputants at this same justice center, where many sat for hours with their retinue of relatives, waiting their turn for justice. Many spoke with pride of the procedures their communities had developed, offering sharp criticisms of state justice. One participant told me:

We see that jail is not the solution for a thief. Right now, for example, many [prisoners] are escaping. Even in jail, there are no guarantees. Another thing is that now they're talking about expanding many of the jails. But what are they going to do with all those people? They're just going to grow and grow and there will be a large number, a large number of prisoners in each jail, and then other problems will erupt inside the jails. So the solution . . . is to educate and train the people, but from the community level. To look for the way to eliminate the root of the problem, and not be looking for the roots up in the branches of a tree that's already grown.

Another man told me:

> We as indigenous people, with the question of crime, we ... have organized our own communities well, and it's the community itself that defends against crime. That's it. We don't have a police or army presence because we know they are the same ones [who are committing crimes]. So what we do is that each community has its own security committee, so that they themselves can get all the crime there is out of their community. I think this is what we're contributing to the entire country, the fact that around here the population organizes itself, and is united, so that in any moment if a group of thieves or a group of criminals enters, they get them out. Only in this way can we change this country, because the government, we've already waited for a long time, and never, never have we seen that they have a solution.

Indigenous justice is thus consciously evoked as an alternative to state law, a vehicle of local empowerment, a way for locally rooted civil society to carve out space formerly monopolized by the repressive state and its formal law. Here, perhaps the archetypal example is the experience of Santiago Atitlán, a Tzutujil Maya village on the shores of breathtakingly scenic Lake Atitlán in the province of Sololá.[10] In 1980, a military base (*destacamento*) was established near the village, and shortly thereafter, *atitecos* (residents of Atitlán) began participating—forcibly—in civil patrols. Tensions between the villagers and military grew as repression escalated and many community leaders were systematically targeted for execution, among them the director of the village's courageous radio station, La voz de Atitlán; the beloved Catholic priest; and many others. In December 1990, the situation came to head following what appears to have been an attempted kidnapping and/or rape of a village resident by soldiers dressed in civilian clothes; although the aggressors retreated to the barracks, angry villagers gathered in the town plaza, ringing the church bell to summon the community to a public discussion. A large crowd numbering into the thousands gathered, and discussion ensued for much of the night until eventually a delegation headed by the community's municipal leaders, and numbering by some estimates as many as fifteen thousand people (Murga Armas 1997), headed to the barracks and asked to speak to the commander. While anxious villagers waited at the gates for the commander to emerge from within, soldiers opened fire into the crowd, killing twelve, injuring twenty-three, and prompting those who could to flee for their lives.

The next morning, a crowd gathered outside the Catholic church in the village center. The leaders drafted a letter to then-President Vinicio

Cerezo, and villagers formed long lines of thousands to sign or leave thumbprints on the document, indicating their support for its demands. The letter asked for an investigation into the massacre and punishment for those responsible; even more boldly, it blamed the military for the incident and insisted that the army withdraw from Santiago Atitlán, leaving the community to provide for its own security. A delegation departed for the capital with the letter, intent on delivering it to the nation's highest authority.

Perhaps more surprising still, the president agreed, issuing orders for the army to leave the village at once and recognizing the community's commitment to govern itself. And indeed, for years thereafter the community governed itself semiautonomously. Although the national police retained a tiny formal presence, they were clearly subordinated to the village authorities, who, organized through the officially recognized Comité Pro Seguridad y Desarrollo (Security and Development Committee), participated in regular nighttime patrols known as *rondas* and resolved conflicts during the day through a participative system of mediation based in Mayan traditions. When I visited the community in 1999, present and former leaders of the *rondas* explained to me that when crimes could not be satisfactorily resolved through the consensus-building mechanisms of Mayan justice, they would be referred to the state legal system through the local justice of the peace. But by all accounts, this was rare; once the army was expelled from Santiago Atitlán, not only politically motivated crimes but common crime declined markedly, and most everyone confirmed to me that they felt safer, because everything was generally calmer (*más tranquilo*) once the army left.[11]

The experience of Santiago Atitlán is often touted as an example for other communities; the Guatemalan sociologist Jorge Murga Armas, in an excellent essay, claims that the case of Santiago Atitlán illustrates the promise of a broader conception of democratic security as inseparable from citizenship. Such a redefinition views not only military challenges but also (and especially) those forces that limit or prevent the free exercise of civil, political, social, cultural, and economic rights as threats to national security. This model, he suggests, could and should be replicated in other communities (Murga Armas 1997). In my discussions with Guatemalan human rights advocates, many made reference to Santiago (and the municipality of Sololá, just across the lake, where, also through grassroots mobilization, residents had rejected postwar plans to convert the notorious Number 14 military base into a military training institute, arguing instead for the establishment of a university extension campus). These examples, many told me, proved that popular mobilization from below was the key to demilitarization and democratization; they pointed to the promise of a new Guatemala, built from the bottom up.

Nor are academics and political activists the only admirers of Santiago Atitlán. Indigenous justice and informalization more broadly have also been embraced by advocates of decentralization and privatization and are increasingly favored by international lending institutions seeking a way to promote the rule of law without involving state bureaucracies in vast experiments in social engineering. It is, by all accounts, more cost-efficient, and probably more effective, to ask communities to resolve their own petty quarrels without tying up state resources in the process. Informal justice, community policing, and other measures that seek to enhance community involvement in everyday crime fighting are thus also a touchstone of justice-sector reformers seeking to trim fat from state bureaucracies under neoliberal mandates to boost efficiency while bringing down expenditures.

At the same time, though, devolving responsibilities on local communities, particularly when so many are plagued with serious internal divisions, is no panacea: it does not necessarily guarantee greater legitimacy or efficiency, and in some cases might amount to little more than passing the buck. Before we embrace the apparent consensus around informal alternatives, then, we should examine when informal law "works" to resolve conflicts without bloodshed and when it degenerates into violence.

Vigilance or Vigilantes?

The stories from Santiago Atitlán certainly offer a promising counterpoint to what might otherwise seem an inordinately bleak picture of law and justice in postwar Guatemala. But what distinguishes vigilance committees from vigilantes? Why, in one community, do the peals of the church bell draw citizens to a collective deliberation culminating in a popular reaffirmation of democracy that rejects violence and reaffirms rights, while in another, they summon the community to a lynching? Not all forms of informal (nonstate) law are liberating: the question thus becomes under what circumstances informal practices offer a valuable alternative to the state justice system, and under what circumstances they merely degenerate into violence.

Though Mayan justice traditions offer a positive alternative perspective grounded in respect for the individual and community, "Mayaness" alone is not enough to ensure that alternative systems avoid violence. Indigenous justice is a slippery concept; in Guatemala, as in most other countries of the Americas, its limitations, methods, and intersection with state justice systems have yet to be specified, and on the ground in many communities, I found a great deal of confusion about what really "counts" as Mayan law. What makes a given sanction or legal proceeding an example of Mayan justice, other than the fact that it is enacted by Mayans? Lynchings do *not* constitute traditional Mayan practice (despite politically motivated accusations to the contrary), yet many Mayan communities engage in them today; and although Mayan leaders are quick to publicly disavow such tactics, many Mayan peasants expressed support for them in interviews with me, even ascribing them legitimacy because they were "Mayan law." As an indeterminate system in which sanctions are not specified nor precedents predetermined, Mayan law can thus be (mis)used to justify violence as well as to repel it: outcomes of collective deliberations, whether or not these are infused with elements of indigenous tradition, can be foundational, or antithetical, to the functioning of a democracy.

Nor is the popular character of the process sufficient to guard against violent vigilantism, for some grassroots assemblies have voted—*voted*, invoking the core practice of participatory governance—to kill, just as others have valiantly endeavored to resolve conflicts through nonviolent means. And much as we might like to think that mob violence is a product of momentary exaltation but "cooler heads prevail" in longer-term deliberations, the difference does not lie in the spontaneous-versus-organized aspect either: I spoke to members of communities where people had elected their executioners in advance. What, then, is the difference between popular justice and vigilantism?

Proposals to strengthen Mayan justice as a way out of lynchings are correct in identifying community cohesion as a potential antidote to collective violence against crime. The provision of alternate fora for dispute resolution may alleviate some of the backlog in the courts, preventing some otherwise unresolved conflicts from spilling over into violence, and provide a more legitimate, culturally contextualized mechanism for social control in Mayan communities, but we should not romanticize away its limitations. First, the success of these institutions relies on the prior existence of some form of social capital among the communities who create them. Because the only effective enforcement such legal systems possess is the sanction of shame, they can only work in communities where ostracism and honor still matter. An unrepentant offender, therefore, is a lost cause: and in an era when Mayan communities contend with competing global value systems, many offenders indeed are unrepentant. Second, such systems will never be capable of reining in the big fish: members of transnational organized crime networks can simply refuse to submit to the jurisdiction of local councils of peasants organized against crime. Nor are they likely to adjudicate disputes of broader social relevance: abusive employment practices by plantation owners against their laborers, for example, or interethnic disputes about land ownership are unlikely to be settled in courts whose jurisdiction can be ignored by powerful individuals outside a geographically rooted peasant community. Such systems may be useful to settle disputes among social equals, but they are ill equipped to tackle legal matters among disputants of dissimilar backgrounds. For this reason, such systems must work to develop vertical ties to the state law as well, to ensure their effectiveness at addressing major crimes as well as minor infractions.

Lastly, in deeply divided communities, such as the many postgenocidal villages of highlands Guatemala where social capital has been systematically obliterated, such mechanisms are likely to be, at best, of limited efficacy, and at worst, vulnerable to quick cooptation by one or another faction vying for political power.[12] On the barren social terrain of some postwar communities, the informalization of justice amounts not just to passing the buck, but lighting the match. Ultimately, informal institutions are no different than any other; they cannot simply be plunked down on the ashes of genocide and expected to confer legitimacy, through their mere presence, on a process enacted in the absence of trust and solidarity. In such settings, even "progressive" or "democratic" institutions can take on perverse or violent characteristics, and civil society itself may behave in decidedly uncivil ways.

Furthermore, none of this is limited to criminal justice in Mayan peasant communities. The movement for *mano dura* more generally is characterized by the same sentiment: in the absence of trust in institutions, violent "justice" becomes the only form of social control considered viable. With the effectiveness of state criminal justice institutions increasingly assailed by populist politicians preaching the gospel of zero tolerance as well as by neoliberal reformers advocating privatization, many support *mano dura* as perhaps the only remaining alternative to widespread lawlessness. When institutional confidence approaches zero, it becomes senseless to suggest preventative criminal justice policies, which if anything legitimate greater state intervention in society over the long term. When citizens are absolutely convinced the system is corrupt to its core, why would they entrust it with such invasive authority? As Guillermo O'Donnell (1993) suggests, suspicion of the state radically shortens the time horizon for expected results; in the sphere of criminal justice, immediate, irreversible "results" can be achieved only through the exercise of violence, legally or illegally, against criminals. This rational calculus dispenses with lofty long-term aims such as justice or rehabilitation, reducing the law to the stripped-down structures of repression: at least, as many respondents told me, death is final.

Ladino Anticrime Organizing in the Capital

In Latin America, concerns about crime cut across classes. As Susana Rotker writes of urban violence across the region: "Potential victims are all of those who could be killed at any given moment because they could fetch a big ransom, because they wear brand-name shoes, because the assailant—who made a bet with his friends—fired his gun by mistake. The potential victim is middle class, wealthy, or poor: it is anyone who goes out and is afraid, afraid because everything is rotting and out of control, because there is no control, because no one believes in anything anymore" (2002: 16–17). Indeed, in Guatemala this sentiment of things being "out of control" was articulated to me by members of some of the country's most privileged families. As the executive director of the country's powerful business lobby, CACIF, said in an impassioned voice:

We've lived through some very difficult times, Angelina. I'm not going to tell you that the private sector has been the most affected, because that's not true, but there has been a lot. There has been a lot. At this table—this is the table of the CACIF, this is where the fourteen directors meet—in less than one year, the mother of the president of the Chamber of Industry was kidnapped, and she was smothered with a plastic bag after her ransom was paid, she died in a shack in Villa Nueva. And the brother of the current president of CACIF, Ricardo Villanueva, was kidnapped by an employee of his—an employee who he had trusted, who he had helped out of poverty by employing him—they kidnapped him, and he turned up chopped into pieces here along the highway to El Salvador. A productive person, I knew him, Angelina, with three children less than eight years old, a man who never did anything to hurt anyone. Really. So I tell you, there's a lot I could tell you, people here really need for justice to be applied. It's terrible. Please, believe me.

Former President Cerezo lamented having to send his children to study outside the country because of fears they could be kidnapped at home. A rancher whose estate in eastern Guatemala once boasted hundreds of head of cattle confessed to me from his house in Guatemala City that in recent years he had let the farm decline because he was literally afraid to visit it:

It's that you expose yourself to [the danger that] they could do something to you, you never know who could lay a trap for you, and I have my people there on the farm but I don't have confidence—it's not that they have done anything to me, to give me reason to not trust them but you hear what has happened to other friends. . . . I have a friend that travels to his farm by helicopter so as not to expose himself to a [potential] kidnapping on the highway, and they've offered [the helicopter] to me but to be honest, it makes me too sad, I prefer not to go. It's something that pains me, that hurts. . . . It's one's patrimony and one can't even go visit it. That's where I grew up, it's where I played as a boy, we used to bathe in the rivers—I'm not a man of the city, you know, I don't like this life. But what can I do?

Not surprisingly, then, a number of middle-class civil society organizations have participated actively in the public security debate. Groups such as Madres Angustiadas (Anguished Mothers), Familiares y Amigos contra la Delincuencia y el Secuestro (Family Members and Friends against Crime and Kidnapping), and Guardianes del Vecindario (Neighborhood Guardians) have been constituted specifically in response to crime. Mainly made up of middle and upper-middle class *ladinos* from the capital, these groups are resolutely pro-democracy, genuinely preoccupied with the country's international image, and for the most part eager to distance themselves from the retrograde right wing, even deliberately refraining from the use of the term *mano dura* (at least when talking to international academics!). At the same time, they are frequent and vociferous advocates for harsher penal sanctions. Among other things, recent press articles cite such organizations as Guardianes del Vecindario as arguing for the elimination of reduced sentences, promoting capital punishment, and attacking widespread corruption in the justice system.

A number of prominent private-sector organizations have also taken positions on crime issues, and without exception they favor a tough law-and-order stance. The former president of the Chamber of Industry, Jaime Botrán, demanded the death penalty for kidnappers: "In cases of kidnapping, where the morality and human rights of those responsible is practically null,[13] there is no other path but that of the death penalty." Guatemalan national legislation, he continued, should prevail over any international treaties. "It's possible that this punishment might not be a deterrent for criminals," Botrán admitted, "but it is a punishment for them. If it can be both, all the better" ("Camara de industria" 1997).

The coffee producers' professional association, ANACAFE (Asociaión Nacional del Café [National Coffee Association]), has also made public pronouncements on the crime issue. In a 1997 security proposal shared with me by ANACAFE's presidential adviser in security matters, the organization writes:

The control of security—minimally—is in the hands of the national police, especially in the rural area, precisely the place where the country's principal economic development is generated. Our economy is based principally in agriculture and we cannot leave it to the mercy of criminals.

For various reasons, the security of the population has been supported in large part by the army. This has been this way because of constitutional law; because of sociopolitical, cultural, and historical reasons; because of its elevated budget; and because of the limited capacity of the civilian security forces. Although positive changes are proposed, nobody can deny that this has been our reality for many years. If the results of this have not always been the best, it is also true that the army, today, is the only institution of the state that has ample experience in matters related to the country's security.

Due to the incipient insecurity that we live in today, we believe the strengthening and modernization of the army is necessary, alongside the modernization and strengthening of the police security forces. It is necessary to be practical, creative, and realistic to combat and eradicate crime. In the short term, the solution does not lie in leaving the army paralyzed while the citizenry suffers the effects of intolerable violence. We urgently need to make positive use of the reservoir of people, knowledge, and experience of the army to solve this problem, which can be done in a combined fashion with the national police. It is necessary to reorganize and channel what we have within our reach. In the short, medium, and long term, this will be more beneficial for all.

Because if it is true that the army has lost prestige for justified reasons, it is also true that the national police lacks credibility; in the majority of cases it is inefficient and lacking in technical equipment and personnel. Also, at different levels it has become corrupted, and it lacks investigative capacity.

At the same time, the tribunals of justice are almost inoperative. The judges find themselves submitted to various pressures. The process is debased because of the constant relation, inherent in the system, between the interested parties and the administrators of justice. The level of corruption is high.

We are sure there are thousands of other obstacles, but our principal proposal is to affirm that there is a great vacuum of authority and of justice, especially in rural areas, and that we are disposed to collaborate with the government to solve this problem. To a large extent, the action of passing internal security to the hands of the National Police has generated this vacuum of authority. We know and understand the reasons for doing so, but we also live day by day with a growing insecurity and the results of having taken such a decision. ("ANACAFE" 1997)

The same document goes on to enumerate the principal problems, from the point of view of coffee producers: "Our concerns: increase in the authority vacuum; deterioration of the regime of legality; increase in levels of violence; complication of self-protection by laws and controls; increase in impunity; proliferation of strongly armed groups in rural areas." It lists recommendations for the state, including the introduction of joint patrols with army and civilian police members—a policy that was subsequently adopted and continues to this day.

A full-page paid advertisement placed by ANACAFE reads:

THE NATIONAL ASSOCIATION OF COFFEE DECLARES:
Guatemala is Bound by the Hands and Feet!

THE DENIAL OF JUSTICE
Weeks ago, the decision made by a judicial instance of appeal favored three kidnappers, by substituting a penalty of fifty years in jail for the death penalty originally imposed. This decision challenges the internal legislation of our country and the national demand that the death penalty be applied.

WHAT ABOUT THE PEOPLE?
On multiple occasions, the people of Guatemala have pronounced themselves, without hesitation, for the application of the death penalty when crimes are committed that legally merit it. No disposition of internal or external nature can be above the popular clamor, especially when it is demanded that Guatemala's legal framework, as a sovereign nation, be respected.

OUR DEMAND
With all due respect, but in a forceful way, we ask the competent authorities to revise their actions and, as the arm defending Guatemalan society, to apply the death penalty in a speedy fashion to those kidnappers who have demonstrated bloodthirstiness, arrogance, opposition to the legal order, inhumanity, and

transgression of the fundamental values of people foreign to criminality: the right to freedom and the right to life.

WITHOUT JUSTICE THERE IS NO PEACE
WITHOUT PEACE THERE IS NO DEVELOPMENT

By far the most significant of private sector crime campaigns, however, was that launched in 1999 by Guatemala's powerful CACIF. Entitled "Guatemala is in mourning" (*Guatemala está de luto*), the campaign featured massive publicity in newspapers and on television. One chilling black-and-white television commercial showed images of swarming rats as an allusion to criminals out of control. The print advertisements also tapped into strong emotions: one depicts a man's fist grasping a doubled belt under the boldface words "It's time to put on the pants" (*Es hora de amarrarse los pantalones*), a heavily gendered expression that refers to taking decisive action. The text below calls on judges—who are listed by name—to dictate a guilty verdict in a specific kidnapping case and gives the name of the child victim and the names of the accused. The image of the belt has a double impact: on one level, it orders the judges to "put on their pants," so to speak, or act decisively; on another, it serves as an easily recognizable allusion to the common paternal practice of disciplining children by hitting them with a leather belt.

Ultimately, these interventions advocate a more restrained, less raw version of *mano dura*. Though they recognize the state's legal institutions as the appropriate entity for handling crime and therefore seek to strengthen these institutions, the measures they espouse ultimately reveal a profoundly limited view of the law. The strengthening they seek is a strengthening of its purely repressive capacity—they want longer sentences, more convictions, more punitiveness. The proposals they advocate ignore social and economic reforms as a potential avenue for change, focusing instead on highly punitive sanctions and a streamlining of the penal process at the expense of the accused. The executive director of CACIF, for example, expressed his view that poverty and crime should be disentangled:

Look, Guatemala is a poor country, Angelina, I don't have to hide it from you that we have the silver medal in illiteracy in Latin America, after Haiti, which is truly shameful, and it's a country with an agricultural economy and still with many outdated structures, with many people who are completely removed from productive life, from economic cycles, from access to services. This is a country that just a few years ago didn't have a network of highways, for example, without services as basic as water, as electricity, in its homes. So the problem of poverty is undoubtedly among the causes [of crime], but it's not the most important one, Angelina. Here I want to underline this and for one simple reason. If I accepted, if I bought the explanation of poverty as the cause of crime, I would be immediately accepting that the poor people of my country are criminal people, and that isn't true.

They also generally sidestep the need for justice in cases of war crimes, pushing exclusively for the resolution of "common crime" cases apparently devoid of politics. Although many of the changes they propose—such as increased accountability in the prison system, professionalization of the police force, and others—would contribute to a more effective and just law-enforcement apparatus, many others, such as the expedited application of capital punishment, are likely to produce outcomes more symbolic than security enhancing. Others—such as the creation of separate tribunals for crimes against tourists, a proposal the Chamber of Tourism told me was being informally considered in 1999, or the creation of private rural armies to secure plantations, advocated by the president of the Chamber of Agriculture in 1999—threaten to produce a bifurcated justice system like those Pilar Domingo Villegas (1995) warns against, whereby certain privileged groups enjoy speedy justice and relative security while the majority of the population is relegated to a second-class system with endemic flaws.

Similarly, the work of such organizations calls attention to certain high-profile, emblematic cases—usually kidnappings of upper- or upper-middle-class Guatemalans—and seeks to apply targeted pressure on the authorities to produce guilty verdicts in those cases. It is thanks in part to such pressures that the clandestine anti-kidnapping Comando unit was created within the Estado Mayor Presidencial, an elite military unit with notorious ties to political killings. Not only does the creation of clandestine structures for crime fighting set a perilous precedent, clearly violating the government's commitments under the peace accords, but it is unlikely to improve the safety of the broader public in the long term.

Nonetheless, they are supported in these efforts by the majority of public opinion, making the state's adoptions of such programs an easy political win. In this sense, despite being historically resented as the powerful symbol of the country's rapacious elites, through crime the CACIF have aligned themselves with popular opinion. Even the executive director of CACIF commented to me:

You know, one thing that really caught our attention, when we put out those bumper stickers,[14] we printed more or less 25,000, it's that CACIF, as a business organization [*cúpula empresarial*], it's like any business organization in the world, Angelina, it's not popular. It's an organization that defends the interests of capital, right, and in whatever country that's seen as, well, let's say, not so good [*Es una organización que recoge los intereses pues del capital, verdad, y en cualquier país siempre eso se mira digamos pues no tan bien*]. But in this case, despite that, and despite the fact that using one of our bumper stickers might represent a challenge to criminals, the people stuck them on. It's incredible to see that even the shoeshine boys, they were out there with their boxes with the CACIF sticker stuck on it—that's what showed us that there was really a need to denounce all that's going on here in Guatemala.

Though there are retrograde authoritarian elements in Guatemala, CACIF, ANACAFE, Madres Angustiadas, and most of the other middle-class organizations attempting to influence state policy on crime are not among them. Rather, the penality these organizations espouse is a neoliberal one, not unlike that supported by private-sector actors in the United States and elsewhere. Despite being formally compatible with democracy, however, such a system may undermine democracy's promise of social justice. Particularly in societies that are deeply divided along class and ethnic lines, this neoliberal version of *mano dura* penality enforces social hierarchies through increased state violence along that border between haves and have-nots. It may in fact reduce crime rates, but it also has the propensity to read popular mobilization itself as crime—something that is not always entirely unreasonable, of course, given the outbreaks of violence discussed earlier.

As a result, the mechanisms of zero tolerance are applied not only to rapists and murderers, but also to striking workers who occupy public space, university students (as in the famous UNAM strike), and others. Although groups such as CACIF explicitly deny that their crackdowns are targeted at the poor, insisting that it's not poverty but immorality that causes crime, poor people's politics are thus increasingly dealt with through the lens of "crime," in what amounts to essentially an attempt to hold down the lid as the "hyper-democratic" pot boils over. Though *mano dura* and zero-tolerance policies appear to promise greater security for all, in fact they prioritize the security of a few and risk making life more insecure for those who fall into the category of possible criminals—the poor, the darker-skinned, the young male residents of shantytowns, those who migrate, those who are unemployed. As increasing numbers of Latin Americans sink into this category, the forms of *mano dura* espoused by both rich and poor alike appear to have set *convivencia* itself on a collision course.[15] It is to this point that I turn in the final chapter of this book.

CHAPTER 6

Convergence at the Poles . . . and Not
on the Polls

FOR THE BETTER PART OF a century, Latin Americans have been encouraged to look to the United States as an image of their potential future. Through modernization and development, the promise of "progress" has been held out as a beacon by well-meaning policymakers, international organizations, and foundations who offered programs and held workshops to train Latin American leaders in "what works," based largely on the U.S. experience.[1]

In the realm of criminal justice, this process is still underway today. Although academics such as Arturo Escobar (1995) pronounced the death of development in the mid-1990s, the news has yet to reach many of those I spoke to in Guatemala, from the rural peasant who told me that he knew executing suspected criminals was an effective approach to criminal justice "because that's how they do it in Texas" to the right-wing politician I interviewed in his office in the Guatemalan Congress, a room somewhat oddly adorned by a large and prominently placed photograph of the U.S. Capitol. Over the past two decades, a wave of support for rule-of-law programs in Latin America continues to import legal training, technology, and ideas from the "developed" world, especially the United States (Carothers 1998, 2003; Fruhling, Tulchin, and Golding 2003; Dezalay and Garth 2002). On matters of crime and punishment, the most visible reminder of this relationship may be the recent high-profile visits of Rudolph Giuliani and William Bratton to Mexico City, Caracas, and other Latin American cities, where they have helped train their Latin American counterparts in the zero-tolerance techniques made famous in New York City.[2] In the context of the U.S.-led but globally waged wars on drugs and on terror-ism, additional pressures encourage Latin American governments to adopt reforms that enhance their ability to collaborate with U.S. law-enforcement agencies; if offers of aid for judicial reform serve as carrots, threats of decertification, exclusion from lucrative trade agreements, and other measures also represent very real sticks.

And although many Latin American governments have consciously sought to incorporate elements of a penal politics "made in the USA" into their arsenal of social control techniques, thus pulling their prac-tices closer to a line initially drawn by U.S. experts, in this chapter I show that a perhaps less deliberate drift has also taken place in the op-posite direction. That is to say, as the U.S. population becomes more po-larized between haves and have-nots and state institutions increasingly position themselves to police this boundary rather than mitigate its ef-fects, the United States has moved closer to a model of governance long recognized by Latin Americans, though perhaps less familiar to many members of a North American society that still considers itself mostly middle class.[3] It is a model of governance characteristic of deeply un-equal societies; some have called it neoliberal penality; yet others have argued against the application of any such unitary term for the con-temporary penal regime, arguing that it is composed of several deeply contradictory strains.[4] Rather than intervening in the debate about how the contemporary regime is termed, my aim here is to observe that in societies characterized by a dwindling set of haves and an ever more numerous (and potentially unruly) group of have-nots, an inexorable pull seems to place criminal justice at the very core of governance strategies. In the U.S. context, Jonathan Simon has referred to this as "governing through crime" (Jonathan Simon 1997). As crime becomes more salient and social control the state's principal project, criminal jus-tice techniques become more aggressive in their enforcement of class and racial boundaries: hallmarks include a widening of the criminal jus-tice net (by broadening definitions of criminal activity, for example) and a deepening of the deprivations visited on those ensnared within it.

The study of crime and punishment in Latin America is inextricably linked to politics. This is a nexus worth examining in its own right, as a means of understanding contemporary realities in the region. But now more than ever, it is also worth examining these elements of the Latin American experience because their study yields lessons increasingly relevant to the contemporary U.S. context. There may be a temptation— a comforting one—for U.S. publics to exoticize the events in this book, to view accounts of horrific abuses committed by authoritarian regimes or the brutality of contemporary lynchings as remote tragedies unfolding in foreign lands, but we should interpret these as extreme manifestations of familiar trends. The differences are of degree, not kind: ultimately, even these most disturbing events should be recognized as reflections of what may be a similar underlying reality.

This is not to say that the challenges faced in these contexts are equal in every way; significant differences continue to separate the political, economic, and military prowess of the United States, as a global hegemon, and the vastly different realities of struggling Central American countries, or even of South American powerhouses such as Brazil. These differences have important ramifications for social and political life, and it would be foolish—if not impossible—to ignore them. The role of the state in penal politics is one particularly salient area of difference. Although citizens in both settings may converge around a punitive model of "just deserts," in the United States few question that the responsibility for punishment should and does lie exclusively with the state, whereas in many Latin American societies the hampered legitimacy and hamstrung effectiveness of the state means that many support private acts of punishment such as lynchings or social cleansing. The distinction here is not trivial: even taking into account the recent erosions of many long-standing rights guarantees in the United States, an accused criminal still enjoys vastly more due-process protections in the U.S. criminal justice system than before most peasant councils–*cum*–lynch mobs in Guatemala (or Venezuela, or Bolivia, or Mexico).

Keeping in mind these differences, however, I focus in the following pages on points of convergence. First, I argue that the rise of penal populism in both settings contains two apparently contradictory currents: support for strengthening state criminal justice systems in order to administer more certain or severe punishments, on the one hand, and support for their being supplanted with private alternatives, on the other. This combination is in many ways a logical outcome of the dueling mandates imposed on states in this era of neoliberal orthodoxy:[5] in order to provide a stable investment climate, states must uphold democracy while at the same time preventing disorder and political upheaval. In countries where political and economic structures are premised on mass exclusion, preserving macroeconomic stability without resorting to massive repression means finding new ways to effectively control the poor. Neoliberal penality does precisely this, restricting the state's activist provision of social services yet augmenting its capacity for repression (through the militarization and buildup of the security forces and the concurrent tolerance—in weak legal regimes—of private stand-ins).

Second, I argue that in confronting the contemporary danger of terrorism through tactics that at least partially rescind core democratic rights, the United States risks repeating mistakes made (under its own advisorship) by Latin American regimes in the recent past. Although the need for swift and effective action to curtail the terrorist threat is beyond question, and the nature of the threat varies in some significant ways from that faced in Latin America, the experience of our southern neighbors provides ample evidence for the dangers of construing security and justice as opposing priorities locked in a zero-sum equation. It is not enough to merely learn the lesson not to resort to mass disappearances, widespread acts of torture, or other egregious human rights abuses; understanding Latin America's poisoned past means more than simply disavowing these most obviously misguided tactics. Rather, we must examine and contest the ways the underlying logics of *both* the war on terrorism and the war on crime perpetuate fuzzy notions of "us" versus "them" that all too easily devolve into racial, ethnic, and class divisions and justify a false security premised on the ever more aggressive policing of these often unspoken boundaries.

Points of Convergence

In this book I have argued that the phenomenon of lynchings forms part of a broader trend popularly known across Latin America as *mano dura*. Under this new penality, crime and punishment have become hot political issues, figuring prominently in campaigns for local and national office across the continent. While politicians and organized civil society groups have clamored for stiffer punishments, including the expansion of the death penalty, the imposition of longer sentences, and the increased intervention of the security forces in daily life—as well as many other measures that seek to strengthen the state's criminal justice apparatus—others have tacitly or overtly taken the law into their own hands, or, in less extreme ways, argued that communities should assume greater roles in crime fighting, precisely because the state cannot be trusted to provide justice and security. As mentioned in chapter 2, though police are often considered corrupt and inept, a special vitriol is reserved for the courts as the site at which law is at its most abstract, enacted in terms of rights, principles, and standards for evidence and procedure that are often seen as stymieing efforts at criminal prosecution.

A similar penal politics has emerged in the United States. Although the popular lynching of criminals is thankfully not a characteristic of the contemporary U.S. penal regime, many of the same trends are evident in less extreme manifestations. The late twentieth century witnessed a fundamental restructuring of punishment and crime control in the United States as the rehabilitative ideal, once the guiding principle of U.S. "corrections," was progressively discredited and largely discarded in favor of a more punitive approach: not only longer sentences for first-time and repeat offenders alike, but increased use of the death penalty, the imposition of deliberately austere conditions and the suspension of educational and other opportunities within prison, and the return of expressive punishments, including public shaming, in some contexts have fundamentally altered the very purpose of punishment in the contemporary United States (for a discussion of these broad changes, see Garland 2001; Jonathan Simon, forthcoming). The most dramatic indication of this change is the nation's skyrocketing prison population, its size in proportion to the population unprecedented in the nation's history (Currie 1998; Caplow and Simon 1999), and its inmate composition, skewed to include disproportionate numbers of ethnic minorities, especially African Americans.

Rather than a unitary set of policies based on a uniform approach to punishment, the new penality is comprised of many complex, and sometimes contradictory, currents. Yet several scholars have suggested that underlying them all appears to be a profound distrust for the state. According to Theodore Caplow and Jonathan Simon (1999), for example, in the United States the scope of the federal government has broadened in the last thirty years as the state has assumed a range of new responsibilities. The perceived failures of many of these programs, trumpeted loudly by antistate conservatives, have led to declining levels of public support for government more generally—and the increasingly pervasive attitude that government social-welfare policies are the source of, rather than the solution for, the crime problem. Caplow and Simon report that in response to the question "How much of the time do you trust the government in Washington to do the right thing?" in 1964, 75 percent answered "just about always" or "most of the time"; in 1995, that number had dropped to only 25 percent. Today, in the wake of the O. J. Simpson trial, the Rodney King beating, numerous police-corruption scandals, and the unrelenting criticism of state justice systems mounted by Democrats and Republicans alike, faith in the U.S. legal system appears to be crumbling—and this leads to a desire to wrest decision-making authority from state bureaucrats, making crime and punishment a matter for public debate and involvement rather than closed-door professional administration by government experts.

One response has been the proliferation of ballot initiatives addressing criminal justice matters. As Zimring, Hawkins, and Kamin (2003) write, "California's Three Strikes is not merely another kind of habitual-criminal legislation; it is rather one step in a campaign to take decision making out of the hands of as many government officials as possible. At its core, then, Three Strikes represents a jurisprudence of mistrust rather than any particular theory of punishment" (174). The authors also cite truth-in-sentencing provisions stipulating the percentage of a sentence that must be served before an offender may receive parole at the discretion of parole authorities; "shall issue" legislation requiring the issuance of concealed weapons permits without special requirements, thus cutting back on discretionary power of local police chiefs; and mandatory sentencing legislation, which limits judges' ability to adapt sentences to specific cases, stipulating instead a set penalty for each offense. All of these types of legislation form part of what these authors call "the politics of mistrust."

In recent decades, the rise of informalization, including the growing popularity of "alternative" models such restorative justice, community corrections, and dispute resolution, may reflect some similar sentiments. At the very least, it reveals a widely shared perception that the formalistic strictures of state justice systems are inadequate to provide "justice" and shows a preference for more contextualized approaches, often implemented by nonstate actors (Abel 1982).

Yet if these various developments suggest a growing suspicion of the state, it would appear paradoxical that in some ways, they have resulted in granting the state ever more sweeping powers (Garland 1996). If popular opinion seeks to repeal rehabilitation and embrace informalization precisely because people don't trust the state, why does the electorate support measures that wind up granting the state more, not less, authority to intervene in social life—precisely at a time when the prevailing neoliberal orthodoxy argues for a slimming of state functions? Even the embrace of such alternatives as mediation and community corrections requires oversight, regulation, and administration by an increasingly complex structure of state bureaucracies. In an era of streamlining state functions, the new politics of penality have led to a massive and unprecedented buildup of state criminal justice bureaucracies, effectively reversing what many imagine to be a shrinking of government since the late 1970s (Beckett and Western 1999).

Indeed, some have suggested that this "politics of mistrust" is really aimed primarily, if not exclusively, at the courts, and that the resultant reallocation of resources really suggests a shifting of state responsibilities from one branch to another rather than any coherent rejection of the state as a whole.[6] Others have argued that support for punitive measures such as California's Three Strikes initiative reflects not an instrumental assessment of the efficacy of any single institution or complex of institutions, but rather an expression of anxiety about social cohesion; in the absence of strong shared norms, many believe only punitiveness can serve as an effective deterrent to criminal behavior (Tyler and Boeckmann 1997).[7]

Whatever the cause of recent changes—whether it is popular disaffection, elite engineering, intra-agency rivalry, or any combination of these or other factors—the effect is clear: in this nation that considers itself a city on a hill, increasingly wide and disproportionately dark-skinned swaths of the population have experienced a sharp deterioration of their civil rights because their social activities, lifestyle choices, neighborhood of residence, or ethnic identity locates them within the sights of an increasingly aggressive criminal justice system.

This aggressiveness is more than merely punitiveness. It comprises at least two central characteristics. First, the net for criminals is cast increasingly wide. Rudolph Giuliani was credited with "cleaning up New York" through the extra-zealous enforcement of "quality of life" crimes; panhandlers and prostitutes, rather than violent sociopaths, are the primary targets of police action under zero-tolerance strategies. Second, there is an increased willingness to deprive those caught in this net of even their most basic rights. A particularly stark example is the practice of felony disfranchisement, whereby individuals convicted of felonies are either temporarily or permanently stripped of the right to vote in many states. In 1998, an estimated 3.9 million Americans (one in fifty people of voting age) had lost the ability to vote because of such laws, which often count any felony conviction—including those for such crimes as shoplifting or drug possession—as grounds for disfranchisement. Nationally, some 13 percent of African American men were affected by such laws; in eight states with particularly restrictive voting laws, one in four black men was *permanently* disfranchised, and in some states—notably Florida and Alabama—black men make up nearly 50 percent of the disfranchised population (Human Rights Watch and the Sentencing Project 1998).

No other industrialized democracies permit such a practice on a massive scale.[8] There is no practical justification for excluding those who have already served criminal sentences from suffrage; their participation in elections cannot be reasonably construed as posing a threat to anyone. Felony disfranchisement has nothing to do with controlling crime; rather, it serves to mark those who have had contact with the criminal justice system as noncitizens, to decrease the permeability of the boundary between "us" and "them," and to push the communities they inhabit into—or beyond—the outer limits of the polity.

Another example is the move to deport lawful residents of the United States for the commission of "aggravated felonies." The 1952 U.S. Immigration and Nationality Act was originally drafted to provide for the deportation of noncitizens convicted of very serious crimes, but in recent decades Congress has steadily expanded the list of deportable offenses, widening the net with the Anti–Drug Abuse Act of 1988, the Immigration Act of 1990, and the 1996 Antiterrorism and Effective Death Penalty Act (AEDPA), which mandated the deportation of lawful permanent residents for crimes as minor as writing a bad check, gambling offenses, shoplifting, mutilating a passport, or transportation for the purposes of prostitution (Cook 2003: 305). Not only does the AEDPA expand the categories of crimes for which deportation is considered, it also sharpens the punishment for getting caught by eliminating discretionary waivers of deportation (prior to 1996, an immigration judge would consider whether deportation of a resident convicted of an aggravated felony would impose an unfair hardship due to family ties, length of residence in the country, and other factors; today, removal is expedited, and such safeguards have been explicitly removed). As a result, noncitizens who have spent virtually all their productive lives in the United States are today remanded to countries of origin where they have no surviving family members, where they may not even be able to speak the language; furthermore, they are prohibited (under the terms of the Illegal Immigration Reform and Immigrant Responsibility Act, passed six months after the AEDPA) from *ever* returning to the United States, even to rejoin spouses and offspring (Cook 2003: 307).

Breathtaking in scope, this legislation also sets strict time limits on appeals filed by death row inmates, imposes unprecedented restrictions on habeas corpus appeals for all defendants, and limits federal court review of state court convictions except in cases where the previous state court decision was found to be unreasonable by the U.S. Supreme Court itself. (These new restrictions on federal review were imposed despite the fact that 40 percent of state death penalty cases carrying have been found by the federal courts to contain harmful constitutional errors that mandate the overturn of capital sentences; *Human Rights Watch World Report 1997*.)

The fear that spawned the AEDPA is inscribed in its very name. Passed amid heightened fears of foreign terrorism in the wake of the bombing of the federal building in Oklahoma City—an act initially attributed by many to Islamic fundamentalists—the act's name proclaims its intention to combat terrorism, yet its content has very little to say about these politically motivated acts of violence. Rather, the legislation assumes that by becoming less tolerant of small crimes like check fraud and petty theft and expelling those who commit such acts where possible (in the case of noncitizens) or relegating them to a penitentiary from which they cannot again emerge, the nation will be safeguarded. This law sets out to shore up security for some by rolling back rights of others. It paints convicts, Americans of foreign origin, and terrorists with the same broad brush, stripping all those who fall into these categories of key rights that form the core of our legal system.

In this sense, it embodies a new penality, then, that purports to buy security at the price of justice—but in which the transaction appears unproblematic, because "our" (law-abiding Americans') security is traded for "their" (criminals', terrorists', foreigners') justice. The system hums along on the strength of two interlocking assumptions: first, that we can reliably distinguish "us" from "them," and second, that we can then strip "them" of certain rights without affecting "our" own.

Neoliberal Penality

The contradictions embedded in recent developments lie at the heart of the neoliberal political project, which advances the notion of the streamlined state even as it relies on increased state involvement in certain sectors (Evans 1997), namely those activities which facilitate investment flows. This is particularly evident in the states of the so-called "developing world", which have long operated without a social safety net: attracting foreign investment requires political stability, formal democracy, and the rule of law, yet the very policies that seek to promote that investment may systematically undercut democracy, law, and order by causing—at least in the immediate short term—deepening inequality and rising discontent among the population. With the harsh, visible exercise of brutal repression to forestall reform now increasingly off-limits for postauthoritarian states, new forms of control are necessary to effectively contain those communities that, by virtue of their mounting numbers and growing desperation, may demand changes that threaten macroeconomic stability.

An increasingly severe penal politics—whether we call it "zero tolerance" or *mano dura*—fits the bill, providing a wedge that can prevent or postpone the realization of democracy's transformative potential. In many countries of Latin America, the reestablishment of democracy suggested that major reforms could be imminent; new constitutions and in some cases peace agreements promised an extension of citizenship rights to the historically marginalized and made available (at least in a formal sense) tools and institutions for the realization (or vindication, *reivindicación*) of those rights. Yet perceiving calls for sweeping social reforms as a threat to their entrenched privilege, powerful sectors in many countries have effectively defused these demands by calling for crackdowns on crime; by playing to popular insecurities accentuated by political and social turmoil, they have garnered support for such positions even from the poor and marginalized classes whose interests they may ultimately undermine. In this way, counterinsurgency has been replaced by crime fighting as the primary justification for a weak yet repressive state. And although zero-tolerance legislation and techniques may be introduced to combat violent crime, once available they are easily deployed to sanction striking workers, prevent public protests, and effectively criminalize social movements of the poor. Such states still boast the formal structures widely regarded as constituent of democracy, but the security forces' enforcement of class-based repression effectively defuses mass movements for political change and leaves only an outwardly visible shell of formal rights that are difficult to mobilize, whether on the barricades or at the ballot box.

As the two most unequal countries in the world's most unequal continent, Brazil and Guatemala provide the most dramatic examples of neoliberal penality. In Brazil, the authoritarian period drew to a close decades ago. Since then, a number of events have emphasized the dramatic changes the country has undergone: the promulgation of a 1988 constitution with broad and historic rights guarantees; the successful sanctioning of corrupt President Fernando Collor de Mello in 1992 without provoking an authoritarian relapse; the popular election of two longtime opponents of military rule, the former exile Fernando Henrique Cardoso in 1994 and 1998 and the Worker's Party leader Luiz Inácio Lula da Silva in 2002; and the creation of a vigorous institutional framework for the defense of human rights, spearheaded by the internationally recognized rights advocate Jose Gregori. But even though political and legal institutions have undergone a dramatic democratization, the reality on the streets, particularly in Brazil's notorious *favelas*, tells a different story.

Since the transition from authoritarianism, concern about crime has skyrocketed. Yet, as Paul Chevigny notes, "it is characteristic of Brazilians that, although they would like to see something done about crime, they have very little faith in the criminal justice system. They see it as slow, ineffective, and skewed in favor of the rich and powerful; many unhesitatingly brand it a 'joke'" (2003: 87). In this climate, there is considerable support for extralegal violence against real or presumed criminals. Death squads, often operating with the participation or at least awareness of the local police and in many cases with considerable public support, regularly target young, dark-skinned male residents of the *favelas*, and street children more generally, for acts of lethal violence. Police brutality is endemic, and in the context of growing concern about crime, some states have implemented policies that encourage abuse by rewarding police who demonstrate "bravery" with promotions and bonuses. All too often, these rewards have been distributed to those who killed criminal suspects under suspicious circumstances (Human Rights Watch 1997), suggesting that violence, not valor, is prized. In São Paulo, police killings of civilians in 1992—the same year Collor was successfully ousted, as Holston and Caldeira (1998) point out—exceeded the per capita number of civilians killed by the New York City Police Department by sixty-one times (Human Rights Watch 1997: 23–24). Also that same year, 111 prisoners were massacred in São Paulo's House of Detention in a move that was widely applauded by the general public (Holston and Caldeira 1998: 267). As Holston and Caldeira show, it is around the issue of responses to criminal violence that the disjunctions of Brazilian democracy are perhaps most apparent.

Loïc Wacquant, writing about Brazil's adoption of neoliberal policing strategies, charges that "deploying the penal state to respond to disorders spawned by the deregulation of the economy, the desocialization of wage labor and the relative and absolute immiseration of large sections of the urban proletariat by enlarging the means, scope and intensity of the intervention of the police and judicial apparatus amounts to (re) establishing a *veritable dictatorship over the poor"* (2003: 200, emphasis in original). Yet as Teresa P. R. Caldeira's (2000) ethnography of "crime talk" among upper-middle-class Brazilians illustrates, such policies are popular. Elites' tolerance for violence by state security forces against shantytown residents amounts to more than merely benign neglect; it is the result, Caldeira shows, of their manipulation of crime as a political issue to benefit their particularistic interests. Understanding crime as an evil that spreads through contamination, infiltration, and infestation (Caldeira 2000: 91), rather than a reflection of socioeconomic conditions, negates the need for real reform, reducing social policy to containment of the criminal threat and justifying the deployment of resources in purely repressive fashion to police boundaries of class, race, and ethnicity.

At the same time, and as part of the same process, the practical impossibility of buying security at this price forces Brazil's privileged to retreat into ever more strongly fortified enclaves where they can avoid contact with the dangers of urban life. Brazil, increasingly, is a society converging on two poles: as ever-greater numbers are plunged into poverty, crime becomes the focus of ever greater concern and social space itself a private commodity. One anecdote illustrates the depth of Brazil's disparities: Fearful of congestion, carjackings, kidnappings, and roadside robberies, increasing numbers of those who can afford it commute via helicopter in São Paulo, a city that boasts more heliports than anywhere else in the world. The most affordable helicopter, in 2000, cost $380,000, or ninety times the annual income of the average São Paulo resident (Romero 2000). Against this opulence, there is violence; although state programs of political murder have subsided in the postauthoritarian period, violence against the poor has quite arguably intensified (Holston and Caldeira 1998).

In Guatemala, too, growing crime talk, segregation, and privatized justice have accompanied what might otherwise appear to be the institutionalization of democracy. The 1996 peace accords commit the government to sweeping reforms of the country's systems of education, land distribution, social welfare, and taxation—to name but a few of the affected areas. Yet not surprisingly, these agreements have encountered significant opposition from agrarian and business elites (Romero 2000). As discussed in chapter 5, in the war's aftermath conservative sectors have played a key role in pressing for a crackdown on crime, diverting attention from the substantive reforms enshrined in the accords and mustering support for militarized policing measures, capital punishment, and other forms of increasingly punitive criminal justice, even where these contravene international human rights norms and/or the accords themselves. Although elites have certainly not manufactured the concern about crime, they have helped to channel existing concerns into exclusively punitive solutions. By focusing on such themes as moral decay, penal leniency, and corruption in the carceral system as causes of the crime wave, opinion leaders have diverted public attention from the serious social problems that the accords aim to address, declaring instead that the pressing problem of crime requires an exclusively repressive solution. In fact, many have claimed that the very human rights provisions enshrined in the accords are themselves the *cause* of crime (see chapter 2). The accords have been virtually set aside in recent years, in large part due to this diversion of attention and resources to crime fighting and the discursive delegitimation of their reformist content.

Yet these developments are not so dissimilar to what other scholars have identified in the United States. Indeed, many have argued that contemporary penal politics can be understood as an attempt to close the political space—the "window" for far-reaching social change—by conservative elite groups. According to this analysis, elite sectors experience anxiety about social order generated by large-scale social transformations such as the extension of rights to previously marginalized groups, including blacks (Beckett 1997) and immigrants (Tyler and Boeckmann 1997), or the globalizing transformation of the economy (Currie 1998). This anxiety is often channeled into concern about crime, fuelling calls for a strong state crime-fighting apparatus that effectively functions as a means of consolidating control of emergent social actors. Thus, although increasingly severe measures of crime control are ostensibly about protecting *all* citizens, they disproportionately benefit privileged sectors by shoring up the status quo against potential popular mobilization and defining the "other" as criminal.

Among the most convincing expositions of this argument is that offered by Katherine Beckett (1997). According to Beckett, the origins of current U.S. anti-crime policy lie in the efforts of conservative Republican politicians to carve out an electoral constituency for themselves following the civil rights movement of the 1960s. In depicting crime as a result of excessive permissiveness and leniency, conservative politicians found a near-perfect platform from which to launch a popularly endorsed dismantling of the welfare state—especially the Great Society antipoverty programs of the 1960s—and a politically successful response to the gains of the civil rights movement. Playing on racial insecurities and fears of the newly empowered black population and equating social protest—including the civil disobedience tactics of civil rights advocates—with lawlessness, conservatives called for a return to individual responsibility and a retreat from the precipice of liberal permissiveness, reframing the crime issue as a question not of inadequate social welfare but of insufficient social control, and, in so doing, reordering the purposes of politics in far-reaching ways.

On both sides of the Rio Grande/Rio Bravo, then, the advent of neoliberal penality has fundamentally altered not only punishment itself, but politics more broadly, undercutting the democratic potential of recent reforms. How do today's tough-on-crime policies achieve such far-reaching political effects? First, they redefine the state's role, not only in relation to punishment, but, more important, in relation to justice. A significant discursive shift occurs whereby expectations of the state shift from positive to negative rights. Although both positive and negative forms of rights (or to put it differently, things the state is obligated *to do for* its citizens—such as providing them with education or health care—and things the state is obligated *not to do to* its citizens—such as torturing or executing them) are enshrined in all liberal democratic constitutions, the neoliberal state is one that restrains, not one that provides. State power may even grow under such a system, but it is exercised in an increasingly reactive, rather than activist, fashion.

The rhetoric goes beyond merely diverting attention from the need for positive rights: it often goes so far as to identify these programs as the *cause* of crime. As Beckett and Sasson write of the United States:

Over the past three decades, conservatives have promoted the view that a variety of social ills including crime, addiction, and poverty, stem not from blocked opportunities linked to class inequality and racial discrimination but rather from "permissiveness" in the forms of criminal justice leniency, tolerance of drug use, and welfare dependency. . . . The conservative effort to frame these issues as a consequence of excessive "permissiveness" and "leniency" was not rooted in public opinion, nor is it consistent with the findings of most sociological research. Instead, these claims-making activities were part of a larger effort to realign the electorate along racial (rather than class) lines and thus forge a new Republican electoral majority. They were simultaneously aimed at shifting the government's role and responsibilities from the provision of social welfare to the protection of personal security. (2000: 73–74)

This stance justifies the dismantling of state structures that protect positive rights and the erection of new, purely punitive structures in their place. Rehabilitative programs for reforming offenders are accused of "mollycoddling" hardened criminals, welfare programs are blamed for "creating" dependency, and needle exchanges are accused of "encouraging" drug addiction. Resources are reallocated from these programs to the construction of more prisons, the financing of longer sentences, and the adoption of new punishment technologies. Even though these state-administered social programs are often deeply flawed, they represent an important effort to address the mechanisms of social exclusion that prevent the types of participation necessary to produce substantive democracy. As such, the removal of programs aimed at "leveling the playing field"—ensuring all citizens the minimum level of education, health, and basic welfare necessary for them to integrate themselves meaningfully into the polity—effectively naturalizes unequal outcomes, implicitly negating the need to address substantive welfare as a component of democracy itself.

By blaming human rights groups and progressive forces for crime, *mano dura* hampers the Left's ability to muster support for urgent social justice reforms. In this way, the advocacy of anything but harsh punitiveness is considered "soft on crime" and becomes untenable as a political position. This same shift makes it impossible, for example, for any serious candidate to national office in the United States to advocate the abolition of capital punishment, say, or the decriminalization of drugs. *Mano dura* thus becomes mainstream, and politicians compete to outdo one another in passionate professions of penal toughness. In such a climate, progressive politics becomes a blind alley that few politicians with national-level aspirations are willing to enter.

Furthermore, neoliberal penality deepens suspicion of the state, which automatically leads to more punitive "solutions." If the state is inherently rent seeking, why entrust it with the broad authority to intervene in the psychic and social lives of society's most dangerous criminals? It makes more sense, under such assumptions, to limit state interventions to the harsh and terminal than to invest state bureaucracies with sweeping authority to render judgments on offenders' potential for recidivism or other matters where subtle judgment is required.

Second, neoliberal penality sanitizes the logic of racial or class-inflected domination by cloaking it in the unassailable rhetoric of universal justice and public safety. These policies lead to greater repression, deployed more selectively against the marginalized, whether that marginalization stems from their skin color, class profile, or their residence in the "high-crime" areas prone to police sweeps and widespread public suspicion. In these areas—or for these people, wherever they may travel—neoliberal penality brings greater insecurity, as ever higher walls (both literal and figurative) prevent their entry into the legal economy. In countries where the security forces are characterized by legacies of abuse and impunity, this represents a particular danger, just as the "war on crime" has justified the rolling-out of the same repressive apparatus responsible for past atrocities, now purportedly in the service of public safety. Not only do the abuses that occur constitute violations of citizens' most basic rights, they also likely dampen political participation by the marginalized classes that are likely to be victimized in such attacks.

Javier Auyero's research in the shantytowns of Argentina, for example, documents how the everyday violence of life turns residents against one another, leaving most more afraid of their neighbors than they are of the state, which periodically invades their neighborhood to shake down drug dealers and beat up petty criminals. These kinds of violence, combined with the endemic unemployment—exacerbated for residents of the *villas*, who are viewed with suspicion and fear by residents of the city they surround—have progressively undermined social capital in the shantytown. Although such settlements have often been the site of political activism in the past, Auyero writes, "state repressive violence and later, the structural violence of unemployment deprived the shantytown dwellers of the means of effective collective control over their own neighborhood and their own lives," leading to a disengagement from broader political struggles (2000: 109).

Under this logic, the democratic "opening" slams shut at its most formal stage, truncating possibilities for future progress by undermining the ability of disadvantaged groups to engage in constructive types of participation. When strikes, protests, or mobilizations of the poor do occur, they are likely to be regarded as acts of lawlessness. In the U.S. context, Beckett describes this merging of crime, political dissent, and race as leading to a perception in the late 1960s that "Negroes who start riots" and "Communists" had provoked a breakdown of law and order; as a result, "most of the federal anticrime dollars allocated in the late 1960s and early 1970s were spent on police hardware and training programs aimed at containing riots and urban protests" (Beckett 1997: 38). Similar processes are underway in contemporary Latin America. In Venezuela, President Hugo Chávez has claimed that *mano dura* against political opponents is necessary and legitimate as a means of upholding peace and order ("Venezuela" 2002). In Ecuador, protests by taxi drivers over rising gasoline costs of led to the declaration of a state of emergency in 1999, and the army was sent to the streets to impose *mano dura* ("La mano dura" 1999); in 2002, university students who mobilized in response to rising transportation costs were repressed by then-President Gustavo Noboa, who declared, "Ten cents [of increased bus fare] do not justify that there should be anarchy in the country and that the extremists . . . try to convert the cities of our country into cities without order" ("Presidente de Ecuador" 2002). In Chile, similarly, in response to protests over the involvement of foreign companies in the government's plan to modernize transportation, the government insisted the Law of State Security—a 1958 law that considers criticism of the authorities a threat to the nation—would be applied to any strikers who attempted to interfere with "the right of the citizenry to be transported" ("Gobierno chileno" 2002). My point here is not to question the wisdom or legitimacy of these specific government interventions, but merely to illustrate the ease with which the rhetoric—and practices— of *mano dura* can be deployed against political mobilizations. There is a particular propensity for perceiving popular mobilization as a threat to law and order when those mobilizing are members of the imagined "dangerous classes."

Yet heavy-handed crackdowns against such events only serve to deepen poor communities' anger at the authorities, increasing the perception that the law itself is an illegitimate force. As Holston and Caldeira warn, "As soon as people perceive that their right to justice lacks institutional consolidation . . . a disastrous chain reaction occurs, as in Brazil, Colombia, or Venezuela in the late 1990s, for example: The justice system and those who defend it become discredited, impunity and violence prevail, and, largely as a result, a culture of vigilantism, exceptionalism, and privatized power predominates" (1998: 283). Hence, the lynchings of common criminals become a reaction not only to crime, but to the law itself. These outbreaks of private violence often serve only to perpetuate the cycle as the ensuing crackdowns by the security forces lead only to more anger and polarization.

As the gap grows between wealthy sectors' use of the law to protect their persons and property (a task that requires more and more repression as social conditions deteriorate) and the impoverished sectors' experience of the law as a violent and violating force, the law becomes simultaneously more punitive and less legitimate. Elite sectors are inclined to support governance based on social control, rather than social welfare, as a way to contain the increasingly pressing concerns of the poor; in areas where such polarization is extreme, the law's legitimacy reaches rock bottom, and widespread support for acts of mob justice is found, particularly among the more marginalized sectors, who are most likely to feel that the law does not speak for them.

In the United States and other "developed" countries where polarization is less pronounced, this cycle has yet to reach the dramatic extremes evident in Brazil or Guatemala; eruptions of mass violence and vigilantism are, thankfully, rare. But growing inequality may imperil legal legitimacy here as well. In the United States, studies have shown that it is not the favorability of outcomes, but the perception of procedural fairness that undergirds citizens' faith in the law (Tyler 1990). Yet as new strategies of crime control are increasingly perceived as targeting poor Americans who become ensnared in the carceral system—whether as suspects, convicts, family members of the incarcerated, residents of the designated high-crime areas where the war on drugs is waged, or merely young men of color—there is danger that growing numbers of these groups may begin to see the law itself as an instrument of domination. Under such circumstances, the probability increases of eruptions of collective violence at the margins.

In the United States, Jonathan Simon has referred to these techniques of social control as "governing through crime" (1997, 2000). Rather than a response to a real crisis in crime, he argues, contemporary penal strategies reflect a crisis in governance as societies reevaluate basic building blocks of government such as health care, public education, welfare, and other social programs. Crime becomes a new form of governance, achieved not only through the control of those increasing numbers of U.S. citizens and residents who form part of the penal population, but rather through a more far-reaching reordering of social relationships involving those who may fill the roles of victims, potential victims, offenders and potential offenders, and others. Simon (2000) maintains that this restructuring of social life has profound implications for the successful functioning of democracy in the twenty-first century; not only does support for an ever more punitive criminal justice regime reveal increasing suspicion of the state, it also encourages a civic culture polarized by exclusive, rather than inclusive, social interactions (Jordan and Arnold 1995) and crisscrossed by fear—a fear that often reinforces class, racial, and ethnic hierarchies.

Harsh punitiveness—a penal politics of "just deserts"—becomes increasingly appealing in such contexts because in its deceptive simplicity and visceral immediacy it promises to dispel the uncertainty that is increasingly characteristic of our times. But it is this engine of fear—not crime itself, nor some elaborate elite conspiracy to keep the poor impoverished—that drives neoliberal penality. It is the everyday fear of the uncertain, augmented in times of dramatic change, expressed as eloquently by my respondents in Mayan villages as by Sparks, Girling, and Loader's (2001) interviewees from "Middle England": fear of adolescent misbehavior, of unfamiliar languages spoken nearby, of traditional values lost in the shuffle. Fear, too, of economic opportunities changing, of a new-found vulnerability to the push and pull of global forces, accompanied by a slipping faith in government as a guardian. In this context, as Simon writes, "Governing through crime . . . might be looked at as a response to this crisis, both a reaching back to real or imagined strategies for maintaining what appears to be a precarious social order, and a reaching forward to new platforms to govern a social order that truly is undergoing remarkable demographic and economic change" (1997:177).

The combination of mistrust of the authorities and support for harsher sentences is not, in fact, so puzzling: there is an illusion of certainty in punitiveness, a finality in executions and life sentences in which the frightened may find solace when it appears all else is lost. As the lynchings tell us (and as I have argued in the foregoing chapters), without trust in institutions—whether the formal institutions of state law or alternative, community-based networks of trust and tradition—the lofty aims of justice are bartered down to their bare repressive backbone. In such contexts, the law serves only to separate, to mark "the limits within which each individual can act without harming others . . . just as the boundary between two fields is marked by a stake" (Marx 1978 [1843]: 42), to excise and eliminate, because seeking justice itself seems too risky in these dangerous times.

Wars Turned Within

This politics of fear is not new to Latin Americans. Throughout the early to mid-twentieth century, countries across the region confronted increasing instability as social movements arose to demand reform of the structures of mass exclusion that had governed these societies since colonialism. And although elites in some countries acceded to demands for reform—most notably Costa Rica, which responded to revolutionary pressures in the 1930s and 1940s by establishing a welfare state—in many more, early architects of authoritarianism responded to such demands by describing their advocates as criminals and defining reform itself as a threat to the nation. Indeed, such claims became easier to make as some reformers turned to increasingly radical tactics, including the use of violence, in their efforts to promote a platform for change. In Argentina, Brazil, Colombia, El Salvador, Guatemala, Nicaragua, Peru, and Uruguay, leftist guerrilla armies emerged asserting increasingly aggressive demands for reform and in some cases seeking to advance their cause through sporadic acts of violence, including high-profile kidnappings and bombings. In most cases the numbers of armed militants were very few, but the presence of multitudinous social movements pushing for reform contributed to a sense of social turbulence and disorder, shared not only by threatened oligarchs but also by everyday citizens confronted with an increasingly uncertain future.

Into this uncertainty stepped men like Augusto Pinochet in Chile, who promised to defend the nation from terrorists and communists, and armed themselves with sophisticated propaganda machines to convince their countrymen that the "enemy within" represented a threat to the very survival of the nation. It is telling that even at the height of the state of siege in 1986, a majority of residents of Santiago reported they were more afraid of crime and drug use than they were of their government's notoriously brutal acts of politically motivated repression (Lechner 1992: 27). This is testament to the fact that

authoritarianism in the Southern Cone [was] the reaction to a long-term process rather than an isolated eruption. Systematic violation of human rights does not alter the fact that large sectors of the population greeted the installment of a regime that promised to restore law and order if not with enthusiasm at least with relief. The so-called authoritarian culture of the region does not account for this acceptance. It was a rational decision: dictatorship appeared as a "necessary evil" or a "lesser evil" compared with the insecurity provoked by the former period of changes and social mobilizations. Why do some people continue to justify a dictatorship even when they know about the death and violence it has brought? Because the dictatorship only deepens fear. The anxiety of losing one's identity, social rootedness, and collective belonging is exacerbated. Because of this fear, the authoritarian regime continues to rely on social support that, albeit of a minority, cannot be explained simply as a means of defending economic privileges. There are other intangible "benefits"—concretely, a certain feeling of security. (Lechner 1992: 30)

It was to this fear that authoritarian regimes appealed. Arguing that "extraordinary times warrant extraordinary measures," states of exception (known variously as states of emergency, states of siege, or security measures) were imposed by dictatorships in Argentina, Brazil, Chile, El Salvador, Guatemala, Uruguay, and elsewhere. Judicial protection, due process, and executive accountability were undermined; military courts or faceless tribunals assumed broad jurisdiction; and various national security laws were introduced to suspend the rights of certain categories of people (namely, those accused of political crimes; Fagen 1992). These measures were taken in the name of safeguarding democracy, and they were measures many citizens supported, or at least tolerated, because they were afraid of the criminals and terrorists that their government told them operated freely in their midst.

As Herman Montealegre has observed, the national security argument permitted various repressive regimes in Latin America to "adopt the extraordinary means established by law to confront dangers to public order: declaration of a national state of war, indictment of citizens on the charge of treason, and attribution of the legal status of enemies of the state to certain persons. . . . This has resulted in an unprecedented and permanent application of traditional provisions of the legal system . . . contained in the juridical codes of Latin America which hitherto had only been employed in cases of actual war between the states" (Montealegre 1979: 3, cited in Schirmer 1998: 4, n. 1). In other words, by declaring a permanent war against subversion, the authoritarian states availed themselves of exceptional legal avenues to handle everyday policing; the war was turned within.

Of course, upholding order and preventing terrorist groups from committing acts of violence are legitimate objectives for government action; under certain circumstances, they even justify the judicious use of force. But the devil lies in the details: How does one discern who is a terrorist? Or who supports terrorism? In Latin America, by the time governments made the fateful policy choices that defined the internal enemy, any measure of transparency had already been lost; military strategies were shrouded in secrecy on the grounds of "national security." At the time the abuses were occurring, most citizens could not have known that health workers, nuns, and literacy promoters were considered national security threats in many nations. In Guatemala, for example, strict control of the media meant that most residents of the capital had no idea that what their government called a "struggle for democracy" meant the wholesale massacre of rural men, women, and children on the basis of their ethnicity alone. Two truth commissions and numerous international inquiries later, many still question why, how, and even whether their government truly committed such atrocities; even among those who acknowledge the abuses, some still argue that such actions were necessary to defend democracy.

In those countries where armed guerrilla movements were engaged in widespread acts of violence, the general population was even more strongly inclined to support government crackdowns. In Peru, for example, the brutal terrorism of the Shining Path (Sendero Luminoso), and to a lesser extent, of the Movimiento Revolucionario Tupac Amaru (MRTA), provoked anger, fear, and frustration that were easily parlayed into support for *mano dura* policies. In May and June of 1992 alone, an average of nine people a day were killed, most of them by the Shining Path; in June and July, there were thirty-three car bombings in Lima alone. So when President Fujimori conducted an "auto-coup" later that year, suspended most legal guarantees (including such basic rights as habeas corpus), and unleashed a vigorous antiterrorist campaign, most Peruvians expressed approval and even relief (de la Jara 2002: 4). The antiterrorist decrees of 1992, however, relied upon imprecise definitions of terrorism that were easily manipulated to allow authorities to arbitrarily arrest and indefinitely detain political opponents, many of whom were brought before "faceless" tribunals in secret proceedings. Suspects were detained in harsh conditions, and some were tortured; most were denied their right to a fair trial. Untold numbers may have been summarily executed; the Truth and Reconciliation Commission concluded in 2003 that an estimated forty thousand to sixty thousand died or disappeared between 1980 and 2000, perhaps half of them at the hands of government forces (Lederer 2003). In total, 21,855 people were detained on charges of "terrorism" between 1992 and 2000; of these, Amnesty International catalogued over 1,100 as either possible or confirmed prisoners of conscience, with no connection to terrorist acts whatsoever (Amnesty International 2003a). Despite these abuses, the government celebrated its "successes" in the war on terrorism by proclaiming ever growing numbers of detained "terrorists" on the nightly news, featuring their photographs in the newspapers, and even placing some of the most prized catches, including Shining Path's leader, Abimael Guzmán, on display in zoolike cages erected in public view.

Despite the harsh tactics, most Peruvians expressed support for their government's strategy, in part because they were afraid for their own lives. As Ernesto de la Jara writes:

They were times in which the terrorism-without-limits of Shining Path— Sendero Luminoso—had managed to terrorize us all, and the majority of the country was inclined to accept anything if it would stop the advance of the death machine that seemed to be the only thing that was in working order in Peru. It wasn't a time for stopping to think that to publicly display people who'd merely been arrested as though they were convicted terrorists was to blow up, in typical Shining Path style, elementary judicial principles and values. Much less was it a time for the luxury of worrying about whether mistakes were being made; whether among those being paraded out in striped suits there might have been not only Shining Path and MRTA members, but also innocent people, victims of circumstance. It was a time in which everybody talked in simple terms about the "costs" of the war. . . . [The state] demanded that we pay the "inevitable cost" of liberties and lives in order to do away with the Shining Path . . . [and] the majority applauded wildly. And when Fujimori invented the principle of *indubio pro societatis* as a justification for violating the rights of a minority in order to protect those of a majority, those who were applauding got to their feet and demanded more, more. It was each person's own security that was at stake. The terrorist threat created a collective willingness to pass over to the dark side of the permissible. It was a sensibility whipped up by the authorities: "We're defending the rights of all Peruvians, not those of the terrorists," they said. (2002: 5)

In part, however, Peruvians also supported these policies because their primary targets were disproportionately poor, uneducated, and in some cases illiterate, unable to defend themselves and unlikely to stir the sympathies of many in Peru's general public. Most cases were simply unknown. Some 75 percent reportedly spoke Quechua as their native language; although about 20 percent of the Peruvian population is indigenous, Quechua speakers usually hail from the poorest, most isolated area of the country). As Amnesty International writes:

The fact that thousands of people were arrested and imprisoned for "terrorism related" crimes they had not committed, with the acquiescence of the majority of the Peruvian population, can be partially explained by the increasing sense of insecurity and fear of violence in the country in the context of the internal armed conflict. This persuaded the majority of Peru's inhabitants that tough measures needed to be implemented to end internal violence. For years the extent of the problem remained irrelevant to most of the Peruvian population because many of those wrongly imprisoned belonged to sectors of the population which historically have been the most vulnerable and discriminated against. (Amnesty International 2003a)

Fujimori fled the country in 2000, leaving thousands still imprisoned on terrorism charges. As the country now struggles to come to terms with abuses committed under Fujimori's rule, the courts have begun the tedious process of reopening terrorism cases. The "forgotten prisoners," it is now clear, number in the thousands, and many never had any ties whatsoever to terrorist groups. In January 2003, the Peruvian Constitutional Tribunal ruled that military trials of civilians for the "terrorism-related" crime of "treason" were unconstitutional, and President Alejandro Toledo has issued a series of decree laws to conform to the tribunal's ruling, including ordering the retrial of all those condemned by the so-called faceless courts (Amnesty International 2003a). But as of March 2003, Amnesty International believed that scores of innocent prisoners remained in Peruvian jails, accused of terrorist acts that they did not commit; thousands of others were disappeared, executed, or tortured as part of the antiterrorism effort. The country will clearly be reckoning with this legacy for years to come.

The popularity of such abusive policies at the time they were enacted shows that public opinion provides no inherent protection against massive human rights abuses, especially in the context of the widespread fear awakened by acts of terrorism (see Holmes and Gutiérrez de Piñeres 2002). And although it may be comforting to assume that Latin American atrocities were perpetrated only by bloodthirsty sociopaths obeying orders from ruthless tyrants, in reality, most of those who carried out orders to kill, maim, and torture in the name of democracy were ordinary people. The recent study by Martha Huggins, Mika Haritos-Fatouros, and Philip G. Zimbardo of police torturers from Brazil's authoritarian period shows that these men were not extraordinary zealots; they were people placed in situations that the authors call "atrocity environments," where the propensity for violence was augmented by structural, institutional, and political circumstances.[9] In both democracies and dictatorships alike, the authors warn, "a sociopolitical climate of public and/or police fear tied to an assumption that police were "at war" against some segment of the population," and a structure of "secret and insular worlds" made—and still makes—ordinary policing activities into potential scenarios for cruel and horrific torture (2002: xx). Today, we recoil—rightly—from stories of massacres of entire villages in the Guatemalan highlands or tortures in the soccer stadium in Chile. But we might do better to recognize the environments for atrocity that exist in our midst, to examine the justifications for their existence, and to consider the lessons from Latin America.

Casting the Net Wide

Extraordinary times warrant extraordinary solutions, the argument goes; rights are a luxury we cannot afford to grant terrorists bent on our very destruction.[10] Yet one clear lesson from Latin America is the danger of casting the net too wide. Despite the righteous conviction in George W. Bush's proclamations that terrorists and those who support them must both face the same fate, the imprecise definition of "support for terrorism" as a terrorist act itself is a slippery (and all too familiar) slope. Argentine President General Jorge Rafael Videla announced in 1978, "A terrorist is not just someone with a gun or a bomb but also someone who spreads ideas that are contrary to Western civilization"; Pinochet warned that minds armed with "envy, rancor and the irreconcilable struggle of classes" were more dangerous, in fact, than weapons (Fagen 1992: 43). And in Guatemala, Ríos Montt explained deaths of civilian noncombatants by saying, "The problem of war is not just a question of who is shooting. For each one who is shooting there are ten working behind him." His press secretary, Francisco Bianchi (a candidate for president in 1999), expanded on the general's statement: "The guerrillas won over many Indian collaborators. Therefore, the Indians were subversives. And how do you fight subversion? Clearly you had to kill Indians because they were collaborating with subversion. And then it would be said that you were killing innocent people. But they weren't innocent. They had sold out to subversion"(Amnesty International 1987: 96).

This logic was not lost on the rank and file. A member of the Guatemalan civil patrols explained the killing of children in an interview: "We have to go finishing them off house by house because the parents pass on the poison [of subversion] to their children. You have to kill the parents and the children of ten, eight, five years, you have to finish them off because they've already heard the things their father says, and the children will do it" (Amnesty International 1987: 99).

Ríos Montt once told President Ronald Reagan that Guatemala's government did not have a scorched-earth policy, "just a scorched-communist policy." This, apparently, was intended to be less troubling, since scorching might be considered an appropriate treatment for communists, though not for "innocent" civilians. Yet even if we accept the use of violence against armed insurgents, this assumes the ability to distinguish between a communist and a campesino—or, in terms relevant to the contemporary United States, a terrorist and a law-abiding Muslim. In Guatemala, the inability to reliably draw such distinctions eventually justified the execution of newborn babies, the brutal slaughter of indigenous peasants considered dangerous by virtue of their ethnicity alone, and other atrocities that defy human understanding.

Fighting Terror with Terror

A second, related lesson is the danger of "fighting terror with terror," or using "dirty" tactics in violation of fundamental human rights to combat an unscrupulous enemy. Although the Bush administration formally denies that U.S. forces today use such tactics as torture and extrajudicial execution, these denials are not really plausible. First of all, the now-infamous photograph of U.S. servicemen and -women with Iraqis in the prison at Abu Ghraib illustrated torture practices for all to see. Second, although the Bush administration initially insisted that these images documented the actions of only a few "bad apples," by the U.S. government's own admission since fall 2001 approximately three hundred instances of alleged abuse by U.S. forces have been reported in Afghanistan, Iraq, and at the U.S. detention facility at Guantánamo Bay (Human Rights First 2004: 1). Moreover, an investigation (known as the Schlesinger Report) commissioned by Secretary of Defense Donald Rumsfeld, concluded in August 2004 that these abuses "were not just the failure of some individuals to follow known standards, and they are more than the failure of a few leaders to enforce proper discipline. There is both institutional and personal responsibility at higher levels." ("Independent Panel" 2004) Furthermore, a confidential report to the U.S. government by the Red Cross, described in a memo leaked to the *New York Times*, stated that U.S. detention and interrogation operations at Guantánamo Bay "cannot be considered other than an intentional system of cruel, unusual and degrading treatment and a form of torture" (N. Lewis 2004).

Reports of multiple deaths have emerged, classified by the medical examiner as homicides stemming from abuses suffered in U.S. custody (Amnesty International 2005). George W. Bush himself alluded to the tactic of extrajudicial execution when he announced, in his 2003 State of the Union address, that "To date, we've arrested or otherwise dealt with many key commanders of al Qaeda. . . . All told, more than 3,000 suspected terrorists have been arrested in many countries. Many others have met a different fate. Let's put it this way—they are no longer a problem to the United States and our friends and allies" (White House Office of the Press Secretary 2003).

Efforts to justify the use of such tactics abound. According to the *Washington Post*, Cofer Black, the head of the CIA's counterterrorist branch, told a congressional intelligence committee in September 2002: "All you need to know: there was a before 9/11, and there was an after 9/11. . . . After 9/11 the gloves come off." Another official, speaking on conditions of anonymity, told the *Post*, "If you don't violate someone's human rights some of the time, you probably aren't doing your job. I don't think we want to be promoting a view of zero tolerance on [torture]. That was the whole problem for a long time with the CIA" (Priest and Gellman 2002). And some scholars have sought to revive the "ticking bomb theory," arguing that under extreme circumstances, torture may be a legitimate weapon against terrorism (Dershowitz 2001).

While not openly advocating torture, the Bush administration has relied on complex legal arguments to elude the applicability of the Geneva Conventions. Washington has called those detained in the war on terror "unlawful combatants," arguing that they are subject to no laws whatsoever. Though the U.S. Supreme Court ruled in 2004 that those detained at Guantánamo Bay cannot be denied access to U.S. courts and the facility has been visited by some outside observers including the Red Cross, only a minority of captives are held there; those detained elsewhere can, according to Washington, be held indefinitely and incommunicado, with no charges brought against them and no access to lawyers; their names, identities, and locations, and the conditions under which they were captured or are being held, are unknown. The Red Cross has been allowed access to detainees on some U.S. bases in Afghanistan, but not during the period immediately after their detention, when abuse was most likely to occur; furthermore, as Amnesty International reported in 2005, "The ICRC is believed still to have no access to detainees held in an unknown number of US Forward Operating Bases in Afghanistan." This places those detained in a legal netherworld where no rights protections apply; effectively, they have been "disappeared."[11]

Within the United States, the war on terrorism has led to a rapid rollback of what many might have imagined to be the country's most cherished civil liberties. Today, even U.S. citizens can be held indefinitely in solitary confinement without access to a lawyer and without charges being brought against them if the Bush administration deems them to be "enemy combatants" based on its own subjective evaluation, which cannot be challenged. At the time of this writing, one U.S. citizen was being held in such a situation—Jose Padilla, whose case went before the U.S. Supreme Court in 2004 but was dismissed on jurisdictional grounds and has now been filed in the lower courts in South Carolina (*Rumsfeld v. Padilla* 2004; A. Lewis 2003). Hundreds more were arrested in the aftermath of 9/11; some were deported, some were detained, but the government has refused to disclose either their identities or the circumstances surrounding their detention or current status. Because most were held as material witnesses rather than criminal suspects, even habeas corpus and the most basic due-process provisions were suspended; requests for information went unanswered. These reports of secret arrests and detentions, of faceless prisoners trapped in a legal limbo, recall the plight of the families of the disappeared in Chile and Argentina, who would ask the authorities where their relatives had gone, only to be greeted with stony silence.

At the same time, suspects—whatever broad justifications are used to label them as such—are not the only people whose rights have been partially rescinded under the war on terrorism. Legislation promulgated in the wake of September 11, 2001, most specifically the USA PATRIOT Act, passed in October 2001, has dramatically undermined such core principles of democratic governance as the right to privacy and the right to an open government, affecting all residents of the United States. In March 2003, the Lawyers Committee for Human Rights reported that

[since] September 11, the executive branch has created initiatives to collect more and more data on all Americans, while providing less and less information about what the government is doing. In the past six months, the executive branch has created initiatives to collect an unprecedented amount of information on Americans and non-citizens who are under no suspicion of having committed a crime. These include initiatives such as the military's Total Information Awareness Program, which would create comprehensive data profiles of everyone; the use of expanded search and seizure powers under the USA PATRIOT Act to seize library, bookstore, and other records; the increased powers to intercept telephone and internet communications; and the lifting of restrictions on the use of special foreign intelligence powers in ordinary criminal prosecutions. (2003: 5–6)

Furthermore, the Bush administration has promoted restrictions on the public's right to know about the activities of its own government. These include dramatic limitations on the Freedom of Information Act— the very legislation that has made information about abuses committed in the context of Latin America's "dirty wars" available to scholars and the general public for the first time, and without which some of the research in this book would have been impossible. Furthermore, the administration has refused to inform Congress about how new antiterrorist legislation—including the USA PATRIOT Act—is currently being implemented, designating such information as "classified" (LCHR 2003: 15). And under secret conditions—and amid official denials—the Department of Justice wrote the so-called PATRIOT II, a draft of which was eventually leaked in early 2003. This proposed legislation would grant even more sweeping powers to the administration, authorizing secret arrests, eliminating court orders issued to prevent police spying, and permitting the extradition of U.S. and foreign citizens without a treaty and the stripping of citizenship as a form of punishment for those deemed to support terrorism (LCHR 2003: 18–20).

. . . With Security and Justice for All

The atrocities committed across Latin America in the name of democracy were not senseless acts of cruelty perpetrated by a few rogue officers, not uncontrollable bursts of violence committed in the haze of the battlefield, but official policy. There was a logic and an order and a reasoning behind them, and entire state bureaucracies were deployed to carry them out. They were not the brutal excesses of one man or one group; they were the work of entire institutions built on secrecy and fear. They are, as such, eminently repeatable.

I do not mean to suggest here that in its war on terrorism the United States is currently perpetrating acts of genocide, nor to imply that today's trends suggest the United States is undergoing some sort of "reverse development" that has brought it to resemble Latin America. Development and social change, as previous generations of scholars have shown us, are not inherently linear processes implying forward or backward motion along a continuum. Profound differences remain between (and within) the countries of the Americas, and we should be cautious about applying terms such as genocide (or, for that matter, democracy) too liberally, thus depriving them of their true meaning or explanatory power.

At the same time, however, comparative analysis can still be illuminating. In the United States, we should recognize that our own society is confronting a danger similar in many ways to the dangers faced by Latin American governments in the twentieth century. We may not be hurtling toward the abyss of mass slaughter, but in the name of defending democracy we may be handily dismantling the building blocks upon which our democracy was built. The terrorist threat is real (as it was, indeed, in Latin America), but if we turn the war within, it may not be the terrorists, but their most zealous hunters, who do us the greatest damage.

The direction the United States has taken in its war on terrorism is, in part, a response to specific world events—most obviously, to the attacks of September 11, 2001—but it is also shaped by concrete social and political structures and ways of understanding the world. Today, crime control and national security strategies converge in bipolar images of the world, in which individuals are either "with us" or "against us" and preemptive actions are justified against those who might one day come to threaten this imagined yet unspecified "us." The policing of this polarization—of the divide between "us" and "them"— becomes more punitive and violent as our societies grow more unequal, as our states retreat further from their positive obligations, and as the legitimacy of our laws becomes evanescent.

Human rights groups have criticized the violations of civil liberties committed by the U.S. government in the context of this new war. And they should; like the police excesses committed in *mano dura* regimes of Latin America, these violations are important and those committing them should be called to account. But across the Americas, human rights groups' advocacy of government restraint in dealing with an unrestrained enemy intent on death and destruction risks casting human rights concerns in a marginal and unpopular role in public debate, as discussed in chapter 2. Indeed, in the absence of a broader critique linking the deprivations of rights to the source of insecurity itself, such criticisms are likely to provoke the dismissive response offered by David Rivkin and Lee Casey in a recent response to Amnesty International's criticism of the U.S. tactics in the war on terror. According to these authors, Amnesty "is trapped in a 20th-century mindset where the greatest threat to individual life and liberty stemmed from the actions of sovereign governments. That is simply no longer the case." NGOs such as Amnesty, they continue, "simply do not consider that the defense of the American population, and the vindication of each individual's right to live without the threat or actuality of terrorist attack, is their problem— and it is time they did" (Rivkin and Casey 2005).

Since 9/11, security appears to have trumped justice and human rights as policy priorities, in the United States and many nations. The human rights movement has been clear and specific in its response, but its critiques have most forcefully denounced the way the war on terror is being fought—the abuses on civil liberties, the conditions of detention—rather than questioning its very premise. As an increasingly wide range of actors around the world appears to be quite openly and comfortably choosing security over justice, the task for human rights could not be more urgent. It is not the task of a watchdog, but of an architect: it is the task of advancing the argument that human rights *are* security. Rather than opposing objectives, dueling priorities between which we must choose, they are intertwined. To attempt to purchase one at the price of another is to doom ourselves to failure. As examples across the Americas unequivocally illustrate, denigrating the rights of others will inevitably destroy our own.

Reference Matter

Notes

1. This is a pseudonym, as are all the names of individual informants in this book.

2. The lynching occurred in a rural hamlet in the municipality of San Jacinto (not its real name), so although she describes the lynching as having occurred "in San Jacinto," she means in one of its outlying villages; the police station is in the municipal center, and this young man rode his bicycle from the village to the municipal center.

3. The use of the phrase *compañeros en la lucha* refers to resistance to state repression. It can be used to refer to involvement in the armed struggle or to participation in political activities organized through civil society groups. The subsequent reference to the lynched men as having been "organized" underscores their involvement in political activities, through participation in a committee named to arrange the introduction of electricity into the village.

4. The informant later clarified that what she means here is that there is no 911 or similar emergency service, and although the police station does have a telephone number, the people in the community do not know what it is, so even those members of the community who had cellular phones had no way to reach the police except by sending a messenger out on bicycle.

5. These names refer to two positions on the mayor's council.

6. An *acta* is a legal document drawn up (in this case) by the community and sealed by its local government officials. It is not infrequent for communities to draw up an *acta* after a lynching as a way of formalizing the execution, as if to "legalize" it, and also to legitimate it by inscribing it in the official record of local government.

7. Xalbaquiej, in the department of Chichicastenango, was the site of a well-known lynching in which eight people were killed in 2000. Circumstances suggest that this lynching may have been politically motivated.

1. Lynchings are here defined as incidents of physical violence committed by large numbers of private citizens against one or more individuals accused of having committed a "criminal" offense, whether or not this violence resulted in the death of the victim(s). Therefore, confrontations between armed groups, military actions, disputes over land which may result in murders, individual settling-of-accounts or vengeance killings, and other types of violence are not considered "lynchings." The numbers of lynchings cited here reflect the number of incidents, not the number of victims; in fact, many lynchings involve multiple victims. The application of the term "lynching" to these acts of violence is not my own innovation but the way they are most frequently described by participants and commentators alike, in various settings across Latin America; the verb *linchar* in Spanish is taken from the English "to lynch."

2. Reliable data on more recent lynchings is hard to come by. MINUGUA closed its offices in 2004 after gradually reducing its presence in the country over the course of several years. In the final years of its operations, owing to reduced capacity the mission was unable to compile data on lynchings as systematically as it had previously.

3. See, for example, Abrahams 1996 on Tanzania; Chabal and Daloz 1999 on Africa more generally; Castillo Claudett 2000 on Ecuador; Vilas 2001 on Mexico; Goldstein 2003 on Bolivia; and Ruteere and Pommerolle 2003 on Kenya.

4. This is not to suggest, however, that the trend does not have deep historical roots in previous periods. See chapter 3 for a discussion of its links to wartime practices of state violence and chapter 4 for an exploration of its origins in the socioeconomic transformations of recent decades.

5. This is not intended to deny that within individual communities, power dynamics may influence which individuals are most likely to be accused of crimes. However, *across cases* I was not able to identify any generalizable characteristics that would suggest the trend itself obeyed a specific racialized or politicized agenda; the victims were not disproportionately members of any specific ethnic, racial, religious, gender, cultural, or class groups.

6. This is because these attacks, though infrequent compared to the many incidents with Guatemalan victims, attract the attention and scrutiny of the foreign media and of the governments of the victims' countries.

7. The well-known 2000 lynching of a Japanese tourist and his Guatemalan tour bus driver in Todos Santos Cuchumatán is one notable exception. This incident, too, has received an exceptional amount of attention from local and international media, tourism boards, the Guatemalan government, and various anthropologists. See Sitler 2001; Barrera Núñez 2005.

8. This is not intended to suggest that in most cases those lynched are actually guilty of the crimes imputed to them or to deny the fact that political motivations also play into many lynchings. For more on this, see chapter 3.

9. In urban settings, street children and homeless youths are frequently the victims of these "cleansings": they are widely associated with criminal activity

and vulnerable to attack because of their public visibility and their extreme marginality. For information on the execution of street children in "cleansing" operations, see the Web site of Casa Alianza, http://www.casa-alianza.org.

10. *Mano dura* is a commonly used term in Latin America; although the term literally translates to "hard-handedness" and is often interpreted as "rule by an iron fist," no true equivalent exists in English. I have decided to use the Spanish term here, not only in an attempt to reverse the usual trend of exporting terms and concepts from English to explain Latin American realities, but also because the Spanish term is much better suited to the concept I seek to get at here than any English approximation.

11. The distinction between polyarchy and democracy was first drawn by Robert Dahl (1971). Others have expressed a similar concept using the terms "political democracy" and "social democracy."

12. Samuel Huntington is perhaps most explicit in this regard: "The existence of . . . private power is essential to the existence of democracy. . . . Political democracy is clearly compatible with inequality in both wealth and income, and in some measure, it may be dependent upon such inequality. . . . Defining democracy in terms of goals such as economic well-being, social justice, and overall socioeconomic equity is not, we have argued, very useful" (1989: 24).

13. For Borón, in addition to the political condition of free competition, two social conditions are required: a minimal level of socioeconomic equality and the effective enjoyment of freedoms, not merely as formal entitlements but as lived experience (1998: 44). Robinson goes further, suggesting that "popular democracy . . . posits democracy as both a process and a means to an end—a tool for change, for the resolution of such material problems as housing, health, education, access to land, cultural development, and so forth. This entails a dispersal of political power formerly concentrated in the hands of elite minorities, the redistribution of wealth, the breaking down of the structures of highly concentrated property ownership, and the democratizing of access to social and cultural opportunities by severing the link between access and the possession of wealth" (1996: 57–58).

14. Przeworski, for example, observes that "to discuss democracy without considering the economy in which this democracy is to function is an operation worthy of an ostrich" (Przeworski 1990: 102, cited in Borón 1998: 45); Diamond has written that "reducing . . . levels of poverty and inequality is one of the paramount imperatives for democratic consolidation in Latin America. As the Inter-American Dialogue trenchantly observes, 'economic exclusion is everywhere the handmaiden of political exclusion'" (1996: 99).

15. See, for example, Augusto Varas: "Democracy is not only the functioning of political systems, but basically a continuous process that is permanently driven by the constant need to extend and institutionalize the rights of citizens in the face of existing or emerging absolute powers. . . . From this perspective, democracy has been a historical process of political change that, by its very nature, has no end. . . . The dynamic element in this long process of democratization has been the permanent social and conceptual expansion of citizenship

and the materialization of a growing number and quantity of citizen rights" (1998: 147).

16. For an excellent discussion of lynchings and their mimetic relationship to state-sponsored violence, see Goldstein 2003: 25. Certainly not all scholars who use the term "popular justice" would consider these to be emancipatory practices, either. Although some studies do explore "people's courts" as positive alternatives to inherently repressive state regimes (see, for example, Santos 1977), even such alternative fora for dispute resolution are shaped by state law; the question is not one of state versus nonstate practices, but rather a recognition of legal pluralism or interlegality, where a variety of forms of legal ordering intersect, coexist, and occasionally conflict. In popular usage, however, particularly in Guatemala, the term *justicia popular* has a strongly normative connotation and expresses approval for a given action; for this reason, I shy away from its use here.

17. In calling attention to support for semiauthoritarian modes of governance among some members of civil society, I do not intend to elide others' participation in groups that actively defend and promote human rights. My point is merely to underscore the fact that civil society is not always or uniformly a progressive force. Human rights advocacy groups such as Amnesty International or Human Rights Watch routinely call on governments like Guatemala's to develop security policies in closer consultation with "civil society" groups. But in Guatemala, many citizens have organized into voluntary associations that promote views directly contradictory to human rights. To give just one example, the Association of Guatemalan Military Veterans (Asociación de Veteranos Militares de Guatemala [AVEMILGUA]) was founded in the mid-1990s with a mission to promote the "honor, prestige, and dignity" of the country's armed forces through analysis of national politics and consciousness-raising about the value of the military in a democratic society. Members of its original leadership were directly implicated in some of the country's most serious human rights crimes. The organization today operates offices in Guatemala City and several departments and played a decisive role in reorganizing the former civil patrols and particularly in orchestrating their support for a specific party (the FRG) in the lead-up to the 2003 elections. (For more on AVEMILGUA, see Peacock and Beltrán 2003.)

To bar such groups from consideration as civil society is to reduce the term itself to a stand-in for "groups whose politics we like" (where the beauty is clearly in the eye of the beholder); yet if we recognize that such groups form part of civil society, we must recognize that calling for participation in civil society is not enough to ensure a socially just outcome or a departure from the genocidal past. This is why purely procedural definitions of democracy are insufficient: in practice, progress toward social justice does not inhere in elections, even "free and fair" ones.

18. Here I refer not to polarization between societies, as in "first-world" or "third-world" countries, but to polarization within societies as socioeconomic inequality increases worldwide.

19. Holston and Caldeira make this point particularly well in their analysis of Brazil's "disjunctive democracy": "The conjunction of political democracy, violence, and judicial discredit we have described—including the abuses of the police, the delegitimation of the justice system, the private measures of justice and security, the generalized disrespect for law, the culture of fear, and the related transformations of public space . . . results in a reproduction of violence, injustice, and inequality. When the state is asked to react to crime by using violence outside of the boundaries of law and does so, when the population supports this illegal and violent action, when many people use the services of private guards and vigilantes and increasingly transform their residences into fortified enclaves, and when even the police deal with violent crime by private vengeance, society turns away from legality and citizenship. It also jeopardizes the possibility of demanding that public institutions of order mediate conflict and restrain violence" (1998: 279–80).

20. See, for example, the various contributions to Jarquín and Carrillo 1998.

21. A noteworthy and highly recommended exception to this is Moser and McIlwaine 2001, a World Bank study of perceptions of violence in urban Guatemala that offers a richly detailed account of how communities regard violence, based on an unusual participatory research design.

22. See http://www.rnw.nl/informarn/html/act001010_laviolencia.html (accessed September 21, 2005).

23. Elton 2000; "Las amargas" 1997.

24. "López Obrador justifica" 2001. See also http://www.diariodemexico .com.mx/2001/julo1/280701/fotos/primera.pdf.

25. See "Flores asturias" 1998; "Falta de juzgados" 1998.

26. I am unaware of any single study that centrally tackles this specific question, but glimpses of how rural residents have historically related to the formal legal system can be gleaned from many of the excellent inquiries into Guatemalan history and anthropology. See, for example, Carmack 1990; Handy 1994; Forster 2001.

27. In Guatemala, this may be partly because those carrying out the more sensational crimes belong to more sophisticated criminal organizations, many of them composed of demobilized former combatants with lingering ties to the state and thus a measure of guaranteed impunity, such that they are beyond the reach of a ragtag band of peasants armed with gasoline; in part it may be because such crimes, though atrocious, are more frequently talked about than they are actually experienced, and thus the stories outpace the opportunities for action in terms of lynchings.

28. Furthermore, if we consider contemporary Latin American lynchings in comparative and historical perspective, the naiveté of equating their eruption to "self-help criminal justice" is yet clearer. For example, in the late nineteenth and early twentieth centuries, lynchings in the U.S. South were often justified by participants and in the local press as necessary to ensure swift, certain justice for black criminals in light of a slow, ineffective, and lenient criminal justice system; yet a wealth of recent scholarship has conclusively shown that these

acts corresponded to boundary management of quite a different sort. Beck and Tolnay, for example, argue that lynchings cannot be explained as reactions to crime, but to other sorts of social and economic insecurity experienced by Southern whites: "Based on accounts of lynchings, it is clear that whites didn't congregate at the gin to lament [economic conditions], then decide to murder a black to relieve their psychological stress. Lynch mobs reacted to some supposed infraction of the norms governing caste relations, whether it be a minor act of racial imprudence or the major crime of murdering a white man. In this sense, it can be argued that black lynchings were a function of crimes committed by blacks. This perspective, however, goes on to argue that the prime reason for lynching was the inability of the existing system of criminal justice to cope with crime, and the motivation of lynch mobs was deeply rooted in a desire to maintain law and order. In the alternative 'black victimization' view, such 'crimes' were only specific triggering incidents that focused and justified outbreaks of violence toward blacks. The powerful dynamics driving these repressive forces originated in the southern economic system" (1990: 537, n. 12).

Although there are many important differences between the U.S. case and contemporary Latin American ones, and a thorough comparison of the two falls outside the scope of my project here, a passing familiarity with the literature on lynchings elsewhere should lead observers of Latin America to be cautious about uncritically accepting presumed connections between crime and contemporary vigilantism. (For more on lynchings in the U.S. South, see, for example, Ayers 1984; Shapiro 1988; Tolnay and Beck 1992, 1995; Brundage 1993; Tolnay, Deane, and Beck 1996.)

29. For a similar argument refuting attempts to describe Mexican lynchings as "traditional," see Fuentes Díaz and Binford 2001.

30. Some commentaries on the Guatemalan phenomenon, including the frequently cited United Nations mission to Guatemala's 2000 report on the topic, use province-by-province breakdowns showing that almost as many lynchings have occurred in the capital city as in rural El Quiché, as a way to dispel the myth that lynchings are somehow a "Mayan" phenomenon. Such arguments are misleading, however, because the numbers are not weighted for population; it is not surprising that in an area with a much larger population, more lynchings would occur. Per capita statistics show a more pronounced concentration of lynchings in the western highlands.

31. Of course, these "traditional" "Mayan" justice practices are themselves a legacy of colonialism and an outcome of the intersection of multiple forms of legal ordering called interlegality by Boaventura de Sousa Santos (and legal pluralism by others); in saying such practices unfold outside the formal legal system, I do not mean to suggest they are ever fully autonomous from it.

32. These figures are taken from an internal document shared with me in 2000. It is important to note, however, that the presence of state authorities in the municipality does not necessarily mean they are easily accessible. In many cases, travel from one's village of residence to the municipal capital, where the closest legal authority is often located, can imply many hours of travel by foot,

bus, pickup truck, or some combination of each. Furthermore, many Mayans do not speak Spanish, the language in which state business is conducted; legal interpreters are sometimes available, but often they are not, and some respondents told me that those who were designated as interpreters acted as merely another layer of officials who needed to be bribed for a case to go forward. Furthermore, entrenched poverty excludes many more, not only by limiting mobility, but by making impossible the payment of legal fees (and bribes) necessary to access the system.

33. It should be noted that estimates of Central American homicide rates are notoriously unreliable and therefore any figure—whether offered by national governments or by international agencies—should be received with skepticism.

34. See, for example, Hendrix 2000 for a discussion of justice centers funded by USAID in Guatemala: "Justice reform in Guatemala will take several generations and will involve a gradual learning process requiring a strategy of incremental progress. Justice Centers are an essential part of this process. . . . As a result of this Guatemalan-led initiative in Justice Center locations, women, the poor, children and indigenous people have greater access to an improved, more transparent, and more efficient justice system. There is a reduction in corruption opportunities and impunity. Service to the community has increased and faith in the system is growing. For these reasons, procedural due process has improved, with corresponding improvements for human rights issues. As the Justice Centers continue the trend toward decentralization, we can expect these positive changes to continue. The challenge will be to maintain this course of reform, with continuous adaptations and adjustments, to assure the rule of law becomes the norm for all Guatemalans" (866–67). Of course, this sounds good, but Hendrix's assessment here is based on his own analysis of the justice centers' programs, not on systematic inquiry into Guatemalans' perceptions of these institutions.

35. For an excellent example of a bottom-up approach to democracy, see Gutmann 2002.

36. They are also the reason I am reluctant to place a single number on the total amount of interviews conducted; in the case of focus groups, typically some people present would participate very actively in discussions, while others might chime in only occasionally with brief comments (or even get up and leave in the middle of the discussion). Unlike one-on-one interviews, these more modest forms of participation are hard to quantify, but they still contributed to my understanding of the research topic and should count toward the overall total.

37. For an insightful discussion of state violence and its effects on language, see Feitlowitz 1998.

38. At the time of this writing, the Guatemalan human rights community is experiencing a renewed wave of politically motivated violence; many admired colleagues and friends have told me this is the worst things have been since the dark days of the early 1980s, when the state's genocidal counterinsurgency

campaigns reached their most feverish pitch. In this time of purported peace, Guatemalan human rights offices are regularly broken into, correspondence is monitored, and activists are attacked and even killed with alarming frequency. For this reason, I have chosen to conceal the identities, institutional affiliations, and regional origins of many of those who collaborated with me in this research, even though at the time some of these interviews were carried out people asked to be identified. They deserve ample credit and recognition for their contribution to this study; unfortunately, however, my concern is for their physical safety, given the gravity of the current situation.

39. Furthermore, because I approached this topic by working with a human rights organization in the former conflict zones, I can only speculate as to what forces might lie behind the lynchings taking place in peripheral urban settings, where this group does not have an organized presence. Although I did interview some people from Guatemala City's marginal neighborhoods about lynchings there, my urban sample was too small to be representative.

40. The only question I asked virtually everyone was their ethnic identity, and even this produced many ambiguous replies.

41. Indeed, in retrospect I believe much of this fieldwork would be more difficult to conduct today. Most of my interviews were carried out in 1999 and 2000, at a time when, although political violence had not subsided entirely, its immediate threat appeared to have receded. In recent years, the climate of fear has returned, and today social activists, journalists, and their collaborators are frequently targeted for death threats and acts of intimidation. Although things hardly seemed relaxed during my fieldwork, in retrospect I realize that I conducted these interviews during a short-lived lull in the storm; given the current wave of violence, I imagine people would be infinitely more reluctant to address sensitive topics today.

42. Freedom House, a U.S.-based nonprofit, publishes an annual assessment of the state of political rights and civil liberties in the countries of the world, in which countries are described as "free," "partly free," or "not free" along specific dimensions of democratic freedom.

CHAPTER 2

1. This is calculated using a measure known as the Gini coefficient, which measures the extent to which income distribution deviates from a perfectly equal distribution. Perfectly equal distribution would have a Gini coefficient of zero. In 2005, Guatemala's coefficient was 59.9 (UNDP 2005).

2. Well over half of the Guatemalan population is indigenous, and the overwhelming majority of these are Mayan; although there are also two non-Mayan indigenous groups, the Garífuna and the Xinca, their populations are very small. In Guatemala, the term *ladino* is commonly used to refer to someone who does not self-identify as indigenous, although, like mestizos across Latin America, Guatemalan *ladinos* themselves are of mixed European and indigenous descent.

3. For a discussion of such figures' limitations, see CIEN, "Investigando la violencia" (n.d.).

4. Not literally: in fact, the palace is now a museum and no longer houses the president's offices.

5. Grupo Pro Seguridad y Justicia 2003; some human rights groups questioned the authenticity of this explosion, arguing that drug-trafficking gangs would not act in this manner.

6. The CICIACS has yet to come to fruition; in 2004 the proposal was ruled unconstitutional.

7. See, for example, "A Country" 2003; Figueroa, *Siglo veintiuno*, August 27, 2000.

8. Alfredo Moreno Molina, a former military intelligence officer and leader of an extensive smuggling ring with links to the Cali cartel and the deputy defense minister among its associates, was among those exposed in a 1996 anti-corruption operation (Arana 2001); Moreno was convicted along with some of his accomplices, although many implicated in these investigations walked free. One of them was Jacobo Salan Sánchez, who was subsequently appointed to head the notorious Presidential Guard (EMP) in 2000; shortly after his appointment, investigations by the Guatemalan daily *El periódico* revealed that he was running death squads from his office, and he resigned. Reporters involved in breaking the story received death threats. At the time of this writing, Salan was among the men under investigation in the inquiries publicly announced by Attorney General de Leon in 2002.

9. By way of comparison, in a 1997 survey the death penalty was endorsed by some 67.4 percent of the male population in Caracas, 58.2 percent of the total population in San Salvador, 47.6 percent in Santiago de Chile, and 43.7 percent in San José, Costa Rica. In the United States, a February 2000 Gallup poll estimated that 66 percent of citizens support capital punishment for convicted murderers.

10. The convention stipulates that state parties should work toward the abolition of capital punishment; though it allows states to continue using the death penalty if it was permitted in their constitutions at the time of their signing the convention, it expressly prohibits their expansion of the practice.

11. Despite pressures on Portillo to fulfill this promise once in office, he did not; at the time of this writing, Guatemala remained party to the convention.

12. For a discussion of these practices, see Amnesty International 1987: 101–13.

13. Victoria Sanford also notes having heard the same interpretation of the FRG's symbol among her respondents in rural highland villages; furthermore, she reports that written death threats received during the war were sometimes accompanied by symbolic drawings of hands (2003: 156); one notorious wartime death squad also went by the name of La Mano Blanca (The White Hand).

14. There are exceptions to this rule, of course; tribunals convened to respond to individual human rights crises, including those at Nuremberg, have

tried individuals; the International Criminal Court is also capable of charging individuals.

15. For an illuminating discussion of this perception among Colombians, see Restrepo 2001. For some discussion of similar trends in Brazil, see Caldeira 2000.

16. The Huelga de Dolores (literally, Strike of Sorrows) is an annual student tradition at the University of San Carlos in Guatemala that dates from 1897. It incorporates acts of social protest and political satire in a weeklong series of activities; university students, wearing hoods to conceal their identities, stage marches and other public events. Some students have taken advantage of the anonymity of the disguise to carry out acts of "justice" against petty thieves in the capital; it is this practice to which the interviewees refer here.

17. The term "the human rights" is often used to refer to the people who promote human rights, as well as the concept itself, as Holston and Caldeira (1998) also note in Brazil. As a foreigner in Guatemala, where foreigners are often associated with human rights work, I have been asked, "Are you one of the human rights?"

18. This is perhaps even true, if one considers that most mechanisms by which crime has historically been combated in Guatemala fall outside the bounds of acceptable law enforcement under human rights standards: true adherence to a human rights regime does imply a fundamental shift in crime control tactics.

19. The Bomberos Voluntarios (Volunteer Firemen) are volunteers who provide emergency services. They operate most of the country's ambulances and are often the first to arrive at the scene of a crime. Because they are volunteers, not a state entity, according to this man they enjoy far greater legitimacy than the police or other authorities.

20. Its official name was changed more than once, but it is most commonly referred to in these terms.

21. *Siglo veintiuno*, September 25, 1997, cited in LaRue, Taylor, and Salazar-Volkmann 1998: 31.

22. *Siglo veintiuno*, February 19, 1998, cited in LaRue Taylor, and Salazar-Volkmann 1998: 31.

23. The Unidad Revolucionaria Nacional Guatemalteca (Guatemalan National Revolutionary Unity [URNG]) is the umbrella organization that comprises the country's main guerrilla groups. The writer is thus claiming that the Children's Code lends support to the guerrillas. *Siglo veintiuno*, February 27 1998, cited in LaRue, Taylor, and Salazar-Volkmann 1998: 31–32.

CHAPTER 3

1. Debates about Mayan peasants' ability to exercise agency, and the extent to which they may be manipulated by outside forces, are not unique to the question of lynchings. For a recent and vigorous debate along related themes, see especially Stoll 1993 and the many responses this work has generated, including

for example, reviews by Painter (1995) and Wilson (1995); and also the responses to Stoll's broader work compiled in Arias 2001.

2. This is the definition adopted by the United Nations Genocide Convention into international law. Many social scientists have used different definitions. For a partial list, see the Association of Genocide Scholars' Web site at http://www.isg-ags.org/definitions/def_genocide.html.

3. As a Kakchiquel woman explained, "The relation between the living and the dead, between the generations, is very linked to the meaning of the sacred places. They are linked in that these sacred places signify the physical places where the grandparents and the ancestors performed their rites. They are places of intergenerational spiritual meeting, between the living and their ancestors. They are sacred spaces like the cemeteries, but more. To violate or burn these places means very much to people; it's a very strong action. They are like the physical structure of spirituality. They are places of deep respect, which demand certain behaviors (for example, one always wears one's best clothes there), certain rites that are passed down between the generations. Their destruction leaves people disoriented because it leaves them without responses. 'What are we going to teach the children?' 'Where are the children going to be taught?' Of course, it also represents an action to leave the people profoundly humiliated. To step on the sacred space or destroy it is to disrespect all the teachings, to violate all that people have cared for in the deepest way. . . . It is to communicate to people that . . . what is most theirs is worthless" (CEH 1999: chap. 3, para. 496).

4. See Oficina de Derechos Humanos del Arzobispado de Guatemala 1998: vol. 1, 129–31; CEH 1999:chap. 3, paras. 500–507, for more thorough discussions of these processes and their effects.

5. Americas Watch 1986: 2. Of course, the army's infiltration of community life was partial and incomplete; participation in the patrols was, after all, coerced, and in many cases individuals and communities resisted incorporation in such structures. An important human rights group, CERJ, was founded precisely to resist forced patrolling. In other cases, men joined the patrol, but did everything in their power to refrain from committing abuses against their fellow townspeople, instead using their position to attempt to protect their loved ones from injury. On the other hand, some individuals were willing participants in the patrols—some may have been motivated by the desire to reap illicit personal gains, certainly, but ethnographic research on the subject has also shown that participation in patrols gave some villagers a sense of sovereignty within their community, a feeling of usefulness in the face of terrible violence (Kobrak 1994, cited in Schirmer 1998: 97; De León-Escribano 1999; Remijnse 2000). Rather than adopting the status of passive victims, residents of some areas embraced the role of active defender of their communities (even if such defense may have been ineffective, since the principal instigator of violence was the Army itself, not the guerrillas against whom the patrols were ostensibly defending). The patrols' legacy, then, is a mixed one.

6. In April 1999, some six hundred marched on the jail in Huehuetenango, attacking guards and then releasing twelve former patrollers who had been

serving twenty-five-year sentences for the murder of the indigenous land activist Juan Chanay Pablo (Amnesty International 2002:10)

7. The name of this individual has been changed.

8. For some time, the speaker explained, her community had been attempting unsuccessfully to organize a committee to raise funds for construction of a school in the village. One of the chief reasons their efforts were unsuccessful, as she explains here, was that Anastasio Choc was among the community leaders, and people were afraid to participate in anything with him.

9. *Licenciado* is an honorary title conferred upon those who have university degrees.

10. *Paja de trigo* is wheat cane that is dried and then used to thatch the roofs of houses in rural Mayan communities. Here the speaker refers to her father hiding in the piles of cane drying outside their home.

11. These comments emerged in the context of the speaker explaining the circumstances behind a very recent lynching in which Anastasio Choc was among those lynched. She insisted that he was lynched because it was discovered that he had been working with a band of thieves operating in the region, not because of his participation in repression during the war. But she did not make any attempt to conceal her satisfaction that he was no longer a threat in her community.

CHAPTER 4

1. "Por radio" 1998; for a more detailed account of this lynching, see Quiñones 2001.

2. Indeed, the Plan Puebla Panama, the Inter-American Development Bank's twenty-five-year, $20 billion initiative in the region and a stepping-stone to Central America's integration in the proposed Free Trade Area of the Americas, promotes precisely this form of development from the nine southern states of Mexico to the southern tip of the Central American isthmus.

3. Some of these processes were directly intertwined with state terror. The Guatemalan army, Carol Smith reminds us (1990), regularly mounted "development" projects on the ashes of Mayan communities; in some cases—as is notably the case with the massacres at Rabinal—the army and/or its paramilitary adjuncts carried out acts of violence against those who refused to surrender their land so that "development" could proceed, viewing all attempts at resistance or contestation as evidence of communism. In this manner, development and modernization often marched in tandem with militarization across the highlands.

4. For an excellent discussion of these developments, see Grandin 2004.

5. For example, in the 1960s landless peasants were given tracts of land in a previously unsettled region of the rainforest in El Ixcán, El Quiché, part of an attempt to ameliorate the agrarian crisis. As a result of this resettlement, many communities in El Ixcán are today made up of residents from various ethnolinguistic groups, each of which has its own language, dress, and set of traditions;

it is relatively unsurprising, then, that such communities face challenges knitting a new, pluralistic social fabric in the wake of the war. For an illuminating study of one such community, see Manz 2004.

6. It also creates a population highly vulnerable to assault: many of my interviewees expressed particularly deep outrage at the activities of criminal bands who lie in wait for peasants returning from the coast, knowing that these men (and occasionally women and children too) will be returning with an entire season's wages, usually in cash. Others spoke of the vulnerability of communities during harvest time, when it was well known that many women and children would be home alone, their husbands and older male children having left to work on the coast.

7. *Cofradías* are traditional religious brotherhoods in Mayan communities. Organized around devotion to a particular saint, *cofradías* are responsible for organizing events to celebrate and honor that saint, but also occupy important leadership roles in highland communities.

8. The speaker is referring to Guatemala's sizable death row, where dozens of convicts await state execution by lethal injection.

9. This is more true of rural than urban lynchings. In urban areas, lynch mobs are generally unable to hold their victims for long stretches of time without some intervention by the authorities. In rural areas, however, the relative isolation of these communities often permits lynchers more time to organize complex rituals and summon large crowds.

10. Though not entirely—obviously, if solidarity reached absolute zero, no collective action of any sort would be possible.

11. It is very important to understand that because of the extreme ineffectiveness of the Guatemalan justice system, potential lynchers can be extremely confident that their actions will go unpunished. (According to MINUGUA, between 1996 and 2003, only twenty-four people were convicted of lynching-related crimes, despite almost five hundred cases of lynchings affecting nearly twelve hundred victims.) This dramatically reduces the threshold of trust required to participate in these forms of collective action.

12. As Andrew Buckser has noted in a similar discussion of lynchings in the postbellum U.S. South, "a lynching which succeeded was not only a victory of the community against the supposed criminal, but also a victory of the community against the government. Justice had been done not by the law but by the communal will; the unofficial realm had triumphed over the official. In a lynching the unofficial white community symbolically regained its authority over the social order" (1992: 25).

CHAPTER 5

1. Although different scholars employ different definitions, a good example of this approach is that offered by Diamond, Linz, and Lipset: "Democracy denotes . . . a system of government that meets three essential conditions: meaningful and extensive competition among individuals and groups (especially

political parties) for all effective positions of government power, at regular intervals and excluding the use of force; a highly inclusive level of political participation in the selection of leaders and policies, at least through regular and fair elections, such that no major (adult) social group is excluded; and a level of civil and political liberties—freedom of expression, freedom of the press, freedom to form and join organizations—sufficient to ensure the integrity of political competition and participation" (1988: xvi). This definition is closely related to the definition of polyarchy suggested by Robert Dahl.

2. In 2003, Amnesty International expanded its original mandate to a much broader mission that embraces the interdependence of all rights, focusing its efforts on "preventing and ending grave abuses of the rights to physical and mental integrity, freedom of conscience and expression, and freedom from discrimination." (www.amnesty.org)

3. These emergent social movements, as Eckstein and Wickham-Crowley deliberately note, understand and advocate rights in their own distinctive and contextualized ways rather than as reflective of a single overarching paradigm of historical progression.

4. Furthermore, the role of civil society becomes even more pivotal in the neoliberal era because although previous generations focused on state-run development strategies to ameliorate social conditions in the region, today such approaches have been largely discredited; decentralized government initiatives are regarded as more efficient in part because they devolve increased responsibility on local actors. The emphasis today is on private sector led growth and governance through "public-private partnerships"; in the realm of citizen security, community policing provides the classic example.

5. The gap between de jure inclusion and de facto exclusion thus mirrors the gap between law on the books and law in society—the awareness of which sparked the law-and-society movement that continues to interrogate related issues today. As various scholars writing in this tradition have demonstrated, this gap is characteristic of all legal systems, which are themselves imbued with and invested in hierarchies of power. Legal structures may be most important at providing opportunities for strategic social and political mobilization rather than at offering legal "solutions" to this gap (Scheingold 1974; McCann 1994). Again, "civil society" is the key actor here; citizens must actively mobilize to make rights real, and law's relation to power imbalances in society means that politically, economically, and socially disempowered groups often operate at a substantial disadvantage in terms of rights mobilization, thus explaining some of the reasons for the gap's endurance.

6. Indeed, though economic restructuring drove subsistence costs up and held wages down in many countries around the world, "no other world region experienced as many protests centering on food and other consumer claimed rights" as Latin America (Eckstein and Wickham-Crowley 2003: 13).

7. Beginning in 1996, several dozen political and intellectual leaders of the Left and center Left in Latin America participated in a series of meetings organized by Roberto Mangabeira Unger and Jorge Castañeda. One product of these

meetings was a 1997 document entitled "Alternativa Latinoamericana," which charted a "third way" for Latin American countries and was widely circulated at the time; it is from this document that I have extracted this phrase. The document refers to "a politics of rolling (or constant) boil (*una política de ebullición constante*). Women, young people, workers, indigenous communities, blacks and mulattoes, minorities of certain sexual preference, oppressed ethnicities, marginalized religious sects and many other groups who lack the full plenitude of their rights and aspirations should be stimulated to mobilize, to conquer spaces and rights and interests." For a copy of this document, see http:// www.latinnews.com/big_issues/bioo-03-s.htm (copy in author's files).

8. There is no generally agreed upon definition for civil society; this is my undoubtedly imperfect attempt to condense a classic liberal understanding in few words. For a useful, detailed discussion of many of the different definitions of civil society, and their attendant problems, see White 1994.

9. Putnam's work has promoted a copious flow of commentary and criticism; several authors have focused on his failure to account for the importance of horizontal forms of social capital. In this regard, see especially Levi (1996). Also relevant to the empirical context discussed here are Perez-Diaz (2002) and Booth and Richard (1998), who argue, along with Levi, that Putnam overlooks the potential "dark side" of social capital. These authors suggest that Putnam's emphasis on collective association as an unambiguously democratic force romanticizes community, ignoring its potential links to violent intolerance and other forces antithetical to democratic deepening.

10. I have reconstructed the following history of Santiago Atitlán drawing on interviews I carried out with residents during a 1999 research trip; Murga Armas 1997; CEH 1999.

11. As the experience of Santiago Atitlán illustrates, Maya justice does not exist in opposition to the formal justice system but often in fact blends with it or relies upon it as a backup. Defensoría Maya, for example, also provides legal advice and representation (within the limits of its capacity) for those who may choose to pursue justice through the state's legal system, especially if previous attempts to resolve the situation using mediation have failed. In this way, while it encourages disputants to arrive at a solution without the courts, it also provides tools for those who may be unable to achieve resolution through extraofficial means.

12. Indeed, even the much-celebrated *rondas* in Santiago Atitlán appeared to have largely ground to a halt when I visited the community in 1999, and controversies and corruption charges surrounding the sitting mayoral council had led to a tense stalemate; after demanding multiple forms of identification from me, questioning who had sent me, and expressing suspicion about the fact that I was not I was not carrying my passport, demanding, "How are we supposed to know you really are who you say you are?" members of the mayoral council agreed to speak with me and ushered me into a back room. There they told me that they themselves had narrowly escaped a recent lynching attempt outside their offices. I later spoke to others in the community about this incident, in

which large numbers of residents angry at the council had gathered in protest and council members had apparently escaped confrontation by exiting through an opening in a back wall; it was unclear that this disturbance was intended to culminate in a lynching, and many community members insisted that such charges were inflammatory and sensational attempts to generate sympathy on the part of council members. Regardless of the incident's outcome or intention, the fact that even in communities with peaceful, independent traditions of semiautonomous governance, dissatisfaction with local leadership can easily spill over into volatile gatherings which may or may not culminate in acts of violence attests to the fragility of informal justice traditions.

13. Botrán, of course, is here missing (or deliberately ignoring) the fact that human rights are universal by definition, and thus even kidnappers have them.

14. The bumper stickers were black and white and bore the slogan "Guatemala is in mourning" and the CACIF logo.

15. *Convivencia* means living together, getting along; it is frequently invoked in the context of discussions of the need for tolerance and dialogue across differences in a diverse society.

CHAPTER 6

1. Certainly development prescriptions did not always mirror actual U.S. experience; sometimes they were derived from more on European models, and sometimes from an imagined path to progress based not on the concrete historical experience of any single country or region, but rather on planners' perceptions and conjectures. A more thorough critique of development projects and their premises lies beyond the scope of this article, but I do not wish to elide its complexity here.

2. See Bratton and Andrews 2001. It is telling that two increasingly familiar terms in the Latin American crime fighting lexicon, *linchamiento* (lynching) and *cero tolerancia* (zero tolerance) are both imported from the English.

3. In fact, this model of governance is not entirely new to the United States either, as the history of lynchings in the postbellum U.S. South (among other examples) would suggest.

4. On this point, see especially O'Malley 1999, in which he argues that the most repressive elements of contemporary penality would more correctly be attributed to neoconservatism—even as they coexist with strains that reflect more neoliberal orientations.

5. In referring to neoliberal policy I mean government policies seeking to foster wealth accumulation, even at the expense of equality or welfare considerations. For a recent overview analysis of these policies and their social effects in Latin America, see Huber and Solt 2004; Walton 2004; Weyland 2004. For a discussion of neoliberal governance in North America, see Rose 1999.

6. I am grateful to Katherine Beckett for bringing this to my attention.

7. There is some indication that the punitive tide may be turning as regards drug offenses; recent ballot initiatives, for example, have decriminalized the use

of marijuana for medicinal purposes and mandated treatment rather than punishment for certain drug offenses. It is too early to say whether these presage more extensive shifts. Nonetheless, though they may represent the beginnings of a popular rethinking of the assumed link between drug use and crime, I am not aware of any evidence suggesting that the more general link between non-drug-use-related criminal behavior and punitiveness is in question.

8. Notably, Chile's 1980 constitution, promulgated under Augusto Pinochet, does impose permanent disfranchisement on convicted felons, many of whom were convicted of political crimes. See Mariner 2000.

9. Philip Zimbardo, one of Huggins's co-authors in this book, is well known for having documented similar findings in a quite different context in the Stanford Prison Experiments. This research, along with Stanley Milgram's *Obedience to Authority*, should dispel any notions that the institutionalized violence experienced in Brazil or elsewhere in Latin America springs somehow from a "culture of violence" unique to such settings.

10. As Rush Limbaugh told his listeners on June 14, 2005, "Let me tell you something, folks, if we are hit again, if we are hit again, we need to hold these people in our country who are undermining our efforts responsible. It ain't going to be the FBI's fault next time. It isn't going to be the CIA's fault next time. It isn't going to be some bureaucracy's fault next time. It's going to be the fault of politicians, left-wing groups and the like who have names and identities and spend their every waking moment trying to obstruct our ability to secure intelligence information for our own national security. You want some names: [Senator Patrick] Leahy [D-VT], [Senator Joseph R.] Biden [D-DE], [Senator Richard J.] Durbin [D-IL], [Senator Barbara] Boxer [D-CA], [Senator Edward] Kennedy [D-MA], [Senate Majority Leader Harry] Reid [D-NV], Newsweek, Time, the *New York Times*, Amnesty International. If we get hit again, these are the names of the people and organizations we need to look at when we're trying to find out why and how it happened" (http://mediamatters.org/items/200506150006 [accessed November 8, 2005]).

11. As Amnesty International reports, "(We are) . . . concerned that the CIA may still be holding people in secret detention in Afghanistan and elsewhere in situations which would amount to "disappearance" (2005).

References

Abel, Richard, ed. 1982. *The Politics of Informal Justice*. 2 vols. New York: Academic Press.

Abrahams 1996.

Albornoz Tinajero, Consuelo. 1995. "Latin America: Human Rights; Hanging and Security." Inter-Press Service. June 21.

Agüero, Felipe, and Jeffrey Stark, eds. 1998. *Fault Lines of Democracy in Post-transition Latin America*. Miami, Fla.: North-South Center Press.

Aguilera Peralta, Gabriel. 1971. *La violencia en Guatemala como fenómeno político*. Mexico: Centro Intercultural de Documentación.

———. 1979. *Violencia y contraviolencia: La violencia y el régimen de legalidad en Guatemala*. Guatemala City: Editorial USAC.

Aguilera Peralta, Gabriel, and Jorge Romero Imery. 1981. *Dialéctica del terror en Guatemala*. San José, Costa Rica: EDUCA.

"Las amargas realidades de la 'justicia' popular." 1997. *Prensa libre*, September 19.

Americas Watch. 1986. *Civil Patrols in Guatemala*. New York: Americas Watch.

Americas Watch and Physicians for Human Rights. 1991. *Guatemala: Getting Away with Murder*. New York: Human Rights Watch.

Amnesty International. 1987. *Guatemala: The Human Rights Record*. New York: AI.

———. 1998. *Guatemala: All the Truth, Justice for All*. London: AI.

———. 2000. *Report 2000*. London: AI.

———. 2001. *Guatemala: Human Rights Community under Siege*. London: AI.

———. 2002. *Guatemala: The Civil Defence Patrols Re-emerge*. London: AI.

———. 2003a. *Peru: The "Anti-terrorism" Legislation and Its Effects: An Unfinished Business in the Transition to Democracy*. London: AI.

———. 2003b. Urgent Action 43/03, AMR 34/006/2003, "Fear For Safety/Threats." London: AI, February 12.

————. 2005. "USA/Afghanistan: More Deaths and Impunity." Public statement. London: AI, October 31. http://web.amnesty.org/library/Index/ENGAMR511722005?open&of=ENG-USA (accessed November 8, 2005).

"ANACAFE y su ponencia sobre la seguridad ciudadana." 1997. Unpublished ms.

"Apresado el violador y homicida de Mariara." 2001. *El universal*, May 14.

"Aprueban en Panamá penas más severas a menores delincuentes." 2003. Xinhua News Service, April 25.

Arana, Ana. 2001. "The New Battle for Central America." *Foreign Affairs* 80, no. 6 (November–December): 88–101.

Archbishopric of Guatemala Human Rights Office (Oficina de Derechos Humanos del Arzobispado de Guatemala). Interdiocesan Recovery of the History of Memory Project (Proyecto Interdiocesano de Recuperación de la Memoria Histórica, REMHI). 1998. *Guatemala Nunca Más*. Guatemala City: ODHAG.

Arias, Arturo, ed. 2001. *The Rigoberta Menchú Controversy*. Minneapolis: University of Minnesota Press.

Auyero, Javier. 2000. "The Hyper-Shantytown: Neoliberal Violence(s) in the Argentine Slum." *Ethnography* 1, no. 1: 93–116.

————. 2001. "Glocal Riots." *International Sociology* 16, no. 1 (January): 33–53.

Ayers, Edward. 1984. *Vengeance and Justice: Crime and Punishment in the Nineteenth Century American South*. New York: Oxford University Press.

Ayres, Robert L. 1998. *Crime and Violence as Development Issues in Latin America and the Caribbean*. Washington, D.C.: World Bank.

Azpuru, Dinorah. 2000. "The Political Impact of Crime: The Case of Guatemala." Paper presented at the 2000 meeting of the Latin American Studies Association, Miami, Fla., March 16–18.

Ball, Patrick, Paul Kobrak, and Herbert F. Spirer. 1999. *State Violence in Guatemala, 1960–1996: A Quantitative Reflection*. Washington, D.C.: American Association for the Advancement of Science. http:/shr.aaas.org/guatemala/ciidh/qr/english/qrtitle.html (accessec November 8, 2005).

Barrera Nuñez, Oscar. 2005. "Imaginaries and Desires: Transcultural 'Love Affairs' in Guatemala." Ph.D. diss., University of Washington, Seattle.

Barry, Tom. 1986. *Guatemala: The Politics of Counterinsurgency*. Albuquerque, N.M.: Inter-hemispheric Education Resource Center.

Beck, E. M., and Stewart E. Tolnay. 1990. "The Killing Fields of the Deep South: The Market for Cotton and the Lynching of Blacks, 1882–1930." *American Sociological Review* 55, no. 4 (August): 526–39.

Beckett, Katherine. 1997. *Making Crime Pay: Law and Order in Contemporary American Politics*. New York: Oxford University Press.

Beckett, Katherine, and Theodore Sasson. 2000. *The Politics of Injustice: Crime and Punishment in America*. Thousand Oaks, Calif.: Pine Forge Press.

Beckett, Katherine, and Bruce Western. 1999. "How Unregulated Is the U.S. Labor Market? The Dynamics of Jobs and Jails, 1980–1995." *American Journal of Sociology* 104, no. 3 (January 1999): 1030–60.

Black, George, with Milton Jamail and Norma Stoltz Chinchilla. 1984. *Garrison Guatemala*. New York: Monthly Review Press.

Bonilla, Adrian. 2001. "The Conflict in Colombia: Implications for Ecuador's National Security." *Foreign Policy in Focus* (July). http://www.foreign policyinfocus.org/outside/commentary/0107ecuador_body.html (accessed April 30, 2003).

Booth, John A., and Patricia Bayer Richard. 1998. "Civil Society, Political Capital, and Democratization in Central America." *Journal of Politics* 60, no. 3 (August): 780–800.

Booth, William. 1994. "Witch Hunt: Babies Are Disappearing, Ugly Rumors Abound, and a Tourist's Life Is at Stake." *Washington Post*, May 17.

Borón, Atilio. 1998. "Faulty Democracies? A Reflection on the Capitalist 'Fault Lines' in Latin America." In *Fault Lines of Democracy in Post-transition Latin America*, edited by Felipe Agüero and Jeffrey Stark. Miami, Fla.: North-South Center Press, 41–66.

Bratton, William, and William Andrews. 2001. "Driving Out the Crime Wave: The Police Methods That Worked in New York City Can Work in Latin America." *Time*, July 23.

Briceño-León, Roberto, Alberto Camardiel, and Olga Avila. 1999. "Attitudes toward the Right to Kill in Latin American Culture." Unpublished ms.

Briceño-León, Roberto, and Verónica Zubillaga. 2002. "Violence and Globalization in Latin America." *Current Sociology* 50, no. 1 (January): 19–37.

Brown, Michael J., Jorge Daly, and Katie Hamlin. 2005. "Guatemala Land Conflict Assessment." Report submitted to the United States Agency for International Development. http://pdf.dec.org/pdf_docs/PNADC728.pdf (accessed November 8, 2005).

Brundage, W. Fitzhugh. 1993. *Lynching in the New South: Georgia and Virginia, 1880–1930*. Urbana: University of Illinois Press.

Brysk, Alison. 2000. "Democratizing Civil Society in Latin America." *Journal of Democracy* 11, no. 2: 151–65.

Buckser, Andrew. 1992. "Lynching as Ritual in the American South." *Berkeley Journal of Sociology* 37:11–28.

Burgos, Elizabeth. 1983. *Me llamo Rigoberta Menchú y así me nació la conciencia*. 1st ed. Barcelona: Argos Vergara.

Buvinic, Mayra, Andrew Morrison, and Michael Shifter. 1999. "Violence in Latin America and the Caribbean: A Framework for Action." Inter-American Development Bank, March. http://www.iadb.org/sds/publication/publication _515_e.htm (accessed November 8, 2005).

Caldeira, Teresa P. R. 1996. "Crime and Individual Rights: Reframing the Question of Violence in Latin America." In *Constructing Democracy: Human Rights, Citizenship, and Society in Latin America*, edited by Elizabeth Jelin and Eric Hershberg. Boulder, Colo.: Westview Press, 197–214.

———. 2000. *City of Walls: Crime, Segregation and Citizenship in São Paulo*. Berkeley: University of California Press.

Call, Charles. 1997. "Police Reform, Human Rights and Democratization in

Post-conflict Settings: Lessons from El Salvador." In *After the War Is Over, What Comes Next?* ed. Nicole Ball. Washington, DC: USAID.

"Camara de industria demanda al OJ inyección lethal para secuestradores." 1997. *Prensa libre*, November 30.

Caplow, Theodore, and Jonathan Simon. 1999. "Understanding Prison Policy and Population Trends." In *Prisons*, edited by Michael Tonry and J. Petersilia. Vol. 26 of *Crime and Justice: A Review of Research*, edited by Michael Tonry. Chicago: University of Chicago Press, 63–120.

"Los carapintada quieren ser presidente." 2003. *Clarín*, May 29.

Carmack, Robert. M., ed. 1988. *Harvest of Violence: The Maya Indians and the Guatemalan Crisis*. Norman: University of Oklahoma Press.

————.1990. "State and Community in Nineteenth Century Guatemala: The Momostenango Case." In *Guatemalan Indians and the State*, edited by Carol Smith. Austin: University of Texas Press, 116–40.

Carothers, Thomas. 1998. "Rule of Law Revival." *Foreign Affairs* 77, no. 2: 95–106.

————. 2003. "Promoting the Rule of Law Abroad: The Problem of Knowledge." Carnegie Endowment for International Peace Working Papers, Rule of Law Series, Democracy and Rule of Law Project, no. 34 (January).

Castillo, Angel Gilberto, Juan de Dios González, Miguel von Hoegen, and Emilio Sequén. 1998. *El sistema jurídico Maya: Una aproximación*. Guatemala City: Universidad Rafael Landívar Instituto de Investigaciones Económicas y Sociales.

Castillo Claudett, Eduardo. 2000. "La justicia en tiempos de la ira: Linchamientos populares urbanos en América Latina." *Ecuador Debate* 51. http://www.lahora.com.ec/paginas/debate/paginas/debate12.htm.

Centro de Investigación y Documentación Centroamericana. 1980. *Desarrollo histórico de la violencia institucional en Guatemala: Violencia y contraviolencia*. Colección Mario López Larrave 6. Guatemala City: Editorial Universitaria de Guatemala.

Centro de Investigaciones Económicas Nacionales. 1999. "Paz urbana: Percepciones de la violencia en Guatemala." Sondeo Urbano Participativo. Colonia Santa Marta, Esquipulas, Chiquimula, and Cantón El Mosquito, San Pedro Sacatepéquez, San Marcos. Unpublished ms.

————. N.d. "Diagnóstico de la violencia en Guatemala: Aproximación cuantitativa y cualitativa." Unpublished ms.

————. N.d. "Investigando la violencia en Guatemala: Algunas consideraciones conceptuales y metodológicas." Documento de discusión para la Red de Centros de Investigación Económica. Unpublished ms.

Chabal and Daloz 1999.

Chevigny, Paul. 1995. *Edge of the Knife: Police Violence in the Americas*. New York: New Press.

————. 2003. "The Populism of Fear: Politics of Crime in the Americas." *Punishment and Society* 5, no. 1 (Spring 2003): 77–96.

Chinchilla, Laura, and José María Rico. 1997. *La prevencion comunitaria del delito: Perspectivas para América Latina*. Miami: Centro para la adminstración de justicia, Florida International University.

Comaroff, Jean, and John L. Comaroff. 1999. "Occult Economies and the Violence of Abstraction: Notes from the South African Postcolony." *American Ethnologist* 26, no. 2 (May): 279–303.

———. Forthcoming. *Policing the Postcolony: Crime, Cultural Justice, and the Problem of Order in South Africa.* Chicago: University of Chicago Press.

Comaroff, John L. 1994. Foreword to *Contested States: Law, Hegemony and Resistance*, edited by Mindie Lazarus-Black and Susan F. Hirsch. New York: Routledge.

Comisión para el Esclarecimiento Histórico. 1999. *Guatemala: Memoria del silencio.* Guatemala City: CEH. http://shr.aaas.org/guatemala/ceh/mds/spanish/ (accessed November 8, 2005).

Comisión para la Defensa de los Derechos Humanos en Centroamérica. 1998. *Informe sobre la situación de los derechos humanos en Centroamérica, mayo–diciembre 1998.* San José, Costa Rica: CODEHUCA.

"Comunidad de Mariara se rebela contra el alto índice de inseguridad." 2001. *El universal*, April 18.

Cook, Melissa. 2003. "Banished for Minor Crimes: The Aggravated Felony Provision of the Immigration and Nationality Act as a Human Rights Violation." *Boston College Third World Law Journal* 23 (Spring): 293–329.

Coordinación de Organizaciones del Pueblo Maya de Guatemala. 2000. *Más allá de la costumbre: Cosmos, orden, y equilibrio.* Guatemala: COPMAGUA.

Corradi, Juan E. 1992. "Toward Societies without Fear." In *Fear at the Edge: State Terror and Resistance in Latin America*, edited by Juan E. Corradi, Patricia Weiss Fagen, and Manuel Antonio Carretón. Berkeley: University of California Press, 267–92.

Corradi, Juan E., Patricia Weiss Fagen, and Manuel Antonio Garretón. 1992. "Fear: A Cultural and Political Construct." In *Fear at the Edge: State Terror and Resistance in Latin America*, edited by Juan E. Corradi, Patricia Weiss Fagen, and Manuel Antonio Carretón. Berkeley: University of California Press, 1–12.

Correa Sutil, Jorge. 1998. "Modernization, Democratization and Judicial Systems." In *Justice Delayed: Judicial Reform in Latin America*, edited by Edmundo Jarquín and Fernando Carrillo. Washington: Inter-American Development Bank, 97–107.

"A Country Turns Upside Down." 2003. *Economist*, May 15.

Currie, Elliott. 1998. *Crime and Punishment in America.* New York: Metropolitan Books.

Dahl, Robert A. 1971. *Polyarchy: Participation and Opposition.* New Haven: Yale University Press.

Dammert, Lucía. 2005. "Mano inteligente contra la delincuencia." *El mercurio*, October 16.

Dammert, Lucía, and Mary Fran T. Malone. 2003. "Fear of Crime or Fear of Life? Public Insecurities in Chile." *Bulletin of Latin American Research* 22, no. 1 (2003): 79–101.

Daniel, E. Valentine. 1996. *Charred Lullabies: Chapters in an Anthropography of Violence.* Princeton, N.J.: Princeton University Press.

Daremblum, Naomi. 2003. "Democracy's Pains." Review of Richard Gott, *In the Shadow of the Liberator: Hugo Chávez and the Transformation of Venezuela*. *New Republic*, February 3.

Davis, Mike. 1990. *City of Quartz: Excavating the Future in Los Angeles*. New York: Verso.

Defensoría Maya. 1999. *Suk'B'Anik: Administración de justicia Maya; Experiencias de Defensoría Maya*. Guatemala City: Defensoría Maya, 1999.

de Janvry, Alain, Elisabeth Sadoulet, and Linda Wilcox Young. 1989. "Land and Labour in Latin American Agriculture from the 1950s to the 1980s." *Journal of Peasant Studies* 16, no. 3: 396–424.

de la Jara, Ernesto. 2002. "Caught in an Anti-Terrorist Web." *NACLA Report on the Americas* 35, no. 4: 4–6.

DeLeón, C. R. 1998. "El fenómeno de los linchamientos y su relación con el tejido social comunitario antes de la firma de la paz." Paper presented at the conference Linchamientos: Diagnóstico y Búsqueda de Soluciones, Panajachel, Guatemala, May.

De León-Escribano 1999.

Dershowitz, Alan. 2001. "Is There a Torturous Road to Justice?" *Los Angeles Times*, November 8.

Dezalay, Yves, and Bryant Garth. 2002. *The Internationalization of Palace Wars: Lawyers, Economists, and the Contest to Transform Latin American States*. Chicago: University of Chicago Press.

Diamond, Larry. 1990. "Beyond Authoritarianism and Totalitarianism: Strategies for Democratization." In *The New Democracies: Global Challenges and US Policy*, edited by Brad Roberts. Cambridge, Mass.: MIT Press, 227–249.

———. 1996. "Democracy in Latin America: Degrees, Illusions, and Directions for Consolidation." In *Beyond Sovereignty: Collectively Defending Democracy in the Americas*, edited by Tom Farer. Baltimore, Md.: Johns Hopkins University Press, 52–104.

———. 1999. *Developing Democracy: Toward Consolidation*. Baltimore, Md.: Johns Hopkins University Press.

Diamond, Larry, Juan Linz, and Seymour Martin Lipset. 1998. Introduction to *Democracy in Developing Countries: Latin America*, edited by Larry Diamond, Juan Linz, and Seymour Martin Lipset. Boulder, Colo.: Lynne Rienner.

Domingo Villegas, Pilar. 1995. "Rule of Law and Judicial Systems in the Context of Democratisation and Economic Liberalisation: A Framework for Comparison and Analysis in Latin America." Documentos de Trabajo del Centro de Investigación y Docencia Económicas, División de Estudios Políticos, no. 25.

Doob, Anthony N. 2000. "Transforming the Punishment Environment: Understanding Public Views of What Should Be Accomplished at Sentencing." *Canadian Journal of Criminology* 42, no. 3 (July): 323–40.

Durkheim, Emile. 1947. *The Division of Labor in Society*. Translated by George Simpson. Glencoe, Ill.: Free Press.

———. 1964. *The Division of Labor in Society*. New York: Macmillan.

Eckstein, Susan Eva, and Timothy P. Wickham-Crowley. 2003. "Struggles for Justice in Latin America." In *What Justice? Whose Justice? Fighting for Fairness in Latin America*. Berkeley: University of California Press, 1–34.

Elias, Norbert. 1982. *The Civilizing Process*. New York: Pantheon Books.

Elizaldo, Triunfo. 1997. "Con el control total, el Ejército agrede a la población civil, advierte." *La jornada*, September 24.

Elton, Catherine. 2000. "Guatemala's Lynch-mob Justice." *Christian Science Monitor*, December 1.

"Encuesta: Reforma electoral con participación." 2000. *Prensa libre*, 25 July.

Epp, Charles. 1996. "Do Bills of Rights Matter? The Canadian Charter of Rights and Freedoms." *American Political Science Review* 90, no. 4: 765–79.

Erikson, Kai. 1966. *Wayward Puritans: A Study in the Sociology of Deviance*. New York: John Wiley and Sons.

Escobar, Arturo. 1995. *Encountering Development: The Making and Unmaking of the Third World*. Princeton: Princeton University Press.

Esquirol, Jorge L. 2003. "Continuing Fictions of Latin American Law." *Florida Law Review* 55, no. 1 (January): 41–114.

Evans, Peter B. 1997. "The Eclipse of the State? Reflections on Stateness in an Era of Globalization." *World Politics* 50, no. 1 (October): 62–87.

Fagen, Patricia Weiss. 1992. "Repression and State Security." In *Fear at the Edge: State Terror and Resistance in Latin America*, edited by Juan E. Corradi, Patricia Weiss Fagen, and Manuel Antonio Carretón. Berkeley: University of California Press, 39–71.

Faiola, Anthony. 2002. "Brazilian Gangs Take Turf Wars out of Slums: Even Upper-Class Areas Invaded by Traffickers." *Washington Post*, December 15.

Fajnzylber, Pablo, Daniel Lederman, and Norman Loayza. 1998. *Determinants of Crime Rates in Latin America and the World: An Empirical Assessment*. Washington, D.C.: World Bank.

———. 2002. "Inequality and Violent Crime." *Journal of Law and Economics* 45 (April): 1–40.

Falla, Ricardo. 1992. *Masacres de la selva: Ixcán, Guatemala, 1975–1982*. Guatemala City: Editorial Universitaria.

"Falta de juzgados motiva a pobladores a tomar justicia por mano propia." 1998. *Guatemala Flash*, March 24.

Feitlowitz, Marguerite. 1998. *A Lexicon of Terror: Argentina and the Legacies of Torture*. New York: Oxford University Press.

Ferrigno, Víctor. 1998. "El estado democrático de derecho frente al conflicto social." Paper presented at the conference Linchamientos: Diagnóstico y Búsqueda de Soluciones, Panajachel, Guatemala, May.

Figueroa, Luis. 2000. *Siglo veintiuno*, August 27.

Fischer, Edward F. 1996. "Induced Culture Change as a Strategy for Socioeconomic Development: The Pan-Maya Movement in Guatemala." In *Maya Cultural Activism in Guatemala*, edited by Edward F. Fischer and R. McKenna Brown. Austin: University of Texas Press, 51–73.

"Flores asturias: Más policias para reducir linchamientos." 1998. *Siglo veintiuno*, December 24.

Foley, Michael W., and Bob Edwards. 1996. "The Paradox of Civil Society." *Journal of Democracy* 7 (July): 38–53.

Forster, Cindy. 2001. *In the Time of Freedom: Campesino Workers in Guatemala's October Revolution*. Pittsburgh, Pa.: University of Pittsburgh Press.

Foucault, Michel. 1977. *Discipline and Punish: The Birth of the Prison*. Translated by Alan Sheridan. New York: Vintage Books.

Fournier, Marco, and Rolando Pérez. N.d. "Autoritarismo y la percepción de la violencia social: El caso de los chapulines." San José: Universidad de Costa Rica, Instituto de Investigaciones Psicológicas.

Fox, Jonathan. 1994. "Latin America's Emerging Local Politics." *Journal of Democracy* 5 (April): 106–16.

Frank, Louisa. 1976. "Resistencia y revolución: El desarrollo de la lucha armada en Guatemala." In *Guatemala: Una historica inmediata*, edited by Susanne Jonas and David Tobis. New York: NACLA, 291–320.

Fruhling, Hugo, and Joseph S. Tulchin, with Heather Golding, eds. 2003. *Crime and Violence in Latin America: Citizen Security, Democracy, and the State*. Washington, D.C.: Woodrow Wilson Center Press.

Fuentes Díaz, Antonio, and Leigh Binford. 2001. "Linchamientos en México: Una respuesta a Carlos Vilas." *Bajo el volcán: Revista del postgrado en sociología de la Benemérita Universidad Autónoma de Puebla* 2, no. 3: 143–54.

"Fuerte SI por pena de muerte." 1998. *Prensa libre*, February 8.

Gardner, Dan. 2000. "Drug Trade Rots Away Mexican Society: Losing the War on Drugs, Part 4, Mexico's War," *Ottawa Citizen*, September 8.

Garland, David. 1996. "The Limits of the Sovereign State: Strategies of Crime Control in Contemporary Society." *British Journal of Criminology* 36: 445–71.

———. 2001. *The Culture of Control: Crime and Social Order in Contemporary Society*. Chicago: University of Chicago Press.

Garth, Bryant G. 2003. "Law and Society as Law and Development." *Law and Society Review* 37, no. 2 (June): 305–14.

Garvey, Stephen P. 1988. "Can Shaming Punishments Educate?" *University of Chicago Law Review* 65, no. 3 (Summer): 733–94.

Gaviria, Alejandro, and Carmen Pages. 1999. "Patterns of Crime Victimization in Latin America." IDB Working Paper no. 408, October 29.

Girard, René. 1972. *Violence and the Sacred*. Baltimore, Md.: Johns Hopkins University Press.

"Gobierno chileno anuncia 'mano dura' a paralizacion del transporte." 2002. *Agence France Presse*, August 10.

Godoy, Angelina Snodgrass. 1999. "'Our Right Is the Right to Be Killed': Making Rights Real on the Streets of Guatemala City." *Childhood* 6, no. 4: 423–42.

Goldin, Liliana R. 1999. "Rural Guatemala in Economic and Social Transition." In *Globalization and the Rural Poor in Latin America*, edited by William M. Loker. Boulder, Colo.: Lynne Rienner, 93–110.

Goldstein, Daniel. 2003. "In Our Own Hands: Lynching, Justice, and the Law in Bolivia." *American Ethnologist* 30, no. 1: 22–43.

————. 2004. *The Spectacular City: Violence and Performance in Urban Bolivia.* Durham, N.C.: Duke University Press.

González, Matilde. 2000. "The Man Who Brought the Danger to the Village: Representations of the Armed Conflict in Guatemala from a Local Perspective." *Journal of Southern African Studies* 26, no 2: 317–35.

Gould, Roger. 1999. "Collective Violence and Group Solidarity: Evidence from a Feuding Society." *American Sociological Review* 64 (June): 256–380.

Grandin, Greg. 1997. "To End with All These Evils: Ethnic Transformation and Community Mobilization in Guatemala's Western Highlands, 1954–1980." *Latin American Perspectives* 24, no. 2 (March): 7–34.

————. 2000. *The Blood of Guatemala: A History of Race and Nation.* Durham, N.C.: Duke University Press.

————. 2004. *The Last Colonial Massacre: Latin America and the Cold War.* Chicago: University of Chicago Press.

Green, Linda. 1998. "The Localization of the Global: Contemporary Production Practices in a Mayan Community." In *The Third Wave of Modernization in Latin America: Cultural Perspectives on Neoliberalism,* edited by Lynne Phillips. Wilmington, Del.: Scholarly Resources Press, 51–64.

————. 1999. *Fear as a Way of Life: Mayan Widows in Rural Guatemala.* New York: Columbia University Press. Grupo Pro Seguridad y Justicia. 2003. "Explota bomba con panfletos." *Prensa libre,* April 5.

Gutiérrez, Edward. 1999. "Leyes favorecen al delincuente." *El diario de hoy* (San Salvador), October 5.

Gutiérrez, Marta, and Paul Kobrak. 2001. "Los linchamientos: Pos conflicto y violencia colectiva en Huehuetenango, Guatemala." Huehuetenango: Centro de Estudios y Documentación de la Frontera Occidental de Guatemala.

Gutmann, Matthew. 2002. *The Romance of Democracy: Compliant Defiance in Contemporary Mexico.* Berkeley: University of California Press.

Handy, Jim. 1994. *Revolution in the Countryside: Rural Conflict and Agrarian Reform in Guatemala, 1944–1954.* Chapel Hill: University of North Carolina Press.

————. 2002. "Chicken Thieves, Witches, and Judges: Vigilante Justice and Customary Law in Guatemala." Paper presented at the Congress of the Canadian Association for Latin American and Caribbean Studies, Montreal, Canada, October 22–24.

Hendrickson, Carol. 1996. "Women, Weaving, and Education in Maya Revitalization." In *Maya Cultural Activism in Guatemala,* edited by Edward F. Fischer and R. McKenna Brown. Austin: University of Texas Press, 156–64.

Hendrix, Steven. 2000. "Guatemalan 'Justice Centers': The Centerpiece for Advancing Transparency, Efficiency, Due Process, and Access to Justice." *American University International Law Review* 15: 813–67.

————. 2002. "Lessons from Guatemala: Renewing US Foreign Policy on the Rule of Law." *Harvard International Review* (Winter): 14–18.

Holmes, Jennifer S., and Sheila Amin Gutiérrez de Piñeres. 2002. "Sources of

Fujimori's Popularity: Neo-liberal Reform or Ending Terrorism." *Terrorism and Political Violence* 14, no. 4 (Winter): 93–112.

Holston, James, and Teresa P. R. Caldeira. 1998. "Democracy, Law, and Violence: Disjunctions of Brazilian Citizenship." In *Fault Lines of Democracy in Post-transition Latin America*, edited by Felipe Agüero and Jeffrey Stark. Miami, Fla.: North-South Center Press, 263–96.

Huber, Evelyn, and Frederick Solt. 2004. "Successes and Failures of Neoliberalism." *Latin American Research Review* 39(3): 150–164.

Huggins, Martha K. 1998. *Political Policing: The United States and Latin America*. Durham, N.C.: Duke University Press.

Huggins, Martha K., Mika Haritos-Fatouros, and Philip G. Zimbardo. 2002. *Violence Workers: Police Torturers and Murderers Reconstruct Brazilian Atrocities*. Berkeley: University of California Press.

Human Rights First. 2004. *Getting to Ground Truth: Investigating U.S. Abusees in the "War on Terror."* New York: Human Rights First.

Human Rights Watch. 1997. *Police Brutality in Urban Brazil*. New York: Human Rights Watch.

———. 1999. *Annual Report*. http://www.hrw.org/spanish/inf_anual/1999/americas (accessed November 8, 2005).

———. 2003. *Informe Annual 2003: Venezuela*. http://hrw.org/spanish/inf_anual/2003/venezuela.html#venezuela (accessed November 8, 2005).

———. 2005. *World Report 2005: Argentina*. http://www.hrw.org/english/docs/2005/01/13/argent9844.htm (accessed November 8, 2005).

Human Rights Watch and the Sentencing Project. 1998. *Losing the Vote: The Impact of Felony Disenfranchisement Laws in the United States*. Washington, D.C., and New York: Human Rights Watch and the Sentencing Project, 1998.

Human Rights Watch World Report 1997. 1997. United States entry. http://www.hrw.org/reports/1997/WR97/BACK.htm (accessed November 8, 2005).

Huntington, Samuel P. 1989. "The Modest Meaning of Democracy." In *Democracy in the Americas: Stopping the Pendulum*, edited by Robert Pastor. New York: Holmes and Meier, 11–28.

"Independent Panel to Review DoD Detention Operations." 2004. Final Report of the Independent Panel to Review DoD Detention Operations, August. http://www.defenselink.mil/news/Aug2004/d20040824finalreport.pdf (accessed November 8, 2005).

Instituto Centroamericano de Estudios Políticos. 1999. *Percepciones de la violencia en Guatemala: Análisis en la actual coyuntura nacional*. Guatemala City: INCEP.

Instituto Interamericano de Derechos Humanos Proyecto "Seguridad Ciudadana en Centroamérica." Informe de Actividades para el año 1998. Unpublished ms.

———. N.d. "Borrador de Diagnóstico Sobre la Seguridad Ciudadana en el Municipio de Villa Nueva (Guatemala)." Unpublished ms.

Intelligence Oversight Board. 1996. *Report on the Guatemala Review*. June 28. http://www.gwu.edu/~nsarchiv/NSAEBB/NSAEBB27/04-01.htm (accessed January 9, 2006).

Inter-American Commission on Human Rights. 2005. Fifth Report on the Situation of Human Rights in Guatemala. http://www.cidh.oas.org/countryrep/ Guateo1eng/chap.5.htm, 2001 (accessed September 21, 2005).

Inter-American Development Bank (IDB). 2003. "Forum on Citizens' Security is Held in Conjunction with Meeting of IDB Governors for Central American Isthmus and Dominican Republic." Press release, February 20.

Jarquín, Edmundo, and Fernando Carrillo, eds. 1998. *Justice Delayed: Judicial Reform in Latin America*. Washington, D.C.: Inter-American Development Bank.

Johnson, Tim. 2003. "Guatemalan Seeks Global Help to Lower Crime in Weary Land." *Miami Herald*, February 9.

Jonas, Susanne. 1991. *The Battle for Guatemala: Rebels, Death Squads, and U.S. Power*. Boulder, Colo.: Westview Press.

———. 2000. *Of Centaurs and Doves: Guatemala's Peace Process*. Boulder, Colo.: Westview Press.

Jordan, Bill, and Jon Arnold. 1995. "Democracy and Criminal Justice." *Critical Social Policy* 44–45 (Autumn): 170–82.

Keck, Margaret E., and Kathryn Sikkink. 1998. *Activists Beyond Borders: Advocacy Networks in International Politics*. Ithaca, N.Y.: Cornell University Press.

Kettmann, Steve. 2003. "Guatemala Fails to Pass US Antinarcotics Test." *San Francisco Chronicle*, February 1.

Kincaid, A. Douglas. 2001. "Demilitarization and Security in El Salvador and Guatemala: Convergence of Success and Crisis." In *Globalization on the Ground: Postbellum Guatemalan Democracy and Development*, edited by Christopher Chase-Dunn, Susanne Jonas, and Nelson Amaro. Lanham, Md.: Rowman and Littlefield, 101–18.

Kincaid, A. Douglas, and Eduardo Gamarra. 1996. "Redefining Public Security in Latin America." In *Latin America in the World-Economy*, edited by Roberto Patricio Korzeniewicz and William C. Smith. Westport, Conn.: Greenwood, 211–28.

Kruijt, Dirk, and Kees Koonings. 1999. *Societies of Fear: The Legacy of Civil War, Violence and Terror in Latin America*. London: Zed Books.

Lagos, Marta. 1997. "Latin America's Smiling Mask." *Journal of Democracy* 8, no. 3: 125–38.

———. 2001. "Between Stability and Crisis in Latin America." *Journal of Democracy* 12, no. 1: 137–45.

———. 2003. "A Road with No Return?" *Journal of Democracy* 14, no 2: 163–73.

LaRue, Frank, Harvey Taylor, and Christian Salazar-Volkmann. 1998. *Can Human Rights Be Denied to Children? Opposition and Defense of the Code for Children and Youth in Guatemala*. Guatemala City: CALDH, 1998.

Lawyers Committee for Human Rights. 2003. *A Test of Justice in Guatemala: The Myrna Mack Murder Trial*. New York: LCHR.

Lechner, Norbert. 1992. "Some People Die of Fear: Fear as a Political Problem." In *Fear at the Edge: State Terror and Resistance in Latin America*, edited by Juan E. Corradi, Patricia Weiss Fagen, and Manuel Antonio Carretón. Berkeley: University of California Press, 26–35.

Lederer, Edith. 2003. "Peru Truth Panel Raises Estimates of Deaths, Disappearances in Past Two Decades." *Associated Press,* June 17.

Lederman, Daniel, and Norman Loayza. 1999. "What Causes Crime and Violence?" In *Violence and Social Capital: Proceedings of the LCSES Seminar Series, 1997–98.* World Bank Sustainable Development Working Paper No. 5. Urban Peace Program Series, edited by Caroline Moser and Sarah Lister. Washington, D.C.: World Bank. 7–11.

Levi, Margaret. 1996. "Social and Unsocial Capital: A Review Essay on Robert Putnam's *Making Democracy Work.*" *Politics and Society* 24, no. 1 (March): 45–55.

Lewis, Anthony. 2003. "The Silencing of Gideon's Trumpet." *New York Times Magazine,* April 20. 50.

Lewis, Neil. 2004. "Red Cross Finds Detainee Abuse in Guantánamo." *New York Times,* November 30.

"Linchamientos: Vecinos de Xalbaquiej justifican muertes." 2000. *Prensa libre,* July 22.

Llorca, Juan Carlos. 2000. "Xalbaquiej visto como masacre encubierta, no un linchamiento." *El periódico,* October 2.

Londoño, Juan Luis, and Rodrigo Guerrero. 1999. *Violencia en América Latina: Epidemiología y costos.* IDB Working Paper R-375, August.

"López Obrador justifica linchamiento." 2001. *El diario de México,* July 28.

López Ovando, Olga. 2000. "Juntas de seguridad en Quiché." *Prensa libre,* May 29.

López y Rivas, Gilberto. 1999. "Zedillo en el país de las maravillas." *La jornada,* 3 September.

Lovell, George W. 1998. "Surviving Conquest: The Maya of Guatemala in Historical Perspectiva." *Latin American Research Review* 23, no. 2: 25–37.

Luna Noguera, Rafael. 1999. "Cada tres días ocurre un linchamiento en zonas populares de Caracas." *El nacional,* September 5.

Macías, Julio César. 1999. *Mi camino, la guerrilla: La apasionante autobiografía del legendario combatiente centroamericano César Montes.* Colonia del Valle, México, D.F.: Planeta.

"La mano dura del gobierno debilito la primera jornada de huelga." 1999. Efe News Services, July 6.

Mamdani, Mahmood. 1996. *Citizen and Subject: Contemporary Africa and the Legacy of Late Colonialism.* Princeton, N.J.: Princeton University Press.

Manz, Beatriz. 1988. *Refugees of a Hidden War: The Aftermath of Counterinsurgency in Guatemala.* Albany: State University of New York Press.

———. 2004. *Paradise in Ashes: A Guatemalan Journey of Courage, Terror, and Hope.* Berkeley: University of California Press.

"Mariara de todos los monstruos." 2001. *El universal,* May 13.

Mariner, Joanne. 2000. "Not Everyone Counts: Florida's 436,900 Missing Votes." *FindLaw's Writ: Legal Commentary,* November 30. http://writ.news.findlaw.com/mariner/20001130.html (accessed November 8, 2005).

Marshall, T. H. 1950. *Citizenship and Social Class.* Cambridge: Cambridge University Press.

Martínez, Francisco. 1999. "Problemática: Sociedad frustrada." *Prensa libre*, August 22.

Martínez, Francisco Mauricio. 1997. "Ejecución extrajudicial o delincuencia común? Reportaje especial." *Prensa libre*, November 3.

Martins, José de Souza. 1991. "Lynchings: Life by a Thread; Street Justice in Brazil, 1979–1988." In *Vigilantism and the State in Modern Latin America: Essays on Extralegal Violence*, edited by Martha K. Huggins. New York: Prager, 21–32.

Marx, Karl. 1978 [1843]. "On the Jewish Question." In *The Marx-Engels Reader*, edited by Robert Tucker. 2nd ed. New York: W. W. Norton, 26–52.

McCann, Michael W. 1994. *Rights at Work: Pay Equity Reform and the Politics of Legal Mobilization*. Chicago: University of Chicago Press.

McClintock, Michael. 1985. *The American Connection*. London: Zed Books.

Melville, Thomas, and Marjorie Melville. 1971. *Guatemala: Another Vietnam?* Harmondsworth, England: Penguin Books.

Mena, Xavier. 1998. "Recomendaciones preliminares sobre la administración de justicia y seguridad." Paper presented at the conference Linchamientos: Diagnóstico y Búsqueda de Soluciones, Panajachel, Guatemala, May.

Méndez, Juan. 1999. "Problems of Lawless Violence." In *The Rule of Law and the Underprivileged in Latin America*, edited by Juan Méndez, Guillermo O'Donnell, and Paulo Sérgio Pinheiro. Notre Dame: University of Notre Dame Press, 19–24.

Merry, Sally Engle, and Neil Milner, eds. 1993. *The Possibility of Popular Justice: A Case Study of American Community Mediation*. Ann Arbor: University of Michigan Press.

Misión de Verificación de las Naciones Unidas en Guatemala. 1999a. *Noveno informe sobre derechos humanos de la misión de verificación de las Naciones Unidas en Guatemala*. Guatemala City: MINUGUA.

———. 1999b. *Suplemento al Noveno Informe Sobre Derechos Humanos de la Misión de Verificación de las Naciones Unidas en Guatemala: Casos de Violaciones a los Derechos Humanos*. Guatemala City: MINUGUA.

———. 1999c. *Suplemento al Noveno Informe Sobre Derechos Humanos de la Misión de Verificación de las Naciones Unidas en Guatemala: Despliegue de la Policía Nacional Civil, Academia de la Policía Nacional Civil, Situaciones Sobre Derechos Humanos*. Guatemala City: MINUGUA.

———. 2000a. *Décimo informe sobre derechos humanos de la misión de verificación de las Naciones Unidas en Guatemala*. Guatemala City, Guatemala: MINUGUA.

———. 2000b. "Los linchamientos: Un flagelo contra la dignidad humana." Guatemala City: MINUGUA.

———. 2002. "Los linchamientos: Un flagelo que persiste." Guatemala City, Guatemala: MINUGUA.

Molina Mejía, Raúl. 2001. "The Resurgence of Violence in Guatemala." *Foreign Policy in Focus*, July. http://www.fpif.org (accessed November 9, 2005).

Monasterios, Rubén. 1999. "El linchamiento nuestro de cada tres días." *El nacional*, September 23.

Montoya, Roberto. 2002. "Linchamientos, un flagelo que sacude Guatemala: Más de 500 personas fueron víctimas de esta alarmante práctica en las comunidades indígenas desde 1996." *El mundo del siglo veintiuno,* December 18.

Morello, Carol. 1994. "Baby Theft Panic Cools Guatemalan Tourism, Adoptions." *Albuquerque Journal,* April 17.

Moscoso, Fernando. 1998. "Buscando los Orígenes del Linchamiento en Guatemala." Paper presented at the conference Linchamientos: Diagnóstico y Búsqueda de Soluciones, Panajachel, Guatemala, May.

Moser, Caroline, and Cathy McIlwaine. 2001. *Violence in a Post-conflict Context: Urban Poor Perceptions from Guatemala.* Washington, D.C.: World Bank.

Murga Armas, Jorge. 1997. "Santiago Atitlán: Organización comunitaria y seguridad de los habitantes; Un reto para la paz." In *Delito y seguridad de los habitantes,* edited by Elías Carranza. Mexico: Siglo Veintiuno Editores, 124–53.

Neild, Rachel. 1999. "From National Security to Citizen Security: Civil Society and the Evolution of Public Order Debates." International Center for Human Rights and Democratic Development. http://www.wola.org/publications/pub_security_civil_society_national_sec_to_citizen_sec (accessed November 8, 2005).

Nelson, Diane. 1999. *A Finger in the Wound: Body Politics in Quincentennial Guatemala.* Berkeley: University of California Press.

"No se modifica la Constitución." 1999. *Prensa libre,* May 18.

"Ocho jinetes apocalípticos sitian al país." 1997. *Prensa libre,* November 2.

O'Donnell, Guillermo. 1992. "Transitions, Continuities, and Paradoxes." In *Issues in Democratic Consolidation: The New South American Democracies in Comparative Perspective,* edited by Scott Mainwaring, Guillermo O'Donnell, and J. Samuel Valenzuela. Notre Dame, Ind.: University of Notre Dame Press, 17–56.

———. 1993. "On the State, Democratization, and Some Conceptual Problems: A Latin American View with Glances at Some Post-communist Countries." *World Development* 21, no. 8: 1355–70.

———. 1997. "Polyarchies and the (Un)Rule of Law in Latin America." Paper presented at the Annual Meeting of the American Political Science Association, Washington, D.C., August 28–31.

———. 1999. "Polyarchies and the (Un)Rule of Law in Latin America." In *The Rule of Law and the Underprivileged in Latin America,* edited by Juan Méndez, Guillermo O'Donnell, and Paulo Sérgio Pinheiro. Notre Dame, Ind.: University of Notre Dame Press, 303–37.

———. 2001. "Democracy, Law, and Comparative Politics." *Studies in Comparative International Development* 36: 7–36.

O'Donnell, Guillermo, and Philippe Schmitter. 1986. *Transitions from Authoritarian Rule: Tentative Conclusions about Uncertain Democracies.* Baltimore, Md.: Johns Hopkins University Press.

Oficina de Derechos Humanos del Arzobispado de Guatemala. 1998. *Guatemala: Nunca más; Informe Proyecto Interdiocesano de Recuperación de la Memoria Histórica.* Guatemala: ODHAG.

Olayo, Ricardo. 1996a. "En Coyoacán, al menos 20 colonias *enrejadas.*" *La jornada,* October 28.

―――. 1996b. "Se respetarán derechos en la presentación de detenidos: PGJDF." *La jornada,* July 18.

Ortiz Moreno, Humberto. 1998. "$300 a policías por cada hampón que consignen con éxito al MP." *La jornada,* September 6.

Painter, James. 1995. Review of *Rigoberta Menchú and the Story of All Poor Guatemalans. Journal of Latin American Studies* 27 (February): 252–53.

Palma Ramos, Danilo A. 1999. *La violencia delincuencial en Guatemala: Un enfoque coyuntural.* Guatemala City: Universidad Rafael Landívar Instituto de Investigaciones Económicas y Sociales.

Pásara, Luis. 1998. "La justicia en Guatemala." *Diálogo (FLACSO)* 2, no. 3 (March): 1–16.

"PDH Registra 68 ataques a defensores de los DDHH." 2005. *La hora,* June 25.

Peacock, Susan C., and Adriana Beltrán. 2003. *Hidden Powers in Post-conflict Guatemala: Illegal Armed Groups and the Forces behind Them.* Washington, D.C.: Washington Office on Latin America.

"Pena maxima." 1999. Editorial, *El nacional* (Caracas, Venezuela), September 7.

Perez-Diaz, Victor. 2002. "From Civil War to Civil Society: Social Capital in Spain from the 1930s to the 1990s." In *Democracies in Flux: The Evolution of Social Capital in Contemporary Society,* edited by Robert D. Putnam. Oxford: Oxford University Press, 245–88.

"Plan de gobierno: FRG propone juntas locales de seguridad ciudadana." 1999. *Siglo veintiuno,* September 28.

Platt, Anthony M. 1995. "Crime Rave." *Monthly Review* 47, no. 2 (June): 35–47.

Poleo Zerpa, Willmer. 1999. "Unos 5 mil reclusos saldrán en libertad en 2 meses." *El nacional* (Caracas, Venezuela), October 1.

Popkin, Eric. 1999. "Guatemalan Mayan Migration to Los Angeles: Constructing Transnational Linkages in the Context of the Settlement Process." *Ethnic and Racial Studies* 22, no. 2 (March): 267–300.

Popkin, Margaret. 1996. *Civil Patrols and Their Legacy: Overcoming Militarization and Polarization in the Guatemalan Countryside.* Washington, D.C.: Robert F. Kennedy Memorial Center for Human Rights.

"Por radio incitaron a sacarlos de la cárcel; desoyeron al gobernador." 1998. *La jornada,* March 27.

Portes, Alejandro. 2001. "Theories of Development and Their Application to Small Countries." In *Globalization on the Ground: Postbellum Guatemalan Democracy and Development,* edited by Christopher Chase-Dunn, Susanne Jonas, and Nelson Amaro. Lanham, Md.: Rowman and Littlefield, 189–206.

"Presidente de Ecuador anuncia mano dura contra protestas." 2002. *Agence France Presse,* January 8.

Priest, Dana, and Barton Gellman. 2002. "U.S. Decries Abuse but Defends Interrogations; 'Stress and Duress' Tactics Used on Terrorism Suspects Held in Secret Overseas Facilities." *Washington Post,* December 26.

Prillaman, William C. 2000. *The Judiciary and Democratic Decay in Latin America: Declining Confidence in the Rule of Law.* Westport, Conn.: Praeger.

Programa Venezolano de Educación y Acción en Derechos Humanos. 2001. Informe Anual 2001. http://www.derechos.org.ve/publicaciones/infanual/2000_01/index.htm (accessed November 9, 2005).

Przeworski, Adam. 1988. "Democracy as a Contingent Outcome of Conflicts." In *Constitutionalism and Democracy*, edited by Jon Elster and Rune Slagstad. Cambridge: Cambridge University Press, 59–80.

———. 1991. *Democracy and the Market: Political and Economic Reform in Eastern Europe and Latin America*. Cambridge: Cambridge University Press.

Pueblo Maya Kaqchikel de Sololá. 1998. *Runuk'ulen ri q'atb'äl tzij kaqchikel Tz'oloj ya' [Autoridad y gobierno kaqchikel de Sololá]*. Coordinated by Julián Cumatz Pecher. Guatemala City: Editorial Cholsamaj.

Putnam, Robert D. 1994. *Making Democracy Work: Civic Traditions in Modern Italy*. Princeton, N.J.: Princeton University Press.

———. 1995. "Bowling Alone: America's Declining Social Capital." *Journal of Democracy* 6, no. 1: 65–78.

Quiñones, Sam. 2001. *True Tales from Another Mexico*. Albuquerque: University of New Mexico Press.

Ramírez, Bertha Teresa. 1998. "Las policías de la capital, utilizadas como 'negocios,' acusa Desfasioux." *La jornada*, February 4.

Remijnse, Simone. 2000. "Civil Patrols, Memories and the Reconstruction of Local Civil Society in Guatemala." Paper presented at the 2000 meeting of the Latin American Studies Association, Miami, Fla., March 16–18.

———. 2003. *Memories of Violence: Civil Patrols and the Legacy of Conflict in Joyabaj, Guatemala*. Utretcht, Netherlands: Rozenberg.

Restrepo, Luis Alberto. 2001. "The Equivocal Dimensions of Human Rights in Colombia." In *Violence in Colombia, 1990–2000: Waging War and Negotiating Peace*, edited by Charles Bergquist, Ricardo Peñaranda, and Gonzalo Sánchez G. Wilmington, Del.: Scholarly Resources, 95–126.

Reuschemeyer, Dietrich, Evelyne Huber Stephens, and John D. Stephens. 1992. *Capitalist Development and Democracy*. Chicago: University of Chicago Press.

Rico, José María. 1999. *La seguridad ciudadana en Centroamérica: Aspectos teóricos y metodológicos, 1998–99*. San José, Costa Rica: Instituto Interamericano de Derechos Humanos.

Rico, José María, and Brenda A. Quiñones. 1998. *Borrador de diagnóstico sobre la seguridad ciudadana en el municipio de Villa Nueva (Guatemala)*. San José, Costa Rica: Instituto Interamericano de Derechos Humanos.

Rivkin, David B., and Lee A. Casey. 2005. "Amnesty Unbelievable: The Human Rights Organization Plays Anti-American Politics." *National Review*, May 27. http://www.nationalreview.com/comment/rivkin_casey200505270804.asp (accessed November 8, 2005).

Robert F. Kennedy Memorial Center for Human Rights. 1994. *Institutional Violence: Civil Patrols in Guatemala*. Washington, D.C.: The Center, 1994.

———. 1996. *Civil Patrols and their Legacy: Overcoming Militarization and Polarization in the Guatemalan Countryside*. Washington, D.C.: The Center, 1996.

Roberts, Julian V., Loretta J. Stalans, David Indermaur, and Mike Hough. 2003. *Penal Populism and Public Opinion: Lessons from Five Countries.* Oxford: Oxford University Press.

Robinson, William I. 1996. *Promoting Polyarchy: Globalization, US Intervention, and Hegemony.* Cambridge: Cambridge University Press.

———. 2001. "Neoliberalism, the Global Elite, and the Guatemalan Transition: A Critical Macrosocial Analysis." In *Globalization on the Ground: Postbellum Guatemalan Democracy and Development,* edited by Christopher Chase-Dunn, Susanne Jonas, and Nelson Amaro. Lanham, Md.: Rowman and Littlefield, 189–206.

———. 2003. *Transnational Conflicts: Central America, Social Change, and Globalization.* London: Verso.

Rogers, Tim. 2000. "The Spiral of Violence in Central America." *Z Magazine,* September.

Romero, Simon. 2000. "Rich Brazilians Rise above Rush-Hour Jams." *New York Times,* February 15.

Rose, Nikolas. 1999. *Powers of Freedom: Reframing Political Thought.* Cambridge: Cambridge University Press.

Rotker, Susana. 2002. "Cities Written by Violence: An Introduction." In *Citizens of Fear: Urban Violence in Latin America,* edited by Susana Rotker. New Brunswick, N.J.: Rutgers University Press, 7–24.

Rueschemeyer, Dietrich, Evelyne Huber Stephens, and John D. Stephens. 1992. *Capitalist Development and Democracy.* Chicago: University of Chicago Press.

Rumsfeld, Secretary of Defense, v. Padilla et al. 2004. No.03–1027 (2d Cir.) cert. argues April 28; decided June 28.

Ruteere, Mutuma, and Marie-Emmanuell Pommerolle. 2003. "Democratizing Security or Decentralizing Repression? The Ambiguities of Community Policing in Kenya." *African Affairs* 102: 587–604.

Salti, Nisreen. 2003. *Public Order in Kosovo: Rapporteur's Report.* A UNA/USA Project Kosovo Roundtable Discussion. http://www.unausa.org/newindex .asp?place=http://www.unausa.org/issues/kosovo/pubord/salti.asp (accessed April 30, 2003).

Sanford, Victoria. 2003. *Buried Secrets: Truth and Human Rights in Guatemala.* New York: Palgrave Macmillan.

Sandoval, Julieta. 1999. "MINUGUA señala que el ejército sólo cerró 9 cuarteles y creó más unidades." *Prensa libre,* December 3.

Santos, Boaventura de Sousa. 1977. "The Law of the Oppressed: The Construction and Reproduction of Legality in Pasagarda." *Law and Society Review* 12: 5–126.

———. 2000. "Law and Democracy: (Mis)trusting the Global Reform of Courts." In *Globalizing Institutions: Case Studies in Regulation and Innovation,* edited by Jane Jenson and Boaventura de Sousa Santos. Aldershot, England: Ashgate, 253–84.

Scarry, Elaine. 1985. *The Body in Pain: The Making and Unmaking of the World.* Oxford: Oxford University Press.

Scheingold, Stuart A. 1974. *The Politics of Rights: Lawyers, Public Policy, and Polit-ical Change*. New Haven, Conn.: Yale University Press.

———. 1984. *The Politics of Law and Order: Street Crime and Public Policy*. New York: Longman.

Scheper-Hughes, Nancy. 1996. "Theft of Life: Globalization of Organ Stealing Rumors." *Anthropology Today* 12, no. 3: 3–11.

Schirmer, Jennifer. 1998. *The Guatemalan Military Project: A Violence Called De-mocracy*. Philadelphia: University of Pennsylvania Press.

———. 1999. "The Guatemalan Politico-military Project: Legacies for a Violent Peace?" *Latin American Perspectives* 26, no. 2 (March): 92–107.

Schlesinger, Stephen C., and Stephen Kinzer. 1982. *Bitter Fruit: The Untold Story of the American Coup in Guatemala*. Garden City, N.Y.: Doubleday.

Schulz, Donald. 2001. "The Growing Threat to Democracy in Latin America." *Parameters* (Spring): 59–71.

Seijo, Lorena. 2003. "86% de la población cree que la justicia es corrupta." *Prensa Libre*, March 18.

Senechal de la Roche, Roberta. 2001. "Why Is Collective Violence Collective?" *Sociological Theory* 19, no 2 (July): 126–144.

Shapiro, Herbert. 1988. *White Violence and Black Response: From Reconstruction to Montgomery*. Amherst, Mass.: University of Massachusetts Press.

Sharckman, Howard. 1976. "La vietnamización de Guatemala: Los programas de contrainsurgencia norteamericanos." In *Guatemala: Una historia inmediata*, edited by Susanne Jonas and David Tobis. New York: NACLA, 321–46.

Sieder, Rachel. 2002. "Recognising Indigenous Law and the Politics of State For-mation in Mesoamerica." In *Multiculturalism in Latin America: Indigenous Rights, Diversity, and Democracy*, edited by Rachel Sieder. New York: Pal-grave, 184–207.

Simon, Jean-Marie. 1988. *Guatemala: Eternal Spring, Eternal Tyranny*. 1st ed. New York: Norton.

Simon, Jonathan. 1997. "Governing through Crime." In *The Crime Conundrum: Essays on Criminal Justice*, edited by Lawrence M. Friedman and George Fisher. Boulder, Colo.: Westview Press, 171–89.

———. 2000. "Megan's Law: Crime and Democracy in Late Modern America." *Law and Social Inquiry* 25: 1111–51.

———. Forthcoming. *Governing through Crime: The War on Crime and the Trans-formation of America, 1960–2000*. Oxford University Press.

Sistema de las Naciones Unidas en Guatemala. 1998. *Guatemala: Los contrastes del desarrollo humano*. Guatemala City: Naciones Unidas.

Sitler, Robert. 2001. "Death in a Mayan Market." *Community College Humanities Review* 22, no. 1 (Fall): 88–97.

Smith, Carol A. 1990. "The Militarization of Civil Society in Guatemala: Eco-nomic Reorganization as a Continuation of War." *Latin American Perspectives* 17, no. 4 (Fall): 8–41.

———. 1990. *Guatemalan Indians and the State: 1540–1988*. Austin: University of Texas Press.

Sparks, Richard, Evi Girling, and Ian Loader. 2001. "Fear and Everyday Urban Lives." *Urban Studies* 38, nos. 5–6: 885–98.

Speed, Shannon, and Jane Collier. 2000. "Limiting Indigenous Autonomy in Chiapas, Mexico: The State Government's Use of Human Rights." *Human Rights Quarterly* 22, no. 4: 877–905.

Spence, Jack, David R. Dye, Paula Worby, Carmen Rosa de León-Escribano, George Vickers, and Mike Lanchin. 1998. *Promise and Reality: Implementation of the Guatemalan Peace Accords.* Cambridge, Mass.: Hemisphere Initiatives.

Stoll, David. 1993. *Between Two Armies in the Ixil Towns of Guatemala.* New York: Columbia University Press.

———. 1999. *Rigoberta Menchú and the Story of All Poor Guatemalans.* New York: Westview Press.

Sullivan, Kevin. 2003. "Street Killings Aim at Honduran Youths: Gang Members Killed in Grisly Violence." *Washington Post*, May 18.

Tinajero Esquivel, Salvador. 1999. "Derechos humanos: Los balbuceos de Ginebra." *La jornada*, August 2.

Tocqueville, Alexis de. 1969. *Democracy in America.* Translated by George Lawrence. New York: Harper and Row, 1969.

Tolnay, Stewart E., and E. M. Beck. 1992. "Racial Violence and Black Migration in the South, 1910 to 1930." *American Sociological Review* 57 (February): 103–116.

———. 1995. *A Festival of Violence: An Analysis of Southern Lynchings, 1882–1930.* Urbana, Ill.: University of Illinois Press.

Tolnay, Stewart E., Glenn Deane, and E. M. Beck. 1996. "Vicarious Violence: Spatial Effects on Southern Lynchings, 1890–1919." *American Journal of Sociology* 102, no. 3 (November): 788–815.

Tonry, Michael. 1999. "Why Are U.S. Incarceration Rates So High?" *Crime and Delinquency* 45, no. 4 (October): 419–37.

Toro, Ivonne. 2005. "Bachelet presenta batería de medidas contra delincuencia y Lavín persiste en sus críticas." *La nación* (Santiago, Chile), October 14.

Torres-Rivas, Edelberto. 1999. "Epilogue: Notes on Terror, Violence, Fear and Democracy." In *Societies of Fear: The Legacy of Civil War, Violence and Terror in Latin America,* edited by Kees Koonings and Dirk Kruijt. London: Zed Books, 285–300.

Trubek, David, and Marc Galanter. 1974. "Scholars in Self-Estrangement: Some Reflections on the Crisis in Law and Development Studies in the United States." *Wisconsin Law Review*: 1062–1102.

Tyler, Tom R. 1990. *Why People Obey the Law.* New Haven, Conn.: Yale University Press.

Tyler, Tom R., and Robert J. Boeckmann. 1997. "Three Strikes and You're Out, but Why? The Psychology of Public Support for Punishing Rule Breakers." *Law and Society Review* 31, no. 2: 237–65.

Ungar, Mark. 2003. "Prisons and Politics in Contemporary Latin America." *Human Rights Quarterly* 25: 909–34.

United Nations Development Programme. 2004. *Democracy in Latin America: Towards a Citizens' Democracy.* New York: UNDP.

———. 2005. *Human Development Report 2005: International Cooperation at a Crossroads: Aid, Trade and Security in an Unequal World.* New York: UNDP.

United Nations Economic and Social Council. 2000. *Report of the Special Rapporteur on the Independence of Judges and Lawyers, Dato' Param Cumaraswamy, Submitted in Accordance with Commission on Human Rights Resolution 1999/31: Addendum, Report on the mission to Guatemala.* E/CN.4/2000/61/Add.1, January 6.

———. 2001. *Report of the Special Rapporteur on the Independence of Judges and Lawyers, Dato' Param Cumaraswamy, Submitted in Accordance with Commission on Human Rights Resolution 2001/39: Addendum, Report on the Mission to Guatemala.* E/CN.4/2002/72/Add.2, December 21.

United States. Department of State. 2000. *Country Report on Human Rights Practices: Guatemala.* Washington, D.C.: Bureau of Democracy, Human Rights and Labor.

———. 2002. *Country Report on Human Rights Practices: Guatemala.* Washington, D.C.: Bureau of Democracy, Human Rights and Labor.

Varas, Augusto. 1998. "Democratization in Latin America: A Citizen Responsibility." In *Fault Lines of Democracy in Post-transition Latin America*, edited by Felipe Agüero and Jeffrey Stark. Miami, Fla.: North-South Center Press, 145–67.

Varshney, Ashutosh. 2002. *Ethnic Conflict and Civic Life: Hindus and Muslims in India.* New Haven, Conn.: Yale University Press.

"Venezuela: Chavez anuncia *mano dura* con la oposicion." 2002. *Deutsche Presse-Agentur*, June 9.

Vilas, Carlos M. 2001. "(In)justicia por mano propia: Linchamientos en el México contemporáneo." *Revista mexicana de sociología* 63, no. 1 (January–March): 131–60.

"El voto no da esperanza." 1999. *Prensa libre*, May 7.

Wacquant, Loïc. 1999. "How Penal Common Sense Comes to Europeans: Notes on the Transatlantic Diffusion of Neoliberal Doxa." *European Societies* 1–3 (Fall): 319–52.

———. 2001. "The Penalization of Poverty and the Rise of Neoliberalism." *European Journal on Criminal Policy and Research* 9, no. 4 (Winter): 401–12.

———. 2003. "Toward a Dictatorship over the Poor? Notes on the Penalization of Poverty in Brazil." *Punishment and Society* 5, no. 2 (April): 197–205.

Walton, Michael. 2004. "Neoliberalism in Latin America: Good, Bad, or Incomplete?" *Latin American Research Review* 39 (3): 165–183.

Warren, Kay B. 1998. *Indigenous Movements and Their Critics: Pan-Maya Activism in Guatemala.* Princeton, N.J.: Princeton University Press.

Weber, Max. 1978. "Bureaucracy." In *Economy and Society*, edited by Guenther Roth and Claus Wittich. Berkeley: University of California Press, 984–85.

Weyland, Kurt. 2004. "Assessing Latin American Neoliberalism: Introduction to a Debate." *Latin American Research Review* 39 (3): 143–149.

White, Gordon. 1994. "Civil Society, Democratization and Development (I): Clearing the Analytical Ground." *Democratization* 1, no. 3 (Autumn): 375–90.

White House Office of the Press Secretary. 2003. "President Delivers 'State of the Union.'" Press release. http://www.whitehouse.gov/news/releases/2003/01/20030128-19.html. January 28 (accessed November 8, 2005).

Wilson, Richard. 1995. Review of *Rigoberta Menchú and the Story of All Poor Guatemalans. Journal of the Royal Anthropological Institute* 1, no. 1 (March): 217–18.

Yashar, Deborah. 1998. *Contesting Citizenship: Indigenous Movements and Democracy in. Latin America.* Palo Alto, Calif.: Stanford University Press.

Yrigoyen Fajardo, Raquel. 1999. *Pautas de coordinación entre el derecho indígena y el derecho estatal.* Guatemala City: Fundación Myrna Mack.

———. 2002. "Peru: Pluralist Constitution, Monist Judiciary: A Post-Reform Assessment." In *Multiculturalism in Latin America: Indigenous Rights, Diversity, and Democracy,* edited by Rachel Sieder. London: Palgrave, 157–83.

Zimring, Franklin E., Gordon Hawkins, and Sam Kamin. 2003. *Punishment and Democracy: Three Strikes and You're Out in California.* Oxford: Oxford University Press.

Zubieta, Celina. 1998. "Guatemala: Victims of Death Squads or Gang Warfare?" Inter Press Service, March 31.

Index

Page numbers followed by "n" indicate notes.

judicial reform, 17, 21; in Latin America, 13; United States' influence on, 151
justice, 11, 78; informalization of, 141, 155; juvenile, 59; law-centered vision of, 21–23; lynchings as alternative form of, 118; military domination of, 24; privatization of, 161–62; security and, 25, 153, 158, 164–65, 179–80; traditional, 20, 37, 98. *See also* Mayan traditional justice
justice of the peace, 20
justice systems: bifurcated, 49–50, 147; Guatemalan, 46–47, 55, 195n10; Guatemalan civil war and, 54
justicia a mano propia, 24, 56, 57; condemnation of by human rights organizations, 69–70
justicia consuetudinaria. See Mayan traditional justice
justicia indígena. See indigenous justice
justicia Maya. See Mayan traditional justice
justicia popular, 186n16
justicia rondera, 134–35
juvenile justice, 59

Kamin, Sam, 155
Keck, Margaret, 66
kidnappings, 46, 50–51, 53, 144
Kincaid, Douglas, 54
Koonings, Kees, 7
Krujit, Dirk, 7

ladinos, 36, 42, 131, 142–49
Lagos, Marta, 125
land distribution, 42, 43
language, 27–29, 34–35, 172; of governance, 35; torture and, 34
Larsen, Melissa, 3, 4
LaRue, Frank, 73–74
latifundias, 42
Latin America: points of convergence with the United States, 153–58, 178–79; weakness of state in, 39. *See also specific nations*
Lavín, Joaquín, 63
law: adherence to legal codes, 20; customary, 98; as democratic binding, 12–13; exportation of legal models, 17; international, 60, 65–66; politics and, 13; presence of, 21; rule of, 13; social capital

and, 35; social context of, 17; violence and, 41
law-and-development movement, 17, 21
law-and-society tradition, 8, 196n5
law enforcement, 56. *See also* police
Lawyers Committee for Human Rights, 177. *See also* Human Rights First
leadership: Maya, 82–83, 83–84, 85, 107, 109, 132; vacuums of, 119
León, Carlos David de, 53
Limbaugh, Rush, 199n10
limpieza. See social cleansing
linchamientos. See lynchings
Linz, Juan, 9, 195–96n1
Lipset, Seymour Martin, 9, 195–96n1
López Obrador, Andrés Manuel, 16
Lula da Silva, Luiz Ignácio, 160
lynchings, 57, 71; as acts of resistance or empowerment, 117, 123–25; agency and, 102; as attempts to rebuild solidarity, 114–17; in Bolivia, 21, 57; in Brazil, 102; community agency and, 101–26; consensus on, 14–25; crime and, 17–20; definition of, 184n1; as a deterrent, 116; in Ecuador, 102; as evidence of underdevelopment, 103; explanations for, 14–25; fear of crime and, 17–18; forced imposition of, 78, 88; as form of governance, 122; as a global phenomenon, 118; in Guatemala, 1, 8–14, 76–100, 124; involvement of political leaders in, 92–93; as a last resort, 119–20; Maya communities and, 84–98; methods of, 95–96; in Mexico, 16, 57, 101, 124; as mimicry of state, 22–23, 118, 123, 166, 186n16; PACs (*patrullas de autodefensa civil*) and, 85–93; in Peru, 102, 124; popular support for, 93–98, 99–100, 124; postwar, 76; as primitive throwback, 16, 20–21; quasi-religious characteristics of, 116–17; remilitarization and, 95–96; rise in, 8; roots in state terror, 34, 76–100; rural, 195n7; significance of, 8–14; in the United States, 2, 187–88n28, 195n12; in urban areas, 20–21; in Venezuela, 57, 101–2, 124; at Xalbaquiej, 91–92

Madres Angustiadas, 143, 148
Maduro, Ricardo, 59
Malone, Mary Fran T., 111